ANALYZING SOCIAL SETTINGS

A Guide to Qualitative Observation and Analysis

Third Edition

John Lofland

Lyn H. Lofland

University of California, Davis

Wadsworth Publishing Company
An International Thomson Publishing Company

Belmont ● Albany ● Bonn ● Boston ● Cincinnati ● Detroit ● London ● Madrid
Melbourne ● Mexico City ● New York ● Paris ● San Francisco
Singapore ● Tokyo ● Toronto ● Washington

Editorial Assistant: Julie McDonald
Designer: Donna Davis
Copy Editor: Lycette Nelson
Production, Composition, & Illustration: Summerlight Creative
Print Buyer: Barbara Britton
Permissions Editor: Jeanne Bosschart
Cover: Cassandra Chu
Printer: Malloy Lithographing, Inc.

Credits for quotations appear on page 268.

Printed in the United States of America
3 4 5 6 7 8 9 10—99 98 97 96 95

For more information, contact Wadsworth Publishing Company:

Wadsworth Publishing Company
10 Davis Drive
Belmont, California 94002, USA

International Thomson Editores
Campos Eliseos 385, Piso 7
Col. Polanco
11560 México D.F. México

International Thomson Publishing Europe
Berkshire House 168-173
High Holborn
London, WC1V 7AA, England

International Thomson Publishing
GmbH
Königswinterer Strasse 418
53227 Bonn, Germany

Thomas Nelson Australia
102 Dodds Street
South Melbourne 3205
Victoria, Australia

International Thomson Publishing Asia
221 Henderson Road
#05-10 Henderson Building
Singapore 0315

Nelson Canada
1120 Birchmount Road
Scarborough, Ontario
Canada M1K 5G4

International Thomson Publishing Japan
Hirakawacho Kyowa Building, 3F
2-2-1 Hirakawacho
Chiyoda-ku, Tokyo 102, Japan

Library of Congress Cataloging-in-Publication Data
Lofland, John.
Analyzing social settings: a guide to qualitative observation and analysis / John Lofland, Lyn H. Lofland. -- 3rd ed.
    p.   cm.
    Includes bibliographical references and index.
        1. Sociology--Research. 2. Social scienees--Research.
3. Sociology--Methodology.   I. Lofland, Lyn H.   II. Title.
HM48.L63 1984
301'.072--dc20   94-25337
ISBN 0-534-24780-6

This book is printed on acid-free recycled paper.

To Fred Davis
1925–1993

We all agree, I think, that our job is to study society. If you ask why and to what end, I would answer: because it is there. . . . [H]uman social life is ours to study naturalistically, *sub specie aeternitatis*. From the perspective of the physical and biological sciences, human social life is only a small irregular scab on the face of nature, not particularly amenable to deep systematic analysis. And so it is. But it's ours. With a few exceptions, only students in our century have managed to hold it steadily in view in this way, without piety or the necessity to treat traditional issues. Only in modern times have university students been systematically trained to examine all levels of social life meticulously. I'm not one to think that so far our claims can be based on magnificent accomplishment. Indeed, I've heard it said that we should be glad to trade what we've so far produced for a few really good conceptual distinctions and a cold beer. But there's nothing in the world we should trade for what we do have: the bent to sustain in regard to all elements of social life a spirit of unfettered, unsponsored inquiry and the wisdom not to look elsewhere but ourselves and our discipline for this mandate. That is our inheritance and that so far is what we have to bequeath.

Erving Goffman
(1983:16–17)

CONTENTS IN BRIEF

CONTENTS

List of Figures

PREFACE TO THE THIRD EDITION

Users of the second edition of this guide may find it helpful for us to summarize how this, the third edition, has or has not been changed. The major continuities and alterations are as follows.

- We have retained the division of the text into the three major parts of gathering, focusing, and analyzing data. Within each of these three parts, we use the same chapters in the same sequence.

- We have dropped the minor Part Four and its single chapter, on guiding consequences, and integrated the points made there into earlier chapters.

- We now place much greater stress on fieldstudies consisting of *three* major activities—gathering, focusing, and analyzing—all of which need to be carried on more-or-less simultaneously even though there is also some sequencing among them.

- Throughout, we have revised the prose, deleted a number of older examples, and called on some of the best of more recent studies and methodological commentaries.

- Responding to the rise of "postmodern" and associated perspectives in social science, we call attention to these developments, evaluate their contributions, incorporate their valid and pertinent insights (most of which we judge to be simply old wine in new bottles), and explicitly reject their nihilistic and sophistic elements.

- Chapter 8, titled "Being Interesting" in the second edition, has been fundamentally reworked and retitled "Arousing Interest." In this chapter, we now give much more attention to the evaluation of field-studies in terms of their trueness, newness, and importance. This attention is part of our response to what we think is a proper question that postmodernists and others have once more brought to center stage: For whom is social science written and why?

- The two chapters of Part Three, on analyzing data, have been greatly expanded, especially as regards the process of coding and memoing and the use of the personal computer in these activities.

- In teaching fieldwork, we have found it very helpful to have students read and "dissect" ethnographic monographs in terms of the scheme of topics we treat in this guide. For that purpose, we have cast that scheme as a set of questions to answer about a published fieldstudy. In the hope that this "dissection guide" might be useful to other instructors, as well as to self-guiding scholars, we have included it here as an appendix.

ACKNOWLEDGMENTS

Numerous colleagues who have not critiqued the draft text of this edition have nonetheless had a great influence on it by means of conversations, admonitions, offhand remarks, publications, and their exemplary behavior in general. For these diverse and diffuse forms of help and for their colleagueship, we express our deep thanks to Patricia Adler, Peter Adler, Mitch Allen, Leon Anderson, Paul Atkinson, Howard S. Becker, Joel Best, Nicole Biggart, Lodewijk Brunt, Spencer Cahill, Kathy Charmaz, Candace Clark, Norman K. Denzin, Gary Alan Fine, Carol Brooks Gardner, Barney Glaser, Kirsten Grønbjerg, Gary Hamilton, Ruth Horowitz, David Hummon, Albert Hunter, John Irwin, Carol Joffe, John M. Johnson, Sherryl Kleinman, David Maines, Richard Mitchell, Robert Prus, Julius Roth, David Snow, Anselm Strauss, Gerald Suttles, Jacqueline Wiseman, and Morris Zelditch, Jr.

In addition, we acknowledge our profound debts to three now-deceased great scholars: Herbert Blumer, Fred Davis, and Erving Goffman. This edition is dedicated to Fred Davis: mentor, colleague, and friend. As our many references to his work testify, Fred was both a consummate practitioner of fieldwork and an astute observer and critic of fieldwork practices. Though we have missed his counsel in doing this edition, we have sought to express his legacy.

A manual of this sort can emerge only out of the accumulated data collection and analytic experiences of generations of naturalistic researchers. We therefore owe a special debt to all the men and women whose writings have formed the "data base" for our efforts. They are listed in the bibliography.

So, also, one best learns about something in the process of trying to explain it to other people. For us, these other people have very importantly been graduate and undergraduate students at UC, Davis. It is largely through our involvements in their struggles and triumphs in fieldstudies that we have formulated our conception of how to do such studies. We thank them for their patience and tenacity in dealing with successive formulations of these materials. Also at UC, Davis, we thank Larry Cohen who, as Sociology Chair, scheduled our teaching in a way that greatly facilitated this revision.

We are enormously indebted to Serina Beauparlant, former Wadsworth Sociology editor, for her enthusiastic support of a third edition and for the detailed reviews that guided us in writing it; these came from

Steven Ballard, University of Maine; Lynn Davidman, Brown University; Patricia Ewick, Clark University; Linda Grant, University of Georgia; Mike F. Keen, Indiana University, South Bend; Sheryl Kleinman, University of North Carolina, Chapel Hill; Keith Pezzoli, University of California, San Diego; Gerry Philipsen, University of Washington; and Juniper Wiley, California State University, Long Beach. The reviews themselves were extremely helpful, and we thank the authors for their very fine work.

Steven Summerlight and associates at Summerlight Creative designed and produced this edition's fresh and crisp new look, and we are highly appreciative of their diligent labors.

THE AIMS AND ORGANIZATION OF THIS GUIDE

This is a book of instructions on how to do a social science fieldstudy—a research genre that is also often labeled "ethnography," "qualitative study," "case study," or "qualitative fieldstudy." While the labels may differ from discipline to discipline, these studies are alike in featuring direct, qualitative observation of natural situations or settings using, mainly, the techniques of participant observation or intensive interviewing, or both.

I. Three Tasks: Gathering, Focusing, Analyzing

The instructions on doing fieldstudies we will provide are grouped into the three parts or *tasks* of:

1. *gathering*—collecting or assembling data;
2. *focusing*—asking social scientific questions about these data; and
3. *analyzing*—developing and presenting a social science analysis of the data.

The order in which we list these three tasks is, in a general and rough fashion, the order in which they are performed in doing a fieldstudy. However, here at the outset and throughout this guide, we must *also* stress that this is only a "general and rough" order. Even though it is true that one must gather data before one can focus and analyze them, it is *also* true that focusing and analyzing are going on *at the same time* as gathering. It is only the linear logic of writing books that makes them *appear* to follow one another and to be separated in time. The reality of fieldstudies is, instead, one of a complex overlapping and interweaving of the three tasks.

Within this understanding of task overlapping and interweaving, we nevertheless find it helpful to think of the first two tasks—*gathering* and *focusing*—as one's two main and ongoing *input* activities. The data one is

1

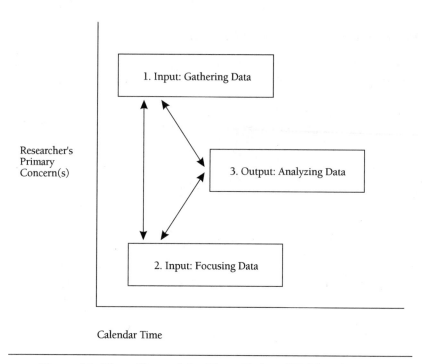

Figure I.1 Flow Chart of the Three Tasks of Fieldstudies

gathering provide *empirical input,* and the focusing questions one is contemplating provide guiding *social science input.* The third task—that of *analysis*—emerges as a synthesis or social scientific *output* of the interaction between gathered and focused data. These relations are depicted schematically in Figure I.1, where gathering and focusing are shown as initial and interacting main activities that give rise to analyzing as an emergent and, at the end, main activity.

The image shown in Figure I.1 is only one among several that can be helpful in conceiving relations among the three tasks of gathering, focusing, and analyzing. A second image that you may find more helpful is that of two banks of a river over which one wants to build a bridge. The gathering of data forms one bank, and social scientific focusing is the other bank. In this image, analysis is a *bridge* between the two. Or, in yet a third way to think of relations among the three tasks, the analysis one develops is an *application* of social science focusing guidelines to one's gathered data.

II. Features and Aspects of Fieldstudies

At the abstract level of performing the three tasks of gathering, focusing, and analyzing data, qualitative fieldstudies are not different from other methods of social research, such as surveys, content analyses, and experiments. Instead, fieldstudies differ from other methods of research in exactly how they treat these three tasks. Specifically, fieldstudies are distinctive in (1) the relation the researcher has to "the data" in *gathering,* (2) the time at which data are *focused,* and (3) the relation of *analysis* to the data and questions of focus. Let us explain each distinctive feature and provide an overview of the chapters in which we treat each in detail.

A. Task One, Gathering Data: Researcher as Witness and Instrument

Qualitative fieldstudy differs from other research methods in that it features researchers themselves as observers and participants in the lives of the people being studied. The researcher strives to be a participant in and a *witness to* the lives of others. This is quite different from other kinds of research in which the investigator is not her- or himself a sustained presence in a naturally occurring situation or setting. Other researchers rely instead on documents, fixed interviews, experimental simulations, and other sources that are at least one level removed from *direct* observation of and participation in independently ongoing natural settings.

The central reason for undertaking this ongoing witnessing of the lives of others is the fact that a great many aspects of social life can be seen, felt, and analytically articulated only in this manner. In subjecting him- or herself to the round of lives of others and living and feeling those lives along with them, the researcher becomes an *instrumentality* or *medium* of the research. The researcher seeks to witness how the studied others perceive, feel, and act in order to grasp these seeings, feelings, and actings fully and intimately. The epistemological foundation of fieldstudies is indeed the proposition that only through direct experience can one accurately know much about social life.

The five chapters of Part One provide guidelines on achieving and managing the researcher's role as witness to lives and instrumentality of the research process.

Chapter 1   Because of the central role of the researcher as both data experiencer and collector and the problematics of achieving this role, fieldstudy people encourage budding researchers to *start where you are*— to use your current situation or past involvement as a topic of research. We discuss the advantages and disadvantages of doing this and related matters in Chapter 1.

Chapter 2   Some settings are more amenable to particular research techniques than others; therefore, a process of *evaluating data sites* in terms of appropriateness and access is necessary. Guidelines for doing this are given in Chapter 2.

Chapter 3   *Getting into* a relevant site is often problematic. The mode of entry must be decided in terms of the social, political, legal, and ethical considerations discussed in Chapter 3.

Chapter 4   Once you have begun, the relationship between the research and its setting will provide a continual array of problems with which you must deal. We consider these problems of *getting along* in Chapter 4.

Chapter 5   The main substantive activity of the researcher is *logging data*. Two principal logging methods are interview write-ups and field-notes. Chapter 5 provides detailed instructions for doing both.

B. Task Two, Focusing Data: Social Science Guidance

Although subjecting oneself as a researcher to the lives of others is indispensable in fieldstudy, that immersion must be guided by the aims and concerns of the social scientific analysis of human group life. We explain the most basic of these aims and concerns in the three chapters of Part Two.

Chapter 6   The first of these basic matters calls attention to how human group life can be viewed as being at different *unit* scales of organization and as possessing different *aspects*. In the analysis stage, you will select one or only a few units and aspects. Therefore, to assist you in deliberating and making these selections, in Chapter 6 we describe ten basic units of social organization in ascending order of "scale," including such familiar entities as social roles, groups, and lifestyles. In addition, we describe three frequently used generic aspects of social situations or settings: meanings, emotions, and hierarchy. Considered together, units and aspects provide possible *topics* of analysis.

Chapter 7   Units and aspects only provide possible objects or topics of focus. In social science analysis, one goes on to *ask questions* about the topics. We outline eight major classes of possible questions in Chapter 7.

Chapter 8   Topics and questions provide the *formal* fundamentals of social science analysis. Decisions that one makes about them anchor one as doing social science analysis. But there is yet a third, albeit more elusive, aspect of social science guidance. This is the question of performing analysis on topics and questions that will *arouse interest* in audiences who read your analysis. Applying and adapting generic criteria for evaluating any intellectual work, we offer suggestions in Chapter 8 on how to arouse audience interest in terms of making one's study *true, new,* and *important.*

Fieldstudies differ from other methods of research in that the researcher performs the tasks of selecting topics, decides what questions to ask, and forges interest *in the course of the research itself.* This is in sharp contrast to many "theory-driven" and "hypothesis-testing" methods of research in which the topics of observation and analysis, the questions about them, and the possible kinds of interest the findings might have are all carefully and clearly specified before one begins to gather data.

This postponing of the process of focusing data to the period of actually collecting the data dovetails with the role of the researcher as witness and instrument (described above with regard to gathering data). Focusing decisions are postponed *because* the researcher is a witness and instrument. The research strategy is to allow the investigator more latitude within the three forms of social science guidance to attend to the setting under study in its own terms—as these interact with the investigator's sensibilities—for the purpose of evolving an analysis.

C. Task Three, Analyzing Data: Emergent Analysis

In so positioning decisions on how to focus data, fieldstudies are inherently and by design *open-ended* regarding the third task, that of analysis. Intellectually and operationally, analysis *emerges* from the *interaction* of gathered data (task 1) and focusing decisions (task 2).

The *purpose* of this process is to achieve analyses that (1) are attuned to aspects of human group life, (2) depict aspects of that life, and (3) provide perspectives on that life that are simply not available to or prompted by other methods of research.

As an open-ended and emergent process, it is inherently more difficult to provide surefire instructions on how to bring gathered data and focusing concerns together and into analysis. Even so, helpful procedures have been identified.

Chapter 9 One set of these procedures focuses on physical operations to perform on the data as aids in deciding on one's topics and questions of analysis. The most basic and central of these are the processes of coding and memo writing. We explain these and other techniques of *developing analysis* in Chapter 9.

Chapter 10 Another set of procedures pertains to features of one's report per se, its elements and their ordering, and the social psychology of writing. We describe these matters and several rules of thumb pertaining to writing in Chapter 10.

III. Audiences

Although by training and practice we are sociologists, in this guide we treat fieldstudies as a trans- or interdisciplinary activity and *not* as the special province of sociologists. Indeed, the research practices we describe are used in at least a dozen theoretical and applied disciplines with excellent effects. Aside from anthropology, political science, and history, the fieldstudy method is used in such diverse fields as administration, education, communications, criminal justice, geography, labor relations, nursing, and social work.

IV. Yet More Labels for Fieldstudies

We use the label *fieldstudies* to denote the method of research explained in this guide. But, as mentioned in the first paragraph of this introduction, not all social scientists use the same labels in the same ways. Social science is a terminological jungle in which many labels compete, and no single term has been able to command the particular domain before us. Often, especially in political science and occasionally in psychology, researchers simply "do it" without worrying about giving "it" a name. Anthropologists provide us with the term for which, historically, the strongest case can be made: *fieldwork*. But as matters have developed in anthropology and other disciplines, fieldwork no longer captures all the salient qualities of this type of study. In sociology, our own discipline, the fieldwork label has some currency, but there are many competitors that connote important additional ideas: *qualitative social research, qualitative methods, fieldwork interactionism, grounded theory, the Chicago school of ethnography,* and *naturalism.*

We point to the existence of this nomenclature chaos in order to help orient those readers who delve into items we cite and into other publications on specific topics being researched. Being aware of the "terminological jungle" should make it possible to look beyond the labels to the activities in which the researchers actually engage. (Histories of this many-labeled tradition include Wax 1971, Ch. 3; Burgess 1984; Emerson, ed., 1988; Denzin 1989; and Vidich and Lyman 1994.)

V. Naturalism

Among the diversity of labels we could use, *fieldstudies* is among the more general, encompassing, and widely accepted; therefore, we use it often in this guide. Personally, however, we have a fondness for the term *naturalism,* or *naturalistic research.* This term has a tradition (e.g., Matza 1969; Blumer 1969; Denzin 1971) and possesses transdisciplinary neutrality. Further, it suggests an appropriate linkage to *naturalist* as that word is used in field biology. From the realms of philosophical discourse, it has acquired the connotation of minimizing the presuppositions with which one approaches the empirical world—a laudable resonance indeed. Moreover, as a literary genre, *naturalism* involves a close and searching description of the mundane details of everyday life, a meaning we seek to foster in the social science context. Both denotatively and connotatively, then, we consider it a richer and more significant label than many other candidate names.

In these chapters, we pay homage to more general usage by referring often to *fieldstudies* and sometimes to *fieldwork*. However, we also frequently use our personal favorite. We trust that these minor inconsistencies will not prove confusing.

PART ONE

GATHERING DATA

F ive aspects of gathering data form the initial task or phase of a fieldstudy. These are:

- the readiness to start where you are (Chapter 1),

- the preference for rich sites of direct, face-to-face engagement where intimate familiarity is acquired (Chapter 2),

- the need to deal with difficulties in entry (Chapter 3),

- the management of relations with the people in the situations or settings under study (Chapter 4), and

- the logging motif of data collection (Chapter 5).

CHAPTER 1

STARTING WHERE YOU ARE

The naturalistic or fieldwork approach to social research fosters a pronounced willingness, even commitment, on the part of the investigator to orient to her or his own extrasocial-scientific concerns; that is, to the concerns that you *bring* to the situation of doing social analysis. Ideally, your concerns will overlap or be related to the codified concerns of social science. But you must first determine what it is you care about *independent* of social science. If that determination coincides with what is already deemed of interest in the relevant disciplines, good. You are in a strong position to do interesting and significant work (see Chapter 8). But if your determination does not so coincide, be of good cheer. Handled deftly, your analysis may well succeed in opening up entirely new avenues of social science interest.

These extrasocial-scientific primary concerns may be of one of two types or both. There are the concerns born of the *accidents of current biography* and those born of *accidents of remote biography and personal history*.

I. Current Biography

A job; a physical mishap; the development, loss, or maintenance of an intimate relationship; an illness; an enjoyed activity; a living arrangement— all these and many other possible circumstances may provide you with a topic you care enough about to study. It is important to emphasize that it is not only that these accidents of current biography may give you physical or psychological access (or both) to social settings (although this is crucial— see Riemer 1977, on varieties of what he calls "opportunistic research"). Such access becomes the starting point for meaningful naturalistic research only when it is accompanied by some degree of *interest* or concern.

Many social science research projects have had their genesis in current biography. Some particularly striking examples are listed in Figure 1.1, where we have also tried to show the variety of situations out of which social analyses grow. (Additional examples are provided by Mitchell 1993, p. 22, fn. 1.)

Figure 1.1 Examples of "Starting Where You Are"

This person:	starting where he or she was:	developed this published social analysis:
Elijah Anderson	a resident of a mixed-class and mixed-race area of Philadelphia	*Streetwise: Race, Class and Change in an Urban Community* (1990)
Alfred Aversa, Jr.	a member and secretary of the "Neptune Yacht Club"	"When Blue Collars and White Collars Meet at Play: The Case of the Yacht Club" (1990)
Fred Davis	working as a cabdriver while in graduate school at the University of Chicago	"The Cabdriver and His Fare: Facets of a Fleeting Relationship" (1959)
Raymond G. DeVries	an expectant parent exploring birthing options	*Regulating Birth: Midwives, Medicine & the Law* (1985)
Judith A. DiIorio and Michael R. Nusbaumer	serving as escorts at an abortion clinic	"Securing Our Sanity: Anger Management Among Abortion Escorts" (1993)
Helen R. F. Ebaugh	a former nun	*Out of the Cloister: A Study of Organizational Dilemmas* (1977) and *Becoming an Ex: The Process of Role Exit* (1988)
Rick Fantasia	working at a small iron foundry when a wildcat strike occurred	*Cultures of Solidarity: Consciousness, Action, and Contemporary American Workers* (1988)
Douglas M. Robins	the human companion of a dachshund named Max	"Dogs and Their People: Pet-Facilitated Interaction in a Public Setting" (with Clinton R. Sanders and Spencer E. Cahill, 1991)
Gerald Suttles	a member of the local planning committee of the Chicago Metropolitan Housing and Planning Council	*The Man-Made City: The Land-Use Confidence Game in Chicago* (1990)
Diane Vaughan	a divorcee after twenty years of marriage	*Uncoupling: Turning Points in Intimate Relationships* (1990)
Jacqueline Wiseman	a long-time patron of secondhand clothing stores	"Close Encounters of the Quasi-Primary Kind: Sociability in Urban Second-Hand Clothing Stores" (1979)
Sharon Zukin	living in a "loft" in New York City	*Loft Living: Culture and Capital in Urban Change* (1982)

II. Remote Biography and Personal History

The concerns you bring to doing social analysis may also arise from accidents of remote biography and personal history—of residence, ethnicity, gender, sexual preference, past identities or experiences, places of residence, family customs, class of origin, religion, and so forth. The fact that most of the work on gender roles is currently being done by women, for example, is hardly coincidental. More specifically, anthropologist Barbara Myerhoff's research for *Number Our Days: A Triumph of Continuity and Culture Among Jewish Old People in an Urban Ghetto* (1978) was motivated in part by a desire to better understand her own Jewish heritage. John Irwin's interest in *The Felon* (1970), in *Prisons in Turmoil* (1980), and in *The Jail* (1985) was intimately related to his own felony conviction at the age of 21 and the five years he spent in a California state prison. And Mary Romero's study of domestic workers (*Maid in the U.S.A.*, 1992) may be said to have had its origins in the fact that as a teenager she had worked as a domestic, as had her mother, sister, relatives, and neighbors; however, in Romero's work, remote biography was also joined with more current experience:

> Before beginning a teaching position at the University of Texas in El Paso, I stayed with a colleague while apartment hunting. My colleague had a live-in domestic to assist with housecleaning and cooking. Asking around, I learned that live-in maids were common in El Paso. . . . The hiring of maids from Mexico was so common that locals referred to Monday as the border patrol's day off because the agents ignored the women crossing the border to return to their employers' homes after their weekend off. The practice of hiring undocumented Mexican women as domestics, many of whom were no older than fifteen, seemed strange to me. It was this strangeness that raised the topic of domestic service as a question and made problematic what had previously been taken for granted. (1992, pp. 1–3)

It is often said among sociologists that, as sociologists, we "make problematic" in our research matters that are problematic in our lives. With the proviso that the connection between self and study may be a subtle and sophisticated one, not at all apparent to an outside observer, we would argue that there is considerable truth to this assertion. In fact, much of the best work in sociology and other social sciences—within the fieldwork tradition as well as within other research traditions—is probably grounded in the remote and/or current biographies of its creators. That such linkages are not always, perhaps not even usually, publicly acknowledged is understandable: the norms of scholarship do not require that researchers bare their souls, only their procedures.

III. Staying Where You Are: A Word of Caution

Of late, a number of sociologists have counseled not only starting where you are, but staying there. That is, some researchers have argued that there is much to be learned by making oneself the (mostly) exclusive focus of one's study, that is, by doing what Norman L. Friedman (1990b) calls "autobiographical sociology" and Carolyn Ellis (forthcoming) refers to as "telling personal stories" (example reports from such studies include Ellis and Bochner 1992, Friedman 1974, and Ronai 1992). We would grant that for some kinds of research concerns (the phenomenology of ongoing emotional experience for example), one's self may be the only available data site (see Chapter 2). And we would grant that in the hands of a skilled analyst and wordsmith, staying where you are may result in meaningful and insightful works of social science. Nonetheless, we strongly advise most researchers, especially beginners, to avoid it. Even when exceptionally well executed, reports analyzing autobiographical data are often viewed by readers as borderline self-indulgence; when only competently executed, they are likely to be labeled "narcissistic" or "exhibitionist" and simply dismissed as uninteresting (see Chapter 8). Although she writes more generally about the "excesses" of self-reflexivity in much recent scholarship, women's studies professor Daphne Patai's criticisms may equally be aimed at autobiographically based research reports.

> But the logical extension of the current academic fascination with self-reflexivity is, unfortunately, that you can never tell *enough.* . . . Will longer passages of identification, then, do the trick? Perhaps, in the end, an entire preliminary autobiography will become *de rigueur*, so that all one's biases and predilections and positionings are made clear to the unwary reader. . . . I doubt that I am the only one who is weary of the nouveau solipsism—all this individual and collective breast-beating, grandstanding, and plain old egocentricity. (1994, p. A52)

IV. Tradition and Justification

Within the fieldwork tradition, the positive evaluation of "starting where you are" has a long history. Speaking of Robert Park, one of the founders of the naturalistic tradition, and his work with sociology graduate students at the University of Chicago in the 1920s and 1930s, Everett Hughes has related that

> Most of these people didn't have any sociological background. . . . They didn't come in to become sociologists. They came in to learn something and Park picked up whatever it was in their experience which he could build on. . . . He took these people and he brought out of them whatever he could find there. And he brought out of them very often something

they themselves did not know was there. They might be Mennonites who were just a little unhappy . . . about wearing plain clothes . . . girls who didn't like to wear long dresses and funny little caps; . . . or children of Orthodox Jews who really didn't like to wear beards anymore (that was a time of escaping a beard, the beard was the symbol of your central Russian origin and you wanted to get it off). And he got hold of people and emancipated them from something that was inherently interesting but which they regarded as a cramp. And he turned this "cramping orthodoxy" into something that was of basic and broad human interest. And that was the case for a lot of these people. He made their pasts interesting to them, much more interesting than they ever thought they could be. (L. Lofland, ed., 1980, pp. 267–268)

As we shall see in following chapters, starting where you are may cause methodological and ethical difficulties. We believe, however, that any such difficulties are a small price to pay for the very creative wellsprings of the naturalistic approach. Starting where you are provides the necessary meaningful linkages between the personal and emotional on the one hand, and the stringent intellectual operations to come on the other. Without a foundation in personal sentiment, all the rest easily becomes so much ritualistic hollow cant. Julius Roth (1966) has written persuasively of the dangers of "hired hand research," of the dismal work performance of alienated labor in the scholarship business (in contrast, see Staggenborg 1988). But alienation is not limited to occasions of following someone else's agenda. If your own agenda is not personally meaningful, you may be alienated as well. Unless you are emotionally engaged in your work, the inevitable boredom, confusion, and frustration of rigorous scholarship will endanger even the completion—not to speak of the quality—of the project.

CHAPTER 2

EVALUATING DATA SITES

H aving identified a personally meaningful interest—in a group, a situation, a setting, a question, a topic, whatever—you must then decide how best (in the sense of "how most fruitfully") to pursue this interest. This requires an assessment of the most appropriate or most feasible "wheres," "hows," and "whens" of the research.

We do not mean to suggest that all decisions regarding the research are, even initially, "up for grabs." As a student, for example, you may be required to write about a particular setting during a specified period; that is, the "where" and "when" of your research may be largely predetermined. Or your interests may logically imply one sort of "how" rather than another.

Nonetheless, regardless of the degree of freedom you have, the process of evaluating data sites is crucial. If it is not crucial in making your own decisions, it may at least be important in terms of understanding the implications of decisions that are already made.

I. The Overall Goal

Your overall goal is to collect the *richest possible data*. Rich data mean, ideally, a wide and diverse range of information collected over a relatively prolonged period of time. Again, ideally, you achieve this through direct, face-to-face contact with, and prolonged immersion in, some social location or circumstance. You wish, that is, to earn "intimate familiarity" with the sector of social life that has tickled your interest.

The naturalistic penchant for *direct* observation and apprehension of the social world reflects a certain **epistemology**, that is, a theory of knowledge. The central tenets of this theory are (1) that face-to-face interaction is the fullest condition of participating in the mind of another human being, and (2) that you must participate in the mind of another human being (in sociological terms, "take the role of the other") to acquire social knowledge. Whatever the barriers to the validity of direct knowledge of others (and they may be numerous), they are as nothing compared to the difficulties engendered by indirect perception. (For important segments of this epistemology, see Blumer 1969, especially pp. 1–89; Schutz 1967, especially Chapter 4 and Sections C and D; Berger and Luckman 1967, especially pp. 28–34; and Cooley 1926.)

Novice fieldworkers, schooled in the "bias avoidance" injunctions of experimental and survey research, often worry that if they become personally involved in their field settings they will "contaminate the data." We want to nip that worry in the bud. You will note that nowhere in the preceding paragraphs have we have said anything about the importance of "objectivity" and "distance." Quite the contrary, we have exhorted researchers to

• collect the richest possible data,
• achieve intimate familiarity with the setting, and
• engage in face-to-face interaction so as to participate in the minds of the settings' participants.

That is, we have counseled involvement and enmeshment rather than objectivity and distance—a counsel that is very much in keeping with the fieldwork tradition, at least as the tradition has developed within sociology. As we shall see in the next chapter, the dual task of raising questions and answering questions does call for a certain internal tension between distance and closeness in the researcher. We shall also see in Chapter 8 that a dispassionate frame of mind is particularly helpful when one is attempting to translate one's amassed data into a sophisticated and interesting analysis. But if one is to collect rich data, the tradition beckons one to "come close." So-called objectivity and distance vis-à-vis the field setting will usually result in a failure to collect any data that are worth analyzing.

As noted in the Introduction, in this guide we shall be concerned primarily with those two interrelated methods most closely associated with the naturalistic preference for direct apprehension: participant observation and intensive interviewing. We recognize, however, that many matters of interest to potential investigators, many questions or topics or settings or situations, will simply not be available through these methods. There will be matters that you cannot "reach" through direct apprehension: historical settings or events, for example, or the actions of very large units, such as political or economic systems. For these research problems, other manuals are to be recommended (see, for example, Allen and Montess 1981; Angrosino 1989; Babbie 1995; Baker 1994; Baker and Bellenge, eds., 1982; Brewer and Hunter 1989; Gilbert 1993; Kyvig and Marty 1982; Skocpol, ed., 1984; Startt and Sloan 1989; Tilly 1984). There will also be matters whose direct apprehension requires neither participant observation nor intensive interviewing, as these terms are traditionally understood. If you are interested in the cultural products of social interaction such as conceptions of the homeless, images of urban life, or beliefs about emotions, you might be best advised to use the built environment, works of art, television broadcasts, autobiographies, transcripts of conversations or public hearings, collections of letters, or magazine advertisements as your data. Or, you may wish to focus on the moment-by-moment flow of emotional experience and have no need to do more than monitor your own subjective states (but see our caution in Chapter 1). For these sorts of research, some of what we discuss in the following pages ("getting in" and "getting along" especially) will be of little value and you will need other guides to fill in the data collection lacunae (see, for example, Altheide 1987; Brunt 1979; Clay 1980; Ellis and Flaherty, eds., 1992; Fields 1988; Mellard 1987; Riessman 1993; Silverman 1993; van Dijk 1985). But most of the matters discussed here should apply equally well to analysts of human cultural *productions* and to researchers of human cultural *producers*.

II. Participant Observation and Intensive Interviewing

Also known as "field observation," "qualitative observation," or "direct observation," **participant observation** refers to the process in which an investigator establishes and sustains a many-sided and relatively long-term relationship with a human association in its natural setting for the purpose of developing a scientific understanding of that association. This may not be the person's sole purpose for being present in the setting, but it is at least an important one. **Intensive interviewing**, also known as "unstructured interviewing," is a guided conversation whose goal is to elicit from the interviewee (usually referred to as the "informant") rich, detailed materials that can be used in qualitative analysis. In contrast to "structured interviewing" (such as opinion polling), where the goal is to elicit choices between alternative answers to pre-formed questions on a topic or situation, the intensive interview seeks to *discover* the informant's *experience* of a particular topic or situation. Among other contrasts, the structured interview seeks to determine the frequency of preconceived kinds of things, while the unstructured interview seeks to find out what kinds of things exist in the first place.

The literature on qualitative methodology has traditionally distinguished rather sharply between participant observation and intensive interviewing, frequently viewing the former as the preeminent method, the latter as a pale substitute (see, for example, Becker and Geer 1970; Goffman 1989; Kleinman, Stenross, and McMahon 1994 challenge this position). We believe this distinction to be overdrawn and any invidious comparison unwarranted. As many anthropological accounts make clear, doing participant observation in another culture involves a great deal of informant interviewing (Golde, ed., 1986; Lutz 1988; Sanjek, ed., 1990; R. Wax 1971). And as W. Gordon West has noted, a review of sociological field reports suggests that "the bulk of participant observation data is probably gathered through informal interviews and supplemented by observation" (1980, p. 39).

Classic participant observation, then, always involves the interweaving of looking and listening, of watching and asking, and some of that listening and asking may approach or be identical to intensive interviewing. Conversely, intensive interview studies may involve repeated and prolonged contact between researchers and informants, sometimes extending over a period of years, with considerable mutual involvement in personal lives—a characteristic often considered a hallmark of participant observation (see, for example, Bogdan 1980; Charmaz 1991; Gold 1989). In addition, many social situations (experiencing grief over the loss of someone or something one cares deeply about, for example) may be masked in everyday interaction and thus be directly apprehensible *only* through intensive interviewing. Therefore, rather than being a poor substitute for participant observation, intensive interviewing is frequently the method of choice.

For these reasons, then, we wish to emphasize the *mutuality* of participant observation and intensive interviewing as the central techniques of naturalistic investigation. In what follows, we shall distinguish between them where it is necessary to do so, but most of our discussion is applicable to both. (A considerable number of general treatments of participant observation, intensive interviewing, or both are available. Among these are Berg 1989; Bernard 1994; Denzin and Lincoln, eds., 1994; Ellen, ed., 1984; Emerson, ed., 1988; Erlandson et al. 1993; Fetterman 1989; Hammersly and Atkinson 1983; LeCompte, Millroy, and Preissle, eds., 1992; McCracken 1988; Morse, ed., 1994; Seidman 1991; Weiss 1994; Whyte 1984.)

III. Detailed Assessment of Data Sites

Assuming, then, that you wish to gather the richest possible data using participant observation, intensive interviewing, or some combination of the two, you need to evaluate potential data sites for appropriateness, access, ethics, immediate risk, and personal consequences.

A. Evaluating for Appropriateness

Questions constrain research locations, research locations constrain questions, methodological preferences and topics constrain both, and so on. The point is that "starting where you are" is likely to set some parameters around what will be appropriate, and these need to be assessed. While the fieldwork tradition in social science puts a premium on flexibility, it is simply a fact that some questions, research locations, topics or methods logically necessitate other questions, locations, topics or methods (Deutscher 1973; Zelditch 1962). If you have decided to rely solely on observation of persons in public places, for example, you will not be able to collect many useful data on emotional states and processes. Or if you are interested in body management strategies in public interaction, intensive interviewing is hardly an appropriate tool, since the data you need are largely outside individual awareness. Doing research with children in a nursery school will yield little of value about day-to-day interaction of school administrators. And you will not be able to learn about the grief experience by participant observation in a group with a low death or other attrition rate.

All of this may seem obvious, if not simpleminded. Yet, as anyone who has read any reasonable number of *unpublished* social science works (by professionals as well as by students) can testify, a fair portion of research appears to proceed without noticeable awareness of, or appreciation for, the problems of appropriateness.

The circumstances of potential research projects are too diverse to yield many specific "principles" of appropriateness. We can, however, offer four general guidelines.

First, using participant observation alone is probably most fruitful when the question, topic, or situation in which you are interested is physically located somewhere, at least temporarily. If you wish, for example, to study the operation of street gangs (Horowitz 1983), to understand the day-to-day lives of the homeless (Snow and Anderson 1993), to explore the way gender is enacted and re-created among children (Cahill 1989, 1986; Thorne 1993), or to detail culture-in-the-making in small groups (Fine 1987), observation will likely yield the richest data most efficiently.

Second, and conversely, you may be interested in what Joseph Kotarba has called "amorphous social experiences—those facets of everyday life that are unique to individuals and not [to] specific kinds of settings . . . [those] existential experiences of self, rich in their social forms . . ." (1980, p. 57). In that event, intensive interviewing (sometimes combined with limited observation) may be the most felicitous, and possibly the *only*, way to proceed. Examples of amorphous social experiences include dissolving an intimate relationship (Vaughan 1990); receiving and giving sympathy (Clark 1987); working in a direct selling organization (Biggart 1989); residing in a small town, city, or suburb (Hummon 1990); being a member of the clergy (Aldridge 1993, 1989); working as a supermarket checker (Tolich 1993); and teaching one's children about sex (Fox et al. 1988).

Third, always consider the possible appropriateness of new or little-used variants of the standard research methods. Zimmerman and Wieder (1977), for example, have reported on the field procedure of the *diary/ diary-interview method*. The technique uses diaries as observational logs maintained by the person being studied; these in turn are used as a basis for intensive interviews. They recommend the technique in situations "where the problems of direct observation resist solution or where further or more extended observation strains available resources . . . [that is,] when the investigator is unable to make firsthand observations or wishes to supplement those already collected" (1977, p. 481). As another example, you might consider *group* or (the more specialized) *focus group interviews* in place of, or as a supplement to, one-to-one interviews (Greenbaum 1993; Morgan and Spanish 1984; Morgan 1988; Morgan, ed., 1993). Group interviewing of whatever sort may be most productive on topics that are reasonably public and are not matters of any particular embarrassment. It has the advantage of allowing people more time to reflect and to recall experiences; also, something that one person mentions can spur memories and opinions in others. Moreover, by allowing moments of not having to talk, of being able to listen to others, group interviewing allows each person to rethink and amend any initial account that, upon reflection, seems in need of amplification, qualification, amendment, or contradiction. In addition, people may not agree with one another on matters of opinion, providing instances of interchange between contrasting perspectives. As a last example, in some settings, at least some of the participants may not be in face-to-face contact but be linked instead via *electronic media* (e-mail, faxes, telephone and video conferences). In such settings, the achievement of intimate familiarity may require that the researcher, too, participate in such disembodied communication networks. John Workman, Jr. (1992), for example, who studied a computer systems firm, found it essential to use electronic bulletin boards to monitor ongoing discussions and debates within the firm and to use e-mail to receive meeting notices and relevant documents, to schedule interviews, and to communicate directly with many of his informants.

Fourth, as will become clear in subsequent chapters, participant observation and intensive interviewing are both highly demanding, laborious methods of data collection. Nonetheless, you should not rule out *ipso facto* the appropriateness of collecting or using (if already collected by others) some quantitative data as well. In recent years, researchers have experimented with adding qualitative components to large-scale survey projects, with generally positive results (Connidis 1983; Morgan 1993). The reverse strategy may sometimes prove equally fruitful. Especially if your research will constitute a "case study"—a holistic investigation of some space- and time-rooted phenomenon—some types of quantitative data may even be essential. If you will be studying a neighborhood or small community, for example, do not overlook the rich and detailed information that census data can make available to you (Myers 1992). Or, as another example, if your focus is a single moderately sized organization, a small survey of the membership may be the most efficient (and possibly the only) way to get a handle on your "cast of characters." (Recent qualitative studies collecting or using various amounts of survey, census, and other quantitative data include Biggart 1989, Grønbjerg 1993, Rosen 1987, and Snow and Anderson 1993. Discussions of the unique features of the case study may be found in Feagin, Orum, and Sjoberg, eds., 1991 and Platt 1988.)

B. Evaluating for Access

As liberals, humanists, cosmopolitans, or whatever, we like to believe that all humans have equal access to the minds of all other humans— that in our shared humanity we are more like than unlike. But a realistic appraisal of any proposed research necessitates our recognizing that, in combination, the attributes of the investigator, of the setting or situation to be studied, and of the people to be learned about may create barriers to the acquisition of rich data. As part of your general task of evaluating data sites, then, you must be concerned with the possible existence of such barriers, with assessing their seriousness, and with considering if or how they can be overcome. In fact, in the literature of qualitative methodology, *access* is probably one of the most written about topics— understandably so, for it remains problematic throughout the entire period of research. As such, we shall encounter it again, especially in Chapters 3 and 4. Even then, however, we shall not have exhausted the topic, for the possible combinations of investigator, setting, and participant attributes generate an almost endless litany of discrete "access situations." Our more limited and realistic goal here and in later pages is to provide you, the investigator considering your own particular access situation, with "food for thought."

In the current context of data site evaluation, we shall consider four problem areas: (1) investigator relationship to setting, (2) ascriptive categories of researcher and researched, (3) large settings, and (4) difficult settings.

1. Investigator Relationship to Setting

In a penetrating, insightful, and now classic essay, Fred Davis (1973) has written about two opposing orientations or stances a researcher might take toward what he or she is studying. Conceived metaphorically as the "Martian" and the "Convert," these stances capture the "dilemma of distance" encountered by all researchers. The Martian sees distance as a passageway to knowing, the Convert views it as a barrier.

> The Martian . . . yearns to grasp the human situation with wholly fresh or, better yet, strange eyes, in a blush of wonderment as it were. In order to do this he wants to divest himself completely of the vast array of unwitting cultural assumptions, rules of thumb, modes of sensibility and—were it somehow possible—the very language, which comprises the "cognitive stuff" of our everyday worlds and beings. . . . In contrast to the Martian's desire to escape and stand wholly outside the social ontological frame of his subjects in order to see how the frame is constructed, the Convert's overriding impulse is to immerse himself ever more deeply *within* the frame so that the distinctive subjective currents of the group may forcibly and directly reveal themselves to him. (1973, pp. 336, 338)

Davis's metaphorical creatures represent very real methodological preferences and debates about those preferences within the social sciences. More profoundly, however, they symbolize a tension that many researchers feel or strive to feel *within themselves.* To ask questions of, to "make problematic," to "bracket" social life requires distance (Martian). To understand, to answer questions, to make sense of social life requires closeness (Convert). The sensitive investigator wishes not to be one or the other but to be *both* or *either* as the research demands.

The point for the prospective investigator assessing for access is simply this: If you are already (or will become) a member in the setting, you almost "naturally" possess (or will possess) the convert stance. You have easy access to understanding. You need, therefore, at least initially, to seek mechanisms for distancing. Conversely, if you are an outsider to the setting, a stranger to the social life under investigation, your access to questioning will be equally natural. You need, then, to seek mechanisms for reducing that distance. The moral is this: Be neither discouraged nor overconfident about your relationship to the setting. Whatever that relationship, it is simultaneously an advantage and a drawback. (See further, Adler and Adler 1987; Horowitz 1986; Monti 1992; Snow, Benford, and Anderson 1986.)

2. Ascriptive Categories of Researcher and Researched

Many social orders define ascriptive categories—such as sex, age, and ethnicity—as important points of difference among people. Therefore, in this limited sense, "who" the researcher is, in contrast to "who" the researched are, may throw up barriers to the acquisition of rich data. Rosalie Wax describes the problem:

> Many tribal or folk societies not only maintain a strict division of labor between the sexes and ages, but the people who fall into these different categories do not converse freely or spontaneously with each other even when they eat, sleep and live in the same dwelling. For example, a young male anthropologist might live in an Indian household and even carry on with the Indian girls and yet learn very little about what women—old or young—think, say or do. . . . Conversely, I, as a middle-aged woman, was never able to converse openly or informally with either the old or the young Indian men at Thrashing Buffalo. The older men, even when I knew them fairly well, would tend to deliver lectures to me; the younger men, as was proper, were always too bashful or formally respectful to say much. With the Indian matrons, on the other hand, I could talk for hours. (1971, p. 46; see also R. Wax 1979)

Wax is writing about a special situation of doing research among traditional groups in rural settings, but her general point is equally applicable to doing research among secular populations in metropolitan areas. If you are African-American, access to white supremacists will, to put it mildly, be severely limited. Nor are you likely to reach the desired "intimate familiarity" if you are male and attempting to study a beauty parlor clique composed of middle-aged women.

During the last ten years or so, the many writings on fieldwork have, with increasing attention and sensitivity, documented the myriad contexts and situations in which ascriptive categories (especially sex) can throw up barriers to the acquisition of rich data (see, for example, Dorn 1986; El-Or 1992; Martin 1978, 1980; Reinharz 1992, Chapters 2 and 3; Warren 1988; Wasserfall 1993; R. Wax 1979). While we applaud these contributions, we must admit to a certain concern that, if viewed en masse, such otherwise sensible warnings may come to reify (give undeserved solidity to) the barrier quality of human physical and other differences. Ascriptive identity categories are, without question, realities—albeit socially constructed ones—and therefore need to be taken into account in planning your research. But they should not be *overemphasized*. (For accounts of the intricacy of the links between sex and access, for example, see Golde, ed., 1986.) Just because you are not "identical" to the persons you wish to study, you should not automatically conclude that such research is impossible or even unusually difficult. The literature of the naturalistic tradition resoundingly contradicts any such conclusion. Being female and Jewish, for example, did not prevent Ruth Horowitz from developing a sensitive analysis of the world of Chicano gang members (1983, 1986). Being adults did not deny Myra Bluebond-Langer, Gary Alan Fine, Nancy Mandell, or Barrie Thorne intimate access to the world of children (Bluebond-Langer 1978; Fine 1987; Fine and Sandstrom 1988; Mandell 1986, 1988; Thorne, 1993). Being an American academic did not prove an insurmountable barrier for Nancy Scheper-Hughes in her attempt to understand the emotional meanings of children and death among impoverished Brazilians (1992). Being white did not prevent Elliot Liebow from producing a classic ethnography of the world of African-American streetcorner men (1967), any more than being a middle-class male prevented him from entering the subjective world of homeless women (1993). Being Jewish did not block Sherryl Kleinman's access to ministerial students of the United Methodist Church (1984), just as being young, white and educated did not block Mitchell Duneier's access to the (mostly) elderly and (mostly) African-American working-class clientele of a South Chicago cafeteria (1992). And, even granting some validity to recent internally generated critiques of the discipline of anthropology (e.g., Clifford and Marcus, eds., 1986; Kuklick 1991; Stocking, ed., 1989), much of its rich literature remains convincing testimony to the human capacity to transcend national and cultural differences.

3. Large Settings

Although fieldwork is traditionally, and perhaps even usually, performed by the "solo operator" (Manning 1977) or "lone wolf" (Florez and Kelling

1984), the size and complexity of some research locales or topics may set up formidable barriers between the single fieldworker and the data she or he is seeking. In these circumstances, the possibility of team research should at least be considered. Unquestionably, very large teams often generate very large problems, especially if many of their members are "hired hands" (Florez and Kelling 1984; Roth 1966; Staggenborg 1988). Even in two- or three-person teams, and even when the members have equal status and responsibility, difficulties of communication and coordination can arise (Shaffir, Marshall, and Haas 1980). Nonetheless, numerous fieldstudies have been successfully accomplished by two or more persons working together (see, for example, Becker, Geer, and Hughes 1968; Becker, Geer, Hughes, and Strauss 1961; Glaser and Strauss 1968, 1965; Snow and Anderson 1993; Snow, Robinson, and McCall 1991).

4. Difficult Settings

Some settings or aspects of social life are easier to research than others. Gathering rich data through observation in open public settings can usually be accomplished with a minimum of misadventure (Cahill 1990; L. Lofland 1985b; Nash and Nash 1994; Ortiz 1994). Doing so in situations of intergroup or intragroup conflict—such as a nation-state defined as "forbidden terrain" by your own government (Fuller 1988, 1987, 1986), during civil war (Joseph 1983, 1978), or amidst the suspicions and violence of the "cocaine culture" (Morales 1989a, 1989b; Williams 1989a, 1989b)—may be extraordinarily difficult. But even in the absence of immediate conflict, pieces of social life may be so shrouded in mystery that even knowing about them, much less gaining intimate familiarity with them, may be problematic. Examples include the day-to-day workings of a segment of the Central Intelligence Agency, the details of the business dealings of the economically powerful, and the arcane rituals of such otherwise innocuous groups as Masons and Greek letter societies.

While we consider it appropriate for the prospective investigator to assess the possible difficulties inherent in the setting of interest, we do not wish to suggest that you should necessarily avoid difficult settings. The difficulty may, on closer inspection, turn out to be illusory. But even if it is real, difficulty does not necessarily equal impossibility, as the preceding citations clearly attest. And if the setting or situation is an especially significant or interesting one, even a partial study of it will be better than none at all. Similarly, the well-known belief in social science that it is easier to "study down" than to "study up" (that is, to study the less powerful rather than the more powerful) probably has some basis in fact. But that belief has also undoubtedly discouraged the execution of studies that would contradict it. Premature foreclosures such as this do a disservice to social science and to social knowledge in general and should be avoided. You should bear in mind that numerous social groups popularly presumed to be difficult to "get to" have been studied well—for example, elite surgeons (Bosk 1979), upper-class women (Ostrander 1984), top business executives (Thomas 1994), nuclear weapons researchers (Gusterson forthcoming), and national defense intellectuals (Cohn 1987).

C. Evaluating for Ethics

Ethical problems, questions, and dilemmas are an integral part of the research experience (especially the naturalistic research experience) as much as they are a part of the experience of everyday life. We shall repeatedly be concerned with ethical matters in the following chapters, for they are especially acute, or at least acutely *felt*, while the research is in progress. Here, in the context of data site evaluation, two critical and closely related questions require the prospective investigator's serious consideration. First, should this particular group, setting, situation, question, or whatever be studied by *anyone?* Second, should this group, setting, situation, question, or whatever be studied by *me?* In asking these questions of yourself, you are assessing the *potential negative consequences* (see below) that the research or its publication might have for various parties (including yourself) and your ethical evaluation of these consequences.

Traditionally, neither question was problematic in social science. Rather, the conventional wisdom held that knowledge was *always* better than ignorance and that, therefore, everything that could be studied should be studied by anyone who had or could obtain access. In the last twenty years, however, that conventional wisdom has come under increasing challenge.

Relative to the question of *anyone* doing a particular study, four kinds of challenges have been made. First, some studies have been called ethically unacceptable because they are "trivial" (for example, aspects of everyday life, Moore 1963) or because the subject matter is "immoral" (for example, the act of mugging, Posner, 1980). Second, some have argued that under conditions of economic and/or political oppression of some populations by other populations, the protection of the less powerful may demand that knowledge about them not be made available to the more powerful (for example, George 1976; Glazer 1972; Sjoberg, ed., 1967). Third, a significant body of opinion in the social sciences holds that, because it involves intentional and continuing deception of the observed by the observer, all (or almost all) covert research is unethical (Bulmer 1982; Bulmer, ed., 1982; Erikson 1967; Kelman 1972, 1970; Warwick 1980, 1975). The American Sociological Association's *Code of Ethics* gives somewhat equivocal support to this position by its injunctions that

> Informed consent must be obtained when the risks of research are greater than the risks of everyday life. Where [even] modest risk or harm is

anticipated, informed consent must be obtained. . . . Sociologists should take culturally appropriate steps to secure informed consent. . . . Special actions may be necessary where the individuals studied are illiterate, have very low status, or are unfamiliar with social research. (1989, p. 3)

And fourth, some feminists have argued (sometimes only implicitly) that research in which there is an absence of equality and full sympathy between researcher and researched violates the tenets of feminist ethics (McNaron, ed., 1985; Oakley 1985, 1981; Ruzek 1978; Stacey 1988; but see Reinharz 1993, pp. 72–75; on the limits on intimacy with informants, see El-Or 1992). A corollary line of thought recommends that, as much as possible, feminist research be collaborative and at the service of the objectives and needs of the researched population (Cancian 1993, 1992).

The first challenge, representing as it does a kind of social science "moral majority" viewpoint, we consider frivolous and—if taken seriously—a threat to free inquiry. However, although we find ourselves in considerable disagreement with them, the other challenges do not seem to us subject to such easy dismissal. Consequently, as we proceed, we will have more to say about the three "undismissed" positions and about the arguments for and against them.

In the face of these varied blanket proscriptions and of the arguments pro and con, how are you to proceed? We would suggest that the decision whether or not you should study some aspect of social life— that is, the answer to the question of whether this group, setting, situation, question, or whatever should be studied by *me*—and the ethical basis or bases for that decision, are matters that must be left to you. This question touches on your particular and personal relation to the group or setting or question, on your values, and on the values of others who are supportive of and significant to you. We urge only that your decision be *consciously* made and that you clearly *articulate* to yourself the basis or bases for making it.

D. Evaluating for Immediate Risk

Earlier in this chapter, in the context of our discussion of access, we pointed to the problems posed by the "difficult" setting—that is, the setting in which international politics, intra- or intergroup conflicts, the power and status of participants, and so forth, may set up barriers to intimate familiarity. But settings may be difficult in another sense as well. Some settings may confront researchers with immediate risks to their physical or emotional well-being (or both). This aspect of the "research adventure," while receiving scant attention in the literature (but see Cannon 1992; Howell, ed., 1990; Kleinman and Copp 1993; Sluka 1990; Wiley 1987; Williams et al. 1992), has certainly been the stuff of fieldworker rumor and legend. One "hears," for example, of a person who had established herself in a setting (say, a cancer ward), but within weeks had found it much too emotionally painful to continue, and simply withdrew. Or, one gets a thirdhand account of the death of someone, who is said to have been murdered in the course of carrying out his studies of the drug culture. Or, as a last example, rumor has it that yet a third person got divorced in the midst of her research because her marriage could not withstand the "problems" she continually brought home from the field. We suggested above that ethical problems are no more prevalent in research than in everyday life, but also no less. Similarly, we would argue that physical and emotional risks are no more prevalent in the research context than in everyday life, but again, also no less. And given that everyday life is, after all, a minefield of dangers, the prudent person will not make a firm commitment to a field setting without first assessing it for risk. Before commencing your research, then, you need to think seriously and realistically (and to talk with others whose judgment you trust) about the level of physical and/or emotional danger you may have to face and about how able and how willing you are to face it.

E. Evaluating for Personal Consequences

Finally, there is the matter of the personal consequences of one's accomplished research to be considered. Because it involves peering into an unknowable future, this kind of assessment is more difficult, more elusive, more a matter of guesswork than are assessments for the proximate issues of appropriateness, access, ethics, or risk. But the fact that personal consequences cannot be known with any certainty does not mean that they cannot be considered and weighed and pondered. Imperfect forethought is better than no thought at all.

The successful completion of a research project is, for most of us most of the time, an occasion for self-congratulations. We have demonstrated that we are the sort of people who are capable not only of gathering data, but also of analyzing them in an interesting manner (see Chapters 8 and 9) and in communicating that analysis to others (see Chapter 10). Such a demonstration is certainly a sufficient reason for feeling good about ourselves. It may also prove a sufficient reason for others—colleagues, the people studied, a broader readership—to feel good about us, to give us their regard, their esteem, their respect. Unfortunately, however, the personal consequences of a completed project are not always or always exclusively so positive. Three examples should give you a flavor of what we mean.

First, there is the possibility that you will experience what might be called an "ethical hangover": a persistent sense of guilt or unease over what is viewed as a betrayal of the people under study. The closer your emotional relationship to those persons, the more you can feel that both in leaving the setting and in transforming your personal understanding of it into public knowledge, you have committed a kind of treason (see, for example, Bluebond-Langer 1978; Heilman 1980; Thorne 1979;

Stacey 1988; Watkins 1983). It is not clear whether there is any way to forestall this experience. In fact, some would argue that it is the "just desserts" of the naturalistic investigator. One veteran fieldworker has eloquently stated the case:

> Even [in field situations] in which the [researcher] openly represents himself to his subjects for what he is (i.e., a person whose interest in them is professional rather than personal), he unavoidably and properly I would hold, invites unto himself the classic dilemma of compromising involvement in the lives of others. Filling him with gossip, advice, invitations to dinner and solicitations of opinion, they devilishly make it evident that whereas he may regard himself as the *tabula rasa* incarnate upon whom the mysteries of the group are to be writ, they can only see him as someone less detached and less sublime. There then follows for many a fieldworker the unsettling recognition that, within very broad limits, it is precisely when his subjects palpably relate to him in his "out-of-research role" self . . . that the *raison d'etre* for his "in-role" self is most nearly realized; they are more themselves, they tell and "give away" more, they supply connections and insights which he would otherwise have never grasped. . . .
>
> It is in large measure due to this ineluctable transmutation of role posture in field situations that, when he later reports, the [researcher] often experiences a certain guilt, a sense of having betrayed, a stench of disreputability about himself. . . . I would hold that it is just and fitting that he be made to squirm so, because in having exploited his non-scientific self . . . for ends other than those immediately apprehended by his subjects, he has in some significant sense violated the collective conscience of the community, if not that of the profession. (F. Davis 1961, p. 365)

As the second example, there is the very small but nonetheless real possibility that your report will be of interest to the criminal-justice system and that you may be called upon to divulge information that you withheld from the final report (the real names of participants, for example) or information that you may have acquired subsequent to the research but that you consider still covered by the confidentiality assurances (discussed just below and in later chapters) given during the research. Consider the case of Rik Scarce, a graduate student at Washington State University who, in 1993, refused to answer a grand jury's questions about participants in the animal rights movement who were the subjects of his 1990 book *Ecowarriors: Understanding the Radical Environmental Movement* (the grand jury was investigating a 1991 raid on a Pullman, Washington research laboratory). As a consequence of his refusal, Scarce was incarcerated in the Spokane County jail for 159 days until a judge ruled that his detention had surpassed the law's intent of "coercion" and instead become "punitive" (Monaghan 1993b). Note that Scarce's decision "not to tell" was anything but idiosyncratic. He argued that he was "bound by the American Sociological Association's code of ethics, one part of which requires that scholars maintain confidentiality 'even when this information enjoys no legal protection or privilege and legal force is applied' " (Monaghan 1993a, p. A9), and the Association supported this argument, filing an *amicus brief* on his behalf (Levine 1993).

Most well-done fieldwork reports seem to be met with praise from at least some quarters and no reaction at all from others. But there is always the possibility of a third sort of negative consequence. In addition to praise and disinterest, your written report may generate a significant amount of approbation from your colleagues (for example, Humphreys 1975; Mathews 1983; Posner 1980), from the people studied (for example, Scheper-Hughes 1981; Vidich and Bensman 1968), or both (for example, Adler, Adler, and Johnson 1992; Whyte 1993, pp. 357–371). Among the myriad possible charges, you may be criticized for betraying your informants, for putting them at risk, for unflattering portraits of them, for not getting the story right, or for getting the story right but not telling it in the right way.

In urging you to give thought to future consequences you cannot possibly predict, we risk being viewed as alarmist, as causing unnecessary and unprofitable worry. But it seems to us that this is one instance in which the following "cliché" truly deserves to be cast as "folk wisdom": To be forewarned *is*, at least to some degree, to be forearmed.

IV. A Concluding Word of Caution

These words of advice, especially those dealing with proximate matters of assessment, should not be construed as suggesting that problems, issues, ethical dilemmas, strategies for surmounting barriers, and so on can all be resolved or determined beforehand and that you can then simply proceed tidily and without difficulty to put your research plan into practice. Nothing could be further from the truth. Naturalistic research is first and foremost *emergent*. Today's solutions may become tomorrow's problems; tomorrow's problems may provide special research opportunities the day after. "Who" you are at the beginning of the research is not necessarily the same "who" that will emerge at the end. Ethical decisions made before entering the field may prove moot; other unforeseen and perhaps unsolvable dilemmas may arise. This emergent character is what gives "being in the field" its edge, its complexity, its vigor, and, for many people, its excitement; it is also what necessitates *flexibility* on the part of the investigator.

You evaluate data sites, then, not because doing so will make your life as a researcher a bed of roses, but because doing so may help to remove a few of the thorns.

CHAPTER 3

GETTING IN

The process of deciding what is meaningful to study and whether you have (or can gain) ethical and appropriate access to rich data may involve conversations and consultations with others, but the decisions themselves are *personal*. When decision is translated into action, when your intention to do research is translated into beginning that research, then you encounter the first truly *social* moment of naturalistic investigation: getting in or gaining the acceptance of the people being studied.

It is one thing to decide for yourself about interest, appropriateness, accessibility and ethics; it is quite another to get all the interested parties to go along with your plan.

In some forms of research, the investigator has considerable power over the research "subjects." Laboratory animal research or medical research with captive human populations are extreme examples. But in the main, naturalistic social research is not one of these forms. In this tradition, you look at and/or listen to people either because the people freely agree to it or because they do not know they are being studied. And since there is little or nothing to stop them from refusing to be interviewed, from denying an observer entree into their lives, or from throwing out or shutting out a secret investigator who is "uncovered," getting in naturally concerns all potential researchers.

The specific form of relationship a prospective investigator has or will develop with the people or setting of interest generates its own set of problems, ethical questions, and solutions regarding the process of entry. The varieties of such relationships have been diversely formulated. Buford Junker's (1960) well-known typology of fieldwork roles—the complete observer, the participant observer, the complete participant, the observer participant—is one example. Schatzman and Strauss (1973) distinguished among watching from the outside, passive presence, limited interaction, active control, the observer as participant, and participation with hidden identity. Adler and Adler (1987) contrast what they see as the more "detached" roles of observer, observer–interactant, observer–interactant–participant, observer–interactant–participant–investigator with the more "involved" roles of peripheral member,

active member, complete member and good-faith member. Such elaborate formulations are quite useful in some contexts, but for our purposes, a simpler set of distinctions will suffice.

We shall consider the "getting in" aspect of naturalistic research as
experienced (1) by *unknown* investigators, either in public and open
settings or in closed settings, and (2) by *known* investigators who are
either full participants in the setting or outsiders whose research role is
primary. We will conclude this chapter by discussing two additional
relevant problems: legal, political, and bureaucratic barriers, and the
question of confidentiality.

I. The Unknown Investigator

Getting in is not really a problem if you are not known as a researcher to
the people you are studying. You simply take up or continue playing a
role in the setting and begin logging data "on the sly." What is problematic is the *ethical status* of covert research itself.

In this section, we consider three types of hidden research. Probably
the least controversial form is research conducted in public and open
settings. Doing research in a closed setting in which you are already a
member is more marginal. The most controversial research arrangement
involves taking on a role in a closed setting for the secret purpose of
researching it.

Two qualifications are in order before we proceed. First, some forms
of naturalistic research cannot be conducted secretly. It *is* possible to
interview persons who do not quite understand your exact role as
interviewer. For example, a number of Rosalie Wax's early interviewees
in a Japanese internment camp believed that she was a sympathetic
newspaper reporter (1971, p. 53). It is also possible to interview "infor-
mally" without fully letting on that one is doing so (Riecken 1969; Snow,
Zurcher, and Sjoberg 1982). However, it does *not* appear possible to do
intensive interviewing (as we define it in Chapter 5) covertly. Therefore,
the following discussion applies only to participant observation.

Second, while the distinctions we make in this chapter are useful for
clarity, actual researchers and settings do not fall into such discrete
categories. In the real world, what is a public and open setting and what
is a closed one may not be all that obvious. Indeed, as we shall see, the
line between open and secret research gets fuzzy when examined closely.

A. Public and Open Settings

If a setting is public and open, that is, defined in law and tradition as a
place where "anyone" has a right to be, it is a very simple matter to enter
it for purposes of doing research. When Lyn Lofland (1985b) observed
public places (for example, waiting areas of bus depots and airports),

she simply entered and sat down. When Spencer Cahill and his students studied public restrooms, their entree "problems" involved only the physical skills necessary to get through the appropriate doors (Cahill et al. 1985). Similarly, Elijah Anderson's "access" to interclass and interracial street interaction required nothing more complex than his physical presence in the public areas of a mixed neighborhood (1990). Partly because getting into public and open settings presents so few problems, such settings are frequently the training sites for untrained and "unleashed" undergraduates, to use James Myers's term (1969, p. 155).

While it can be argued that such research is clearly unethical (it does, after all, involve deceit by omission if not commission) serious ethical debate seldom lingers on this research situation. Presumably the impossibility, if not the ludicrousness, of removing the deception is one reason. As Julius Roth has noted, "When we are observing a crowd welcoming a hero, it is obviously absurd to say that we should warn everybody in the crowd that a sociologist is interpreting their behavior" (1970, p. 279). The presumption that no harm can come to any of the people observed is another reason. A third, perhaps, is the frequent "ho-hum" attitude of people when they learn they are being researched. Natalie Allon's experience is typical:

> When I expressed my intellectual curiosity about the [singles] bars, quite a few male and female patrons laughed me off. They said that I had a most sophisticated, protective defense if I did not wind up meeting a man whom I liked and who liked me. After all, whether or not I succeeded in meeting a man, I would always succeed in collecting information. Some said that doing research was a most clever introductory greeting, and they were going to try such a line as they met others. Some told me to relax and take it easy—I was single and drinking and so a member of the scene just like everybody else. They said that everybody in the scene had ulterior motives and mine happened to be research. (1979, pp. 68–69)

B. Closed Settings

The serious ethical questioning about covert research begins when the researcher moves out of the public realm and into the private, that is, into a closed setting, access to which is not granted to just "anybody." Gary Fine has referred to this situation as "deep cover":

> In research studies in which subjects are not aware that they are under investigation, the position of the researcher is structurally equivalent to that of the undercover intelligence agent, although presumably there is a different set of motives. In that situation, the researcher may witness a wide variety of behaviors but simultaneously may find it difficult to inquire about any of these behaviors without the cover being suspect. A

cover that is blown in such a situation—when subjects discover that their *new member* is actually a professional observer—may have profound implications. This uncovering discredits not only the research . . . but [also] the researcher . . . , and perhaps the entire scientific enterprise. (1980, p. 124, emphasis added)

It is precisely the "spy" quality of covert research in closed settings that raises questions about its propriety in social science. In fact, as we noted in Chapter 2, some people argue that an investigator who takes a position for the purpose of secretly researching the setting is committing the most unethical research act in the naturalistic tradition. Certainly the high value that feminists place on equality and sympathy between researcher and researched is badly and baldly compromised by the knowledge imbalance inherent in covert research. To concur with Sheryl Ruzek (1978, pp. xi–xii) that "presenting an identity other than [the researcher's] own violates the ethos of many groups and individuals" is necessarily to eschew whatever advantages "deep cover" might offer.

Interestingly enough, for some persons at least, if the research project arises after you have become part of the setting—a frequent corollary of "starting where you are"—the moral onus seems less severe (e.g., Bulmer 1982). Thus some social scientists who equivocate about secret research in settings where one is already "in place" and who find no moral difficulties with doing it in public and open settings are adamant that entering a setting for the purpose of secret research should not be allowed (Erikson 1967; Gibbons and Jones 1975, Ch. 9; Warwick 1982). Julius Roth's comments on what might be viewed as moral hair-splitting among social scientists are apt:

Does the manner in which one comes to be a secret observer affect the morality of the situation? Is it moral if one gets a job in a factory to earn tuition and then takes advantage of the opportunity to carry out a sociological study, but immoral to deliberately plant oneself in the factory for the express purpose of observing one's fellow workers? If the outcome is the same—e.g., if the manner in which the observations are used is the same—I for one see no moral difference in these two situations, but I find some of my colleagues do not agree with this position. (1970, p. 279)

Our view is that there are very serious, perhaps damning, ethical problems in *all* covert research *if* the presumed immorality of deception is the overriding concern. Deception is no less present in public and open-setting research than in preplanned, "deep-cover" research in closed settings. On the other hand, if other concerns are also important (for example, lack of harm to those researched, or the theoretical importance of a setting that can never be studied openly), then we can find no more justification for abolishing *all* deep-cover research, preplanned or not, than for abolishing secret research in public settings. We must admit also to the view that a portion of these adamant calls for the pristine purity of openness are just a touch naive. Among many other complexities, ethnographic researchers do not, despite the presumptions of the moralists, have complete control over "who" the researched will take them to be. As Richard Mitchell has noted:

> Qualitative investigators . . . may seek to present themselves in one manner or another . . . , but subjects can and usually do reinterpret, transform, or sometimes altogether reject these presentations in favor of their own. During his 2-year research sojourn to acutely segregated South Africa in the early 1960s, [Pierre] van den Berghe attempted to act, according to the dictates of his conscience, as if race was of no consequence. This behavior was accounted for in a variety of ways by the South Africans. He was viewed by Whites as a Communist agitator, an odd foreigner who had not yet learned to "handle the Natives" (van den Berghe, 1967, p. 189), or as merely socially inept. Blacks classified his behavior as that of a police informer, agent provocateur, missionary do-gooder, or paternalist (van den Berghe, 1967, p. 190). Virtually no one, White or Black, understood his actions as expressions of the nonmaterialistic Gandhian socialism to which he was personally committed (1993, p. 12). (See also Hilbert 1980; Punch 1986, Chs. 2 and 4; Friedman 1990b provides an account of the advantages of, as well as particular obligations incurred by, covert research.)

As in all other ethical dilemmas of naturalistic research, we believe that the ethically sensitive, thoughtful, and knowledgeable investigator is the best judge of whether covert research is justified. The key words here, however, are *sensitive, thoughtful,* and *knowledgeable.* We would suggest that you undertake no covert research (at least none in closed settings) before you have acquainted yourself with the problems, debates, and dilemmas associated with such research. You should, at minimum, be familiar with the code of ethics (if any) of your discipline and you should know how covert research is viewed by the theory groups or other subdisciplinary clusters with which you identify (e.g., feminist sociologists). Beyond that, the following books and book chapters are recommended as useful introductions to the issues:

Secrecy and Fieldwork by Richard G. Mitchell, Jr. (1993).

Chapter Six on "Ethical Issues and Concerns" in Bruce L. Berg, *Qualitative Research Methods for the Social Sciences* (1989).

Handbook on Ethical Issues in Anthropology edited by Joan Cassell and Sue-Ellen Jacobs (1987).

The Politics and Ethics of Fieldwork by Maurice Punch (1986).

Chapter Nine on "Ethical Problems, Ethical Principles and Field Research Practice," in Robert G. Burgess, *In the Field: An Introduction to Field Research* (1984).

Social Research Ethics edited by Martin Bulmer (1982).

Chapter XIII on "Deceptive Social Science Research," in Sissela Bok, *Lying: Moral Choice in Public and Private Life* (1978).

"Sociological Snoopers and Journalistic Moralizers: Retrospective on Ethical Issues," in Laud Humphreys, *Tearoom Trade: Impersonal Sex in Public Places* (1975).

II. The Known Investigator

Writers on naturalistic methodology generally conceive the major entry problems of the known investigator to be *strategic* rather than ethical, implying a rather sharp distinction between open and covert research. For the sake of clarity, this distinction is a useful one. However, it is also essentially artificial. Once again, it is Julius Roth who has stated the case most succinctly:

> All research is secret in some ways and to some degree—we never tell the subjects "everything". . . . So long as there exists a separation of role between the researchers and those researched upon, the gathering of information will inevitably have some hidden aspects even if one is an openly declared observer. The following are at least some of the reasons for this.
>
> 1. The researcher usually does not know everything he is looking for himself when he first starts out and structures his study to some extent as he goes along. Some of the things he finds of interest to study as the research goes on are things which the subjects might have objected to if they had been told about it in the beginning.
>
> 2. In many types of studies of social behavior, the researcher does not want the subject's behavior influenced by his knowledge of what the observer is interested in.
>
> 3. Even if the subjects of a study are given as precise and detailed an explanation of the purpose and procedure of the study as the investigator is able to give them, the subjects will not understand all the terms of the research in the same way that the investigator does. The terms used have different connotations to them, their experiential contexts differ, and their conceptions of the goals of the study are likely to be different. . . . (1970, pp. 278–279; see also Fine 1993; Hilbert 1980)

And, Roth might have added, all research is secret to some degree because the people under study do not always believe and/or remember that the researcher *is* a researcher (Mitchell 1993, pp. 12–13 and Ch. 5; Peneff 1985; Thorne 1980, 1979).

Bearing in mind, then, that the ethical dilemmas engendered by covert research have not disappeared with the decision to be a known investigator but have merely been muted, let us concentrate on the strategic problem of entry. This differs somewhat depending on whether one is already a full participant in the setting.

A. The Participant Researcher Role

The principle of "starting where you are," as we have seen, leads many naturalistic investigators to do research in their own "nests," as it were. If they decide to conduct that research openly, they have the task (as do outside researchers) of making their intentions known, gaining cooperation from the setting participants, and, depending on the character of the setting, perhaps seeking formal permission. The participant researcher, however, has the advantage of already knowing the "cast of characters." The outside researcher must discover whom to ask or tell, whom to ask or tell *first*, whether formal permission is required, whether a letter is necessary, and so forth. To the participant researcher, such knowledge is part of the badge of membership and easily (if not always successfully) put to use.

B. The Outside Researcher Role

The major strategic problem of getting in, then, falls to the outsider seeking admission to a setting for the purpose of observing it or access to individuals for the purpose of interviewing them. Researchers deal with a wide range of topics, settings, and situations, and the types of people who might stand between them and their research are necessarily much too varied for the strategies of getting through or around them to be succinctly codified. The experiences of many fieldworkers over the years, however, suggest that you are more likely to be successful in your quest for access if you enter negotiations armed with *connections, accounts, knowledge,* and *courtesy.*

1. Connections

There is a great deal of wisdom in the old saying, "It's who you know that counts." Gaining entry to a setting or getting permission to do an interview is greatly expedited if you have "connections." For example, the anthropologist Joan Cassell writes of the considerable difficulty she had gaining access to surgeons: a year's negotiation with a representative of the Department of Surgery where her ex-husband was an attending physician resulted only in a denial of access; six months of wrangling to obtain an interview with a representative of the American College of Surgeons led only to the advice that she become

> active in the Ladies Auxiliary of your husband's hospital. . . . Eventually, at almost the last minute, when a reviewer for the agency that eventually

funded my study asked for proof that I had access to surgeons, a friend of my ex-husband said I could do research in the hospital where he was Chief of Surgery (and wrote a letter to that effect). (1988, p. 94)

Sometimes, the initial contact may be at some social distance from the desired research setting but still able to link the prospective investigator to marginals who, in turn, link her to central actors. Susan Ostrander's experience in this regard is almost a "textbook case" and is worth quoting at some length.

> For a period of months before beginning my project on upper-class women, a project that began as my Ph.D. dissertation, I talked with my fellow graduate students and professors about my plans. One day, a fellow graduate student told me she had worked on an electoral campaign with a woman she thought met the criteria for upper-class membership that I was intending to use. . . . I contacted this woman and told her of my interest in "learning about the role of women in some of the old and influential families in town." As is often true of first contacts, this woman was somewhat marginal to her class. . . . She nonetheless met the criteria of upper-class membership and, even more important, was known and respected by others. . . . She told me that it was important to "go in the right order. You have to start at the top." . . . She offered to call three of these [top] women for me and arrange their consent. She was successful, and I interviewed them, explaining my project by telling them that people knew a great deal about what men in families like theirs did with their lives but that very little was known about what women did. At the end of the interviews, I asked if they could refer me to other women like themselves, with similar backgrounds, and if I could use their names. They agreed and offered to call the women they mentioned to say they had spoken with me. I was in. (1993, pp. 9–10)

These examples are by no means exceptional. It seems quite typical for outside researchers to gain access to settings or persons through contacts they have already established. They cast about among their friends, acquaintances, colleagues, and the like either for someone who is already favorably regarded by the person or persons with access control or for someone who can link them to such a person. This is, of course, the major principle involved in what, in interview studies, is called "snowball" or "chain-referral" sampling: a method that "yields a study sample through referrals made among people who are or know of others who possess some characteristics that are of research interest" (Biernacki and Waldorf 1981, p. 141). Thus, as we can see from the above quotation, after having been put in touch with her initial informant by a colleague, Susan Ostrander then asked that woman to recommend others to whom she might talk, beginning the snowball or chain-referral process. In short, then, wherever possible, you should try to use and/or build upon *preexisting relations of trust* to remove barriers to entrance.

2. Accounts

It is well worth your while to expend time and effort developing a careful explanation or account of the proposed research. Whether you are using the method of intensive interviewing or of participant observation, you are asking people to grant access to their lives, their minds, their emotions. They have every reason for wanting to know why they should allow such an intrusion. Judging from the testimony of veteran fieldworkers, the best accounts are brief, relatively straightforward and appropriate to their audience.

- Most listeners are not going to be interested in the details of the researcher's "pet" enthusiasm. What they want is a *brief* and direct answer to the question, "Why should I let you _____?" and not a scholarly treatise. As we saw in the Ostrander quote above, a simple and nontechnical account will often suffice. Many researchers find it unnecessary, at least initially, to say little more than "I am writing a book on _____" (Horowitz 1989; Williams quoted in Williams et al. 1992, p. 349). However, should you be asked for more detail, you must certainly be prepared to supply it. (In bureaucratic settings, for example, a written research proposal may be requested.)

- While appreciating the truth of Julius Roth's assertion (quoted above) that "we never tell the subjects 'everything,'" it is nonetheless advisable to provide an account that is as *straightforward* as you can make it. If you have decided to do "open" research, there is no point in complicating an already complicated situation by starting out with evasions or outright lies, or with promises (for example, censorship rights) you will not keep. There will be plenty of difficulties in getting along in the field despite the best of intentions and plans. Setting yourself up at the outset for later charges of deceit is simply begging unnecessary trouble. Still, it must be admitted that "fudging" one's account a bit—what Fine (1980) calls "shallow cover"—seems a fairly widespread practice (as when sociologists claim to be compiling "a recent history" rather than doing a sociological investigation). Perhaps the best advice was proffered by Erving Goffman: "I like a story such that if they find out what you are doing, the story you presented could not be an absolute lie. If they don't find out what you're doing, the story you presented doesn't get in your way" (1989, p. 127; see also Fine 1993; Mitchell 1993).

- Finally, accounts should be *appropriate to their audience:* The way the story is told (not the story itself) should be tailored to the people hearing it. What you tell the director of a nursery school and what you tell the children cannot be identical if you wish to be straightforward with both the director and the children (on "accounting" to children, see Fine and Glassner 1979; Fine and Sandstrom 1988; Mandell 1988).

While your account is supposed to help you gain initial access to the research site and is thus deserving of care in its preparation, it would nonetheless be an error to attach too much importance to it. As Rosalie Wax reminds us:

> Most sensible people do not believe what a stranger tells them. In the long run, [the investigator's] hosts will judge and trust him, not because of what he [initially] says about himself or about his research, but by the style in which he lives and acts, by the way he treats them. (1971, p. 365)

3. Knowledge

As we shall see in the next chapter, one tried-and-true strategy for getting along in the field is to adopt a "learner" or even "incompetent" role. Since you are seeking to learn, it makes sense to act accordingly; the know-it-all or expert is not likely to be "taught." Like all good things, however, this strategy can be pushed too far, and when it is, it becomes a liability. The getting-in stage of research is one point where overplaying the learner can have negative, perhaps fatal, conse-quences. If you are to avoid being perceived as either frivolous or stupid and dismissed as such, you should have enough knowledge about the setting or people you wish to study *to appear competent to do so.* How much knowledge will be enough will vary, of course. If you wish to study the "mothering" experience, it may be enough to know that the persons from whom you are requesting interviews are, in fact, females and mothers. On the other hand, as George Moyser advises, if you are studying elites, your background research may need to be quite extensive.

> [I]f the researcher is to realize to the full the benefits of an open-ended and flexible exchange then the ground must indeed be worked over very thoroughly ahead of time. This involves, first of all, the researcher be-coming acquainted with the relevant elite procedures, symbols and ter-minology, as well as significant events, dates and personalities of the moment. As these will form the reference points of responses, the re-searcher must be able quickly to appreciate their significance and to use them in questions with an air of familiarity. This will in turn help both to build the necessary degree of seriousness and rapport with the respon-dent and to avoid being fobbed off with trite, standardized or superficial answers.
>
> To the same general ends, relevant background information concern-ing each particular respondent must also be obtained. (1988, p. 123; see also Thomas 1993)

Age and other personal statuses may also affect how much prior knowledge is "enough." We suspect, for example, that younger re-searchers may be granted more leeway in this regard, since their lack of knowledge is compatible with their age. However, in some settings (highly technical ones, for example) younger researchers may need to demonstrate *more knowledge* than would their older counterparts in order to appear competent because youth itself may be taken as a negative indicator. And when "incompetent" statuses are compounded, so trouble may be. For example, researchers who are young and female and therefore "unthreatening" are often granted easy entree to research settings. But in some of these (highly technical and highly masculine ones, for example) this advantage may prove a double-edged sword. If "unthreatening" translates into "unserious," one may find oneself merely humored by participants, resulting in one's data collection efforts being seriously hampered (Gurney 1985).

4. Courtesy
Last, and perhaps most important, you will enhance your possibilities for gaining entry if courtesy enters the negotiations. Consider the following:

- It is courteous to seek interviews by writing or phoning (or both) the prospective interviewees to request their cooperation and to inquire about a convenient time and place, rather than by showing up unannounced at their homes or offices.

- It is courteous to inform interested parties of your research, even if you do not need their immediate cooperation and they are not going to be part of the group studied.

- It is courteous to take the task of getting permission from dependent or subordinate populations you wish to study (children or the hospitalized mentally retarded, for example) as seriously as the task of getting permission from their caretakers.

- It is courteous to help others know who you are through connections, to provide them with a reasonable account of what you want to do, and to demonstrate enough knowledge to suggest your competence to do it.

III. Political, Legal, and Bureaucratic Barriers

Recent political and legal trends around the world have exacerbated the already highly problematic character of "getting in," rendering some naturalistic studies exceedingly difficult, if not impossible. In the main, the difficulties emanate not from the most directly interested parties—the persons to be researched or their immediate caretakers or supervisors—but from the political, legal, or bureaucratic units of the nation-state.

For example, Third World leaders increasingly perceive Western anthropologists as representing cultural, political, and/or economic imperialism and therefore deny them access to many Third World societies (Glazer 1972; Sjoberg, ed., 1967). In Great Britain, the Official Secrets

Act of 1911, with its "potentially draconian sanctions" has, according to George Moyser, made access to

> civil servants (and . . . to official documents) very difficult (see Campbell, 1983, p. 357–61). Arthur (1987), indeed, claims that the Act constitutes an "invisible barrier" which "the tenacious researcher constantly confronts—becoming more visible the more sensitive the agenda of the research." (Moyser 1988, pp. 119–120)

And in the United States, some research sites—Cuba, for example—have been turned into "forbidden terrain" by government officials acting to protect what are defined as foreign-policy interests (Fuller 1988; Warren and Staples 1989).

As another example, some investigators have been subject to defamation and libel suits, or the threat of them, by persons they have studied (for example, Cavendish 1982, preface; Punch 1986, Ch. 3; Wallis 1979, Ch. XI), as well as to other sorts of harassment (Beckford 1983). The chilling effect of this situation may pose yet another barrier, as social researchers question whether they can risk access in the first place.

Finally, as a last example, in the United States since the 1970s social research has been increasingly subject to the regulation of federal and local bureaucracies. Based upon the model (which many researchers regard as totally inappropriate) of medical research with human "subjects," local institutional bodies (often referred to as Institutional Review Boards, or IRBs) have administered federal regulations that involve assessments of risks and benefits, procedures for "subject" protection, and guarantees of informed consent. In early 1981, as a consequence of heavy lobbying by social research interest groups, most social research, especially naturalistic research, was presumptively exempted from regulation. Murray Wax and Joan Cassell described the changes:

> Compared to the previous [Department of Health, Education, and Welfare] regulations . . . , these are better tailored to social research. Investigations that pose little or no risk and in which informed consent is implicit in the nature of the research interaction (as in a social survey) have been eliminated from compulsory review. There is a clear delineation of the investigative conditions which lead to genuine risk and which so require monitoring; there is recognition that the very procedures for validating informed consent might themselves generate risks by creating records that link participants to questionable activities. (1981, p. 224)

However, Wax and Cassell go on to warn that

> the revision of the regulations does not guarantee alterations in conduct by local . . . IRBs. The new regulations do not prohibit IRBs from continuing to enforce more stringent standards; nor do they prohibit them from insisting upon reviewing projects not funded by the federal govern-

ment, but rather encourage institutions to broaden the range of their reviews. (1981, p. 224)

At this writing, Wax and Cassell's concern that the new regulations would engender little change appears to have been justified. As before the revision, just how much of a barrier the regulations pose to naturalistic research seems to vary from institutional setting to institutional setting and from IRB to IRB. In some universities, all research—even unfunded and undergraduate research—is subjected to regulations and review; in other settings, only funded research is affected. Similarly, some IRBs interpret informed consent so literally that "covert" research in public places is eliminated as an option; other IRBs exempt such research from informed consent mechanisms on the grounds of "no risk." And so on, through a confusing array of interpretations and applications. In the face of this complexity, the only advice we can give is to suggest that before beginning your research, you acquaint yourself both with your campus's IRB policies and with the extent to which local researchers take them seriously.

Despite the undoubted negative consequences of political, legal, and bureaucratic difficulties surrounding access in recent years, these difficulties have been accompanied by (and have probably contributed to) an intensified, and in some instances, exaggerated concern among naturalists about the ethics of their activity. Exaggerations aside, we view this as a generally positive occurrence. (For further discussion, see the books and articles referenced in Section I.B. above and the citations in this section, as well as Berg 1989, Ch. 6; Galliher 1980; Wax and Cassell, ed., 1979.)

IV. The Question of Confidentiality

In social research, what is commonly called the "assurance of confidentiality" is the promise that real names of persons, places, and so forth either will not be used in the research report or will be substituted by pseudonyms. This practice has long been taken for granted in the naturalistic research tradition. Of course, it is understood that confidentiality, like secrecy, is a matter of degree. In intensive interview studies, public-place observations, or studies of fluid social groupings, individuals may be able to identify quotations from or descriptions of themselves. They are extremely unlikely to be able to identify anyone else. In studies of stable communities or ongoing groups, however, pseudonyms are unlikely to prevent any of the participants from recognizing, or at least making pretty accurate guesses about, "who's who" (Scheper-Hughes 1981; Vidich and Bensman 1968; Whyte 1993, Appendix). Despite this potential for slippage in the cloak of confidentiality, confidentiality itself is standard operating procedure for both known and unknown researchers. For known researchers, in fact, the guarantee of confidentiality (and thus the protection) of the people being researched is often viewed both as an essential technique for "getting in" and, once entree has been accomplished, as a sacred trust, even in the face of imprisonment or threats of imprisonment (Brajuha and Hallowell 1986; Levine 1993).

Beyond the matter of protection for the people being studied, there is another consideration that argues for confidentiality as a standard practice. At their best, social researchers are neither muckrakers nor investigative reporters (although these are, of course, important societal roles). Their goal *as researchers* should, in our view, be neither moral judgment nor immediate reform, but *understanding*. The absence of names or the use of pseudonyms (if names, per se, are necessary for clarity) helps both the analyst and the reader to focus on the generalizable patterns emerging from the data and to avoid getting deflected into telling or hearing a "juicy" human-interest story.

There are, however, some negative voices among this general consensus on the advisability of confidentiality. Some researchers have argued that for studies of publicly accountable behavior or of large, powerful organizations, the guarantee of confidentiality is inappropriate (Rainwater and Pittman 1967; see also Duster et al. 1979; Galliher 1980). Others have suggested that it may, in fact, impede social scientific (especially social historical) knowledge:

> The ideal of scientific documentation is that of full disclosure of evidence essential to critical interpretation and ultimately replication. The burden of proof that names are not essential to social science field reports should be on the investigator. (Colvard, 1967, pp. 343–344)

Similarly, Malcolm Spector has reported that in research with public figures, who are used to being quoted and may prefer to speak "on the record," the guarantee of confidentiality may impede rather than facilitate access to rich data (1980, pp. 103–105). And, finally, some researchers believe that their personal ethical responsibility to give "voice" to their informants may, under some circumstances and with some persons, necessitate the use of real names (Scheper-Hughes, 1992, p. 19).

Before giving any promise of confidentiality, you might wish to review these arguments, as well as the code of ethics of your academic discipline and any current federal and state statutes relative to privacy. For, while we judge these arguments to raise serious questions about the inevitable advisability of confidentiality in *all* research situations, we also believe, in contrast to Colvard, that the burden of proof that names *are* essential to social science field reports or to the larger scientific endeavor should be on the investigator. When in doubt, the best advice remains: Disguise or obscure.

Having, by hook or by crook, finally gotten access to the data, you must work at maintaining your position: You must deal, that is, with the problem of "getting along."

CHAPTER 4

GETTING ALONG

L ike life, being "in the field" is never static. As we have suggested, research in the naturalistic tradition is very much an emergent affair. New problems continually arise; new solutions are continually necessary. Cooperative people may turn nasty. Uncooperative people may become superior sources of data. A bad beginning in a setting may unexpectedly prove to be an advantage, or a good beginning may turn sour. Quiescent difficulties may erupt at any time. Expected difficulties may never materialize.

The course of research is no more controllable than the course of a marriage, or the course of a friendship, or the course of a life. On the other hand, the course of research is also no less controllable. As in all activities, knowing a bit about what to expect, learning from the successes and failures of others, anticipating and thus guarding against pitfalls, and so forth should help reduce the difficulties of the field experience to manageable proportions.

In what follows, we subdivide our discussion of "getting along" into three tasks: getting along *with self,* getting along *with members,* and getting along *with conscience and colleagues.* First, we shall be concerned with the emotional stress that investigators may encounter; second, with the problem of achieving continual access to rich data; and third, with the ongoing ethical dilemmas that must be faced. In reality, this is an artificial division, but one that is useful for exposition. We ask you, then, to bear in mind that these three tasks are profoundly interrelated.

I. Getting Along with Self: Emotional Stresses

Being a researcher can be an emotionally stressful experience. As Rosalie Wax has described it,

> the person who cannot abide feeling awkward or out of place, who feels crushed whenever he makes a mistake—embarrassing or otherwise—who is psychologically unable to endure being, and being treated like, a fool not only for a day or week but for months on end, ought to think twice before he decides to become a participant observer. (1971, p. 370)

In the introduction to their *Experiencing Fieldwork*, William Shaffir and Robert Stebbins are no more optimistic:

> Fieldwork must certainly rank with the more disagreeable activities that humanity has fashioned for itself. It is usually inconvenient, to say the least, sometimes physically uncomfortable, frequently embarrassing, and, to a degree, always tense. (eds. 1991, p. 1)

Although Wax is thinking particularly of participant observation by a known observer, and Shaffir and Stebbins are speaking more generally, all are pointing to the fact that being an investigator can be personally difficult.

There is obviously no way to catalog every source of emotional or psychological difficulty ever encountered by fieldworkers. Such a cataloging probably would not be very useful anyway and would certainly discourage many people from even attempting naturalistic research. (Consider that if humans *really* anticipated all the difficulties they would encounter in any enterprise, very little, if anything, would occur.) In the belief that some forewarning may help you cope, however, we will look at four common situations of emotional distress: (1) deception and the fear of disclosure, (2) loathing and the desire to withdraw, (3) sympathy and the impulse to help, and (4) marginality and the temptation to convert.

A. Deception and the Fear of Disclosure

The perception that you, the researcher, are deceiving the people you are studying and the resulting anxiety over possible disclosure of that deception seems to be the emotional stress situation most characteristic of unknown investigators. From published reports, however, it seems clear that known researchers experience this as well. Because the people you are studying openly cannot know everything about what you are doing, there is always the fear that a direct and discomforting challenge is just around the corner.

- Did X remember that I was a researcher when she told me that? And if not, when she does remember, will she be angry or upset?
- Is this person I'm interviewing, who seems to be getting restless, about to ask me more about my research aims than I really want to tell right now?
- Is the person in charge of this group I'm studying going to notice that my research interests have shifted since I received permission to do the research, and if he does, will he still approve?

Unknown observers in open and public settings may also suffer from a nagging concern that "someone will find out." Even though the people in such settings are often not upset when they do find out, such knowledge does not necessarily prevent the investigator from worrying. When Lyn Lofland was observing in public waiting rooms, she was always vaguely fearful that someone would challenge her continued and repeated presence. On only one occasion—in an airport—was she approached; although the official who discovered she was doing research had no objection to her remaining, she was so uncomfortable that she left almost at once and never returned (see also Karp 1980).

Unknown observers in closed settings have written little about the emotional stress of deception and the fear of disclosure. But from the reports of investigators in milder situations of deception (for example, Klatch 1987) and, more directly, from the evidence of people in nonresearch "passing" situations (spies, "closet" homosexuals, and so forth), there is evidence that for many the fear of being unmasked (and of the attendant possibilities for humiliation, embarrassment, and abuse) is a constant companion. And the fear is not unjustified. Gary Larson's humorous depiction of the covert observer's nightmare (see Figure 4.1) seems less humorous when a real researcher lives it.

> Then Firth butted in. "We have several people in intelligence in the group . . . we've read your diary. . . ." At this point the elaborate plotting going on behind my back became clear, and I couldn't think of anything to say. It was apparent now they [members of a black-magic group] considered me some kind of undercover enemy or sensationalist journalist out to harm or expose the Church, and they had gathered their evidence to prove this. . . . "So now, get out," Lare snapped. "Take off your pentagram and get out." As I removed it from my chain, I explained that I had driven up with several other people and had no way back. "That's your problem," she said. "Just be gone by the time we get back." Then threateningly she added: "You should be glad that we aren't going to do anything else." (Scott 1983, pp. 132–133)

B. Loathing and the Desire to Withdraw

Few researchers have confessed to loathing the people they study or interview. Presumably, very few do. After all, if your discomfort, distaste, or dislike is too strong, you are going to be spending most of your time hiding your true feelings, leaving little energy for the data logging and analysis tasks that are the point of the research in the first place. Or you are simply going to leave the setting. (Numerous fieldworkers have noted, however, that you may learn a great deal from people whom you dislike; for example, Kleinman and Copp 1993.) Thus, most investigators do not even attempt research with people whom they already know they will thoroughly despise.

Perhaps the most forthright confession of loathing is to be found in passages from Bronislaw Malinowski's private journals, published as *A Diary in the Strict Sense of the Term* (1967). Available in print only many

THE FAR SIDE   By GARY LARSON

"So, you're a *real* gorilla, are you?
Well, guess you wouldn't mind munchin' down
a few beetle grubs, would you? ... In fact,
we wanna see you chug 'em!"

Figure 4.1 Gary Larson on Covert Observation. FAR SIDE copyright

years after the famed anthropologist's death, the diary, kept during his
researches with the Trobriand Islanders (among other groups), reveals
what one reviewer, Patrick Gallagher, called "a magnificent lack of
rapport" (1967, p. 23):

> Even more embarrassing, he confesses to despising his subjects ("young
> females, blackened, with shaven heads, one of them . . . with an animal-
> like brutishly sensual face. I shudder at the thought of copulating with
> her"), to distrusting them ("They lied, concealed and irritated me. I am
> always in a world of lies here"), and even to abusing them ("I was enraged
> and punched him in the jaw once or twice"). (Gallagher 1967, p. 25)

It is not surprising that under the circumstances, Malinowski also admits to withdrawing—if not from the field altogether, at least from contact with the "natives": "He also confesses, repeatedly, to chronic dissipation of time in reading 'trashy' novels . . . and, as frequently, to preoccupation with sexual daydreams and 'lecherous' acts" (Gallagher 1967, p. 25).

Anthropologists continue to debate whether these expressions represent Malinowski's more persistent feelings toward the peoples he studied or whether they are the honest, and very human, expressions of episodic rage and loathing under extraordinarily difficult field situations. Whatever the case, Malinowski's candid revelations of self stand as a strong reminder to all naturalistic researchers that entry into a research setting does not transform an ordinary human being into a saint. Unless you can honestly say that you have never in your life met a person you did not "love," you need to be prepared for the possibility that you will encounter in the field people you will loathe.

To speak only in the polarities of loathing and loving, however, is to ignore the emotional contexts in which the vast majority of fieldworkers find themselves. Notwithstanding recent pronouncements about the ethical necessity for feelings of "deep respect," "full sympathy," and "authentic caring" toward the people studied (see Chapter 2, Section III.C), researchers typically report feelings that are mixed, shifting, ambivalent, and complex. Certainly, unless they restrict themselves to the study of homogeneous groups of whom they thoroughly approve and with whom they completely identify (which would render a significant portion of social life "off limits"), researchers must anticipate experiencing at least some negative emotions. And even settings that seem fully congenial will not guarantee a steady diet of bonhomie. Some fieldworkers tell of discovering only after their project is well launched that their informants or their settings are not as sympathetic as they had expected them to be (for example, Koonz 1987, Lee 1992). Some tell of field situations in which a section of the people they were observing or interviewing turned out to be most congenial, but another portion were barely tolerable (for example, Brunt 1975, Daniels 1983). There are stories of changing situations or changing relationships in the setting profoundly altering the fieldworker's view of its participants (for example, Johnson 1975, Taylor 1987, Wasserfall 1993). There are other stories of finding oneself "tarred with the same brush" as the stigmatized population one is studying and, as a consequence, coming to feel, at minimum, ambivalent about the group (for example, Warren 1977). In sum, many investigators some of the time and some a good portion of the time dislike the people and the setting and wish they were someplace else altogether. (See also Fine 1993, Kleinman and Copp 1993, Reinharz 1993.)

C. Sympathy and the Impulse to Help

People everywhere tend to need help, and it is not at all unusual for investigators to provide some forms of mundane assistance to the people they are studying (see the discussion of trade-offs below). But sometimes researchers encounter a more difficult situation of need in which the people being observed or interviewed face severe difficulties that would require a full-time commitment to alleviate. Naturalistic researchers (known or unknown) must often struggle with the personally painful question of whether to throw in the towel on doing research and give themselves over entirely to "helping" or to remain in the field as a chronicler of the difficulties.

D. Marginality and the Temptation to Convert

If deception and the fear of disclosure is the characteristic stress situation of the unknown observer, then marginality and the temptation to convert (to cease all research and fully join the group) is the characteristic stress situation of the known observer (especially participant observers). This is not to say that other researchers do not also experience marginality. Unknown observers may experience it simply out of the knowledge that they have another self (researcher) whom none of their setting companions knows about. And persons doing intensive interviewing may find themselves feeling that it would be far more comfortable to stop the interview and just have an informal and unrecorded conversation. But it seems to be the known participant observer (either as participant researcher or as outside researcher) who most typically experiences discomforting moments of truth about marginality. Barrie Thorne writes of a time when members of the draft resistance movement in which she was involved and which she was studying were being asked to commit themselves to an act that might result in arrest. Her account provides an especially poignant example of these "moments of truth."

> As M. began the invitation, I felt fear in my throat. Fear, shame, guilt—both a desire to join the group that surged forward after M.'s invitation and a (stronger) reluctance since I didn't feel I could risk arrest and realized that the pressures compelling me to go forward were of a group rather than an individually thought-through kind. But that realization didn't seem to minimize the emotion. People began leaving their pews and going forward. Eventually there seemed to be only a few scattered people remaining in the pews. M. commented over the microphone, "There seem to be more up here than down there." I felt all eyes were upon me; I was sure my face was flushed; I found myself fingering my purse, almost in readiness to run up. But I didn't. . . . The group—more like a community given its size and solidarity—stood in a solid bunch,

spilling out over the sides and the front of the chapel, but clearly demarcated from those of us, scattered and far from constituting a group, who remained in the pews. The spatial arrangements dramatized the gap between the committed and the uncommitted. (Thorne, 1979, p. 80)

While such dramatic moments highlight the difficulty of being a participant observer, marginality is more commonly experienced as a chronic sense of loneliness, anxiety, and perhaps even alienation. There can be a continual, often subtle, but always painful sense of separation between the observer and the observed. It is as if, daily, one were being told, "You are here and you know a lot about us, but you are not really one of us." For a creature as sociable and as desirous of acceptance as Homo sapiens, this can be hard indeed.

E. Dealing with the Stresses

In the face of these possibilities for emotional stress, what are you to do? As we said initially, simply knowing that such possibilities can occur may lessen their impact. But not inevitably. You may instead conclude that your research is not worth living with deception and the fear of disclosure and so confess and depart. You may decide that continued association with persons you find loathsome is unbearable. You may come to feel that the needs of the people you are studying are compelling above all other commitments. And you may come to believe that community with the group being researched is far better than colleagueship with other researchers. Some fieldworkers have, in fact, made such decisions and judgments.

However, for those who hope to come through these and other emotional difficulties of "being in the field" without giving up their research role, two newer developments in fieldwork suggest at least partial strategies. First, relative to the sympathy–helping quandary, participatory research—"a radical type of activist social research in which the people being studied, or the intended beneficiaries of the research, have substantial control over and participation in the research" (Cancian 1993, pp. 93–94; see also Stoeker and Bonacich, eds., 1992, 1993)—may be of some use. Here the investigator collaborates with setting participants to find answers to questions that concern *them,* thus presumably researching and helping at the same time. Unfortunately, this type of research also has its drawbacks. It not only generates personal and professional dilemmas of its own (see Cancian 1993, Hammersley 1992), but also offers "help" that is or is almost as long-term as the help wrought by traditional social scientific work. In the face of truly dire need, the participatory investigator will find herself coping with the same emotional tug-of-war as her more profession-oriented colleagues. Second, both participatory research and feminist ethnography (with its injunction to researchers to be "as one" with the members) would seem to offer a loophole to the marginality clause in the fieldworker's "contract." To the degree that the requisite level of identification with the researched can be achieved, these research options seem promising. But as we noted relative to "loathing," full identification is an elusive goal. And even when it seems to have been achieved, the researcher—as the one who is writing things down, who will eventually write it all up, and who almost inevitably will go away—must admit to distance, however microscopic, between herself and the "friends qua collaborators qua brothers and sisters" she encounters in the field. As feminist sociologist Judith Stacey has written,

> Many . . . feminist scholars share the view that ethnography is particularly appropriate to feminist research. . . . [yet my ethnographic research] placed me in situations of inauthenticity, dissimilitude and potential, perhaps inevitable betrayal, situations that I now believe are inherent in fieldwork method. . . . The lives, loves, and tragedies that fieldwork informants share with a researcher are ultimately data, grist for the ethnographic mill, a mill that has a truly grinding power. (1988, pp. 22–23)

Despite their imperfections as solutions, both participatory research and feminist ethnography do seem capable of reducing at least a portion of fieldwork's inevitable emotional stresses—at least for some people, some of the time.

However, to those of you who, like us, are unattracted by these options, the advice we have culled from the literature is simple: Keep in contact with fellow researchers and/or friends with whom these problems can be discussed, placed in context, and weighed. Or, if that option is not available, take a cue from Malinowski: Perhaps a diary is in order.

II. Getting Along with Members: The Problems of Continuing Access

As we have seen, you—as a researcher—may be an important barrier to rich data. If emotional difficulties prove great, they can deflect energy and time from the primary task of data collection or lead to abandoning the research altogether. Nonetheless, the major problem of access in the field ordinarily involves the researcher's relations with members; that is, the people who are being researched are generally the more serious potential barrier to data.

We noted in Chapter 2 that access is one of the most widely discussed topics in the literature of qualitative methodology, and this remains as true in the "getting along" stage as it was in the earlier phases of the research process. We deal here with only certain issues raised in that literature (those we judge to be the most central). If you wish to pursue particular issues more extensively or are interested in topics not covered here, you might consult the books referenced at the end of Chapter 2, Section III.

When in the field, investigators are concerned to act toward the people being studied so as to maximize the information that is coming to them. Let us consider how they might do this with regard to *stance, style,* and *situations.*

A. Stance: Trust or Suspicion

Dictionaries commonly define *stance* as an "intellectual or emotional attitude." The naturalistic tradition is of two rather different minds regarding the most appropriate attitude to take toward the folk. We will let Rosalie Wax speak for what is certainly the more traditional, and possibly the majority, view:

> I find it difficult to reproach myself or my fellow fieldworkers for our disposition to regard the people we intend to study as good, honorable, and innocent. . . . I know that there are many societies that have developed elaborate and ingenious devices for relieving any stranger of his money and of his general confidence in human nature. I also know that no respondent or stranger has ever treated me as vilely as have some of my fellow social scientists. On the other hand, I know that *one cannot live with human beings in the field or out of it without trusting them. The great feat in most field expeditions, as in life, is to find the areas in which a mutual or reciprocal trust may be developed.* (1971, p. 372; emphasis added)

Jack Douglas has provided an articulate statement of the opposing stance:

> The investigative paradigm is based on the assumption that profound conflicts of interest, values, feelings and actions pervade social life. It is taken for granted that many of the people one deals with, perhaps all people to some extent, have good reason to hide from others what they are doing and even to lie to them. *Instead of trusting people and expecting trust in return, one suspects others and expects others to suspect him. Conflict is the reality of life; suspicion is the guiding principle.* (1976, p. 55; emphasis added; see also Hoffman 1980 on "camouflaging" intent in intensive interviewing situations.)

We have juxtaposed these passages to highlight the contrast between them. But in truth, the authors are not as far apart as their words suggest. Wax is well aware that the people she is researching often lie, by commission and by omission, sometimes unintentionally and sometimes quite deliberately. Her accounts in *Doing Fieldwork* are filled with instances of such problems. And Douglas, in a later passage of *Investigative Social Research,* softens the tone of his earlier assertion:

> It is all too easy for anyone . . . to conclude that we see all of society as [conflict-ridden and secretive] and therefore reject all cooperative methods in studying society. This would be completely wrong, as will be clear in our later discussion. . . . But to avoid any such misunderstandings we should emphasize from the beginning that we see society as being mixed and are proposing a mixed strategy of researching it. (1976, p. 56)

We should understand the contrasting statements by Wax and Douglas as representing opposite ends of a continuum. Which end you tend toward will depend on what and who you are researching and upon your personal position regarding the necessity for full sympathy and identification with the researched. In a very factionalized setting where issues of enormous import are being struggled over and whose participants view you with suspicion, you should undoubtedly keep a copy of Douglas's book in hand. But if you are interviewing people with whom you deeply sympathize, who seem to trust you and who want to talk about the topic at issue, viewing them as "unfriendly or hostile witnesses" is not only unnecessary but also unwise. Judging from their own accounts, most fieldworkers adopt a stance that is somewhere in the middle of the continuum: trust combined with a heady dose of skepticism; suspicion mixed in with large portions of faith.

B. Style: Presentation of Self

Unknown investigators do not need to worry about whether they are behaving in acceptable investigator *style.* They simply behave in a manner appropriate to the role they occupy. Known researchers, however, must determine how to act or present themselves so as to keep the flow of information coming.

Obviously we do not refer here to donning a persona totally at odds with your natural demeanor. We are speaking, rather, of asking yourself questions such as an employer might ask herself about her behavior relative to her employees or a teacher might ask about his behavior relative to the children in his classroom. In many sectors of social life, goal achievement revolves in part around self strategies. In naturalistic research, based on the cumulative experience of many fieldworkers, two complementary methods of self-presentation offer a particularly felicitous personal style: absence of threat and acceptable incompetence.

1. Absence of Threat

Granting but ignoring the exceptions, the first counsel one might offer a prospective investigator is to be nonthreatening to the people being researched, or at least to keep any potential threat within reasonable limits. We do not primarily mean threatening in any physical sense. Rather, we refer to threats to beliefs, self-confidence, and existing social arrangements by means of argument, ridicule, sarcasm, disinterest, and so forth. In most interview and observation situations, the investigator who is supportive, cordial, interested, nonargumentative, courteous, understanding, and even sympathetic will receive a good deal more information than one who acts in the opposite fashion (Vaughan 1990; on exceptions, see Gordon 1987, Punch 1986).

This advice, however, may be considerably more difficult to put into practice than you might think. Consider how frequently in normal interaction many of us are more interested in talking than in listening, in telling than in learning, in convincing than in understanding, and so on. In fact, many researchers find this continual openness to others and suppression of self exhausting and an additional source of emotional and psychological stress.

Being nonthreatening also means being sensitive and attentive to matters of appropriate grooming and dress. What is appropriate depends, of course, on the relation between the researcher as a person and the setting itself. Forty-year-old researchers observing adolescents undoubtedly make themselves and the young people appear ridiculous if they copy the latter's dress. Conversely, the casual student garb of jeans and shirt is not an appropriate costume for interviews with corporate executives. A guiding principle for appearance is to dress and groom yourself in a manner that shows respect for yourself and for your hosts.

2. Acceptable Incompetence

A naturalistic investigator, almost by definition, is one who does not understand. She or he is "ignorant" and needs to be "taught." This role of watcher and asker of questions is the quintessential *student* role. Now it happens that the idea of the ignorant student who has to be taught is a commonsensical and widespread notion. People almost everywhere feel they know and understand that role. Thus, the investigator who assumes the role of *socially acceptable incompetent* is likely to be accepted. In being viewed as relatively incompetent (although otherwise cordial and easy to get along with), the investigator easily assumes the role of one who is to be taught. Such persons *have* to be told and will not take offense at being instructed about "obvious" things or at being "lectured to." That is, such persons are in a good position to keep the flow of information coming smoothly (for example, Stebbins 1987; on children as research aides, see Cassell, ed., 1987).

The advantages of being acceptably incompetent may be limited or nullified, of course, by particular research settings, situations, questions, and relations. We have already noted that acting too incompetent may endanger entry to a research setting in the first place and have quoted George Moyser on the need to be knowledgeable when interviewing elites. There are also settings where even conventionally acceptable incompetents are not tolerated, where one may need some special bond and expertise in order to develop intimate familiarity. For example, investigators studying the world of crime who themselves have criminal backgrounds probably have an edge on those who lack that commonality with the researched (again, an advantage of starting where you are).

There are unquestionably many other situations where the role of the acceptably incompetent would be a hindrance (see, for example, Gurney 1985, Williams et al. 1992). And certainly, like being nonthreatening, many investigators will experience being acceptably incompetent as stressful, especially over the long run. Nonetheless, for those who are in appropriate settings and who can tolerate being what a naturalistic researcher generally *is*—a nonthreatening learner—the rewards of information received can be considerable. You might well keep in mind the admission of Agatha Christie's intelligent and successful detective, Hercule Poirot. When asked why he, a Belgian by birth, sometimes spoke good and at other times broken English, even after many years of residence in England, he replied:

> It is true that I can speak the exact, the idiomatic English. But, my friend, to speak the broken English is an enormous asset [for a detective]. It leads people to despise you. They say—a foreigner—he can't even speak English properly. It is not my policy to terrify people—instead I *invite their gentle ridicule*. (1934, p. 174; emphasis added)

C. Situations: Threats to Access

The naturalistic investigator encounters many *situations* in the field that endanger continuing access to rich data and therefore require solutions. The number of these may be as great as the number of possible research sites or questions, but we will describe only the four that seem to recur with greatest regularity: factions, trade-offs, closed doors, and insider understandings.

1. Factions

Almost any social setting is likely to contain factions, cliques, or quarrels of some kind. In fact, some internal distrust and dissent seems almost universal in human groupings. *Unknown* observers must necessarily align themselves, at least to some extent, with whatever faction or clique or side of a quarrel is dictated by the nature of their role. Thus, for them, the problem of factions is somewhat simplified. And the intensive interviewer of people who have no personal connection with one another is even more exempt. But the known observer in a stable setting and the researcher interviewing socially connected people (the political leaders of a small community, for example) must cope with the problem of how to maintain neutrality in the midst of divisiveness. Such researchers must at least avoid appearing so excessively loyal to one group that they will be denied access to the other (or thrown out of the setting altogether).

One typical way to protect against these dangers is to align yourself with a single grouping, to remain relatively aloof from intragroup dissensions, and to be on "your group's" side in any conflicts within the setting. For example, Rick Fantasia's study of *Cultures of Solidarity* (1988) brought him into intimate association with the coalitions of workers involved in labor struggles but required little or no contact with management. Similarly, Becker, Geer, Hughes, and Strauss (1961) and Becker, Geer, and Hughes (1968) studied medical students and undergraduates, respectively, but *not* medical faculty or college professors. And in both of the educational settings, the researchers attempted to make clear their interest in students as a category, not in the smaller divisions within the category.

Of course, in the early days of a fieldwork project, you may unintentionally make what later prove to be unfortunate alignments. The advice of Weinberg and Williams, which deals with individuals, applies to the problem of factions as well and remains as sound today as when it was proffered nearly twenty-five years ago.

> In the early phases of field work, when one feels most alone, it is easiest to associate with those held in disrepute; so one learns to keep on the move and neither spend too much time with those whose company is most pleasureful nor avoid those whom one finds least amicable. (1972, p. 172)

On the other hand, researchers have studied disputes between or among factions quite successfully, moving—as interviewers, as observers, or both—among the conflicting parties (for example, Heirich 1971, Horowitz 1983, Joseph 1983, Kornblum 1974, Morales 1989b, Shupe and Bromley 1980, Williams 1989a). As much as we can garner from their accounts, success in this difficult enterprise is partially a function of:

- the perception by the participants that the researcher is truly an outsider to the dispute;
- the continued perception of the researcher's impartiality relative to the dispute;
- the researcher's scrupulous honesty about the fact of studying both sides, combined with scrupulous confidentiality regarding the content of each side's private views and strategies (that is, not playing double agent); and
- possession of a great deal of accurate information about what each side knows of the other throughout the life of the conflict.

2. Trade-Offs

As we indicated in Chapter 3, the investigator is able to conduct research only because the people in the setting either consent to being observed or interviewed or don't know that research is going on. Thus, the issue of trade-offs is a legitimate component of the naturalistic process. Unknown researchers in closed settings are already contributing to their respective settings through their roles in them, of course, and in public-place research, researchers are largely irrelevant. But the people who are tolerating a known observer or an interviewer in their midst have every reason to ask, What do I get in return? What's the trade-off?

Among fieldworkers, the most common answer has been mundane assistance of one or another sort. Sometimes the assistance has an ephemeral quality, as when observers "ratify a moral community" by "witnessing" its activity (Bosk 1985) or when interviewers truly listen to a person talk about something she wants to talk about (an infrequent occurrence in social life). But interviewers and observers may also trade off with more concrete provisions: by offering rides or loans, delivering messages, serving coffee, giving advice and opinions, holding illegal goods, offering physical defense, telling lies, and so on through the entire range of normal "friendly" relations typical of organized social life. For example, Ruth Horowitz tell us the following:

> When one of the Lions [a youth gang she was observing] was arrested, not only did I make a small contribution to his bail but, as the only person over 21, I signed for him. I was asked and began to contribute small sums to the group's funds for beer and wine. . . . (1986, p. 416)

In a similar vein, Kathy Charmaz writes of attending "several weddings as well as several memorial services of people I had interviewed. . . . I had tea with elderly women, visited elderly men, admired pictures of spouses, grandchildren, and boyfriends . . . and met family members, friends, and housemates" (1991, p. 274). And Charles Bosk relates that he served the surgeons who allowed him to hang around by being "an 'extra pair of hands' and a 'gofer.' During the time of my fieldwork, I became very proficient at opening packages of bandages, retrieving charts, and fetching items from the supply room" (1989, p. 137).

Although less common, the assistance may be in the form of more esoteric goods and services. For example, during his participant observation in an Italian neighborhood, William F. Whyte found himself voting four times (once in his own name, three times under assumed names) in a single local election (1993, pp. 313–317). In the context of actual field situations, you must decide for yourself where to draw the line at helping. On reflection, Whyte rejected the propriety of this helping behavior:

> I knew that it was not necessary; at the point where I began to repeat, I could have refused. There were others who did refuse to do it. I had simply got myself involved in the swing of the campaign and let myself

be carried along. I had to learn that, in order to be accepted by the people in a district, you do not have to do everything just as they do it. In fact, in a district where there are different groupings with different standards of behavior, it may be a matter of very serious consequences to conform to the standards of one particular group.

I also had to learn that the field worker cannot afford to think only of learning to live with others in the field. He has to continue living with himself. If the participant observer finds himself engaging in behavior that he has learned to think of as immoral, then he is likely to begin to wonder what sort of person he is after all. Unless the field worker can carry with him a reasonably consistent picture of himself, he is likely to run into difficulties. (1993, pp. 316–317)

You must, then, draw an appropriate line. But unless you wish to be seen as odd and cold, and perhaps risk being completely shut out from the research setting, you cannot forego the helper role altogether: It is your trade-off for access.

3. Closed Doors

Even when you have achieved entry to a setting or successfully begun a series of interviews, you are still in no way guaranteed that all aspects of the setting you wish to observe or everyone you wish to interview will be available. In the face of such "closed doors," experienced fieldwork-ers frequently make use of *allies*. These may be some of the same people who helped you "get in" (see Chapter 3, Section II.B.1), or they may be people you have met during the course of the research itself who have indicated a desire or willingness to assist. For example, almost from the moment she entered her research setting (a small charitable foundation), Susan Ostrander was invited to attend meetings of the donor committee, but she had difficulty gaining access to donors who were less active in the foundation. That access finally was accomplished "through my es-tablishing connections with a few donors initially at meetings and, especially I believe, in early interviews, which donors perceived as being personally valuable in sorting out a number of issues. *These donors told this to others who then wanted to be interviewed*" (1993, p. 17; emphasis added).

Perhaps the most famous ally within the naturalistic tradition of sociology is William F. Whyte's "Doc." Whyte had been "fiddling" (the only appropriate word) around Cornerville (his pseudonym for the Italian neighborhood he was attempting to study) for some time and getting nowhere. Finally, he went to a local settlement house.

In a sense, my study began on the evening of February 4, 1937, when the social worker called me in to meet Doc. . . . "I want to see all that I can. I want to get as complete a picture of the community as possible," . . . [Whyte said.] [Doc replied:] "Well, any nights you want to see anything, I'll take you around. I can take you to the joints—gambling joints—I can take you around to the street corners. Just remember that you're my friend. That's all they need to know. I know these places, and if you tell them you're my friend, nobody will bother you. You just tell me what you want to see and we'll arrange it." (1993, p. 291)

But insider-allies such as Doc can do more than open doors to other people or parts of the setting. They can also open doors to understanding.

4. Insider Understandings

We pointed out in Chapter 2 (Section III.B.1) that while outside researchers have the requisite distance from the setting to ask questions, they lack the closeness necessary to understanding the setting in the way the participants do. We suggested that persons in such situations should therefore seek mechanisms for reducing the distance. Allies are one such mechanism. When allies are important guides to insider understandings, they are generally referred to as **informants** or **key informants**. (In intensive interviewing, all interviewees may be thought of as informants; especially articulate ones are sometimes thought of as key informants.) The understandings of these helpers may, of course, be erroneous or misleading, and the wise investigator is never too gullible. As a general rule, reliance on multiple informants (as is always the case in intensive interviewing) is probably preferable to reliance on only one. Whatever the potential dangers in their use, however, it is unlikely that many richly empirical and deeply understanding studies could have been achieved by outside researchers without the assistance of articulate, wise, knowledgeable and helpful informants. If you are an outside researcher, then, the cultivation of informants is virtually imperative.

D. Getting Along While Getting Out

As the Richter and Bakken cartoon (Figure 4.2 on the following page) suggests, there comes a time when it is "appropriate" to leave the field. On occasion, the appropriate moment is decided by one's hosts, and one is simply and unceremoniously ordered to depart. This is what happened to Gini Scott, whom we quoted above, when her purposes for being in the black-magic group were challenged. This is also what happened to John Lofland (1977), when the local leader of an aspiring "new" religion decided that Lofland's sociological interests (which he had declared from the outset) were more sincere than his religious interests and that, despite his vague murmurings to the contrary, he was never going to convert.

More typically, however, it is the researcher who makes the decision to go—because her grant money has run out, because the course that required the research effort has come to an end, because the boat to take him home has arrived, because she does not seem to be learning anything new, because the number of amassed interviews has grown too large to handle, and so forth and so on through a myriad of possible

*"Actually, I'm a participant-observer collecting data
for a definitive study of rodent behavior."*

Figure 4.2   Richter and Bakken on Leaving the Field.   Reprinted by
permission of Mischa Richter and Harald Bakken.

motivations for exiting. Whatever the motivation, the handling of these
voluntary departures probably deserves more careful thought and pre-
planning than fieldworkers have traditionally given to it. Writing in
1980, David Snow pointed out that "the disengagement process has
received scant attention in published discussions of [fieldwork]. . . . To
be sure, a number of works allude to dis-engagement as one of the
'phases' or 'stages' of [fieldwork] . . . but with few exceptions . . . it is
typically glossed over in a paragraph or two" (p. 101; see also Maines,
Shaffir, and Turowetz 1980). In the same article, Snow discussed both
"legitimate" reasons for exiting and factors that might pressure the
researcher to leave prematurely or to prolong her stay unnecessarily, but
he did not directly address the issue of getting along with members
during or after departure.

Clearly, this issue is personally or professionally irrelevant in some
research situations. For example, if the (known or unknown) researcher
has come to dislike the setting participants, he may be delighted simply
to walk away and not look back. Similarly, unknown researchers in
public and open settings usually do not have to deal with the issue at all.
It is typical for them to have formed no personal relationships, and, even
if they have, their research locales are often of the sort in which people
are expected to drift in and out. But for those investigators (known or

unknown) in more stable settings who—because of close personal ties with the researched or because of future research agendas—want to leave open the possibility of a return, the issue is a live one indeed. And, as with many live issues in fieldwork, the advice implied or proffered by what literature exists on it (see, for example, Carpenter et al. 1988; Shaffir and Stebbins, eds., 1991, Part IV) is not unlike the advice one might give or receive in everyday life—in this instance, advice specifically about the etiquette of departures:

- Inform people of your plans ahead of time and try to avoid leaving or appearing to leave abruptly.
- Explain why and where you are going.
- Say your goodbyes personally.
- Promise to keep in touch.
- Where appropriate, keep in touch.

III. Getting Along with Conscience and Colleagues: Ongoing Ethical Concerns

All of the personal and strategic problems we have discussed in this chapter can also be or become ethical problems. These problems may arise from a researcher's conscience, colleagues, or both. For example:

- Is it ethical to talk to people when they do not know you will be recording their words?
- Is it ethical to get information for your own purposes from people you hate?
- Is it ethical to see a severe need for help and not respond to it directly?
- Is it ethical to be in a setting or situation but not commit yourself wholeheartedly to it?
- Is it ethical to develop a calculated stance toward other humans, that is, to be strategic in your relations?
- Is it ethical to take sides or to avoid taking sides in a factionalized situation?
- Is it ethical to "pay" people with trade-offs for access to their lives and minds?
- Is it ethical to "use" people as allies or informants in order to gain entree to other people or to elusive understandings?

And so on through the catalog of every conceivable fieldwork situation.

Much attention has been lavished on questions such as these in recent years by fieldworkers agonizing over their own behavior and relationships and more generally by specialists in ethics. (References to key writings are listed in Chapter 3, Sections I.B and III.) Without in any way denigrating these efforts or belittling the honestly expressed moral anguish of some researchers, we believe that too much can be made of the special and particular ethical problems involved in the fieldwork setting. In our view, the fieldwork situation is no more (although certainly no less) difficult ethically than everyday life. Particularly when the situation involves voluntary agreements and relations between researcher and researched and when it is one of essentially equal power, its ethical dilemmas come close to those faced daily by morally sensitive individuals:

- If I don't tell my husband *everything* about my deeds or even about my thoughts, am I lying, and is my relationship thus somehow unethical?
- If, because I don't want to alienate my spouse and I need my mother-in-law as a baby-sitter, I don't reveal to her that I dislike her intensely, am I being immoral?
- I know about the starvation in Somalia. If I do not give up my job and try to do something directly, have I failed as a moral person?
- I've been through twelve "scenes" in the past six years. What sort of person am I?
- If I try to "dress for power" and I am learning to be assertive, does my strategic view of interaction make me inauthentic?
- I'm staying out of the battle between two of my colleagues at work. Should I?
- I sometimes use flattery to try to get my students to be more interested. Is that improper?
- My father helped me to get my first job and told me a lot about the world I'd be entering. Should I have let him do that?

And so on through the catalog of every conceivable situation in everyday life.

These daily ethical dilemmas are no more readily resolved than the similar dilemmas of field research. But then, why should there be a difference? Fieldwork is not detached from ongoing social life, and the continuing ethical dilemmas of social life seem an inexorable part of the human condition. A few researchers, faced with the disconcerting realization that one can act with total ethical purity *or* do fieldwork but not both, have wondered out loud if perhaps it is not fieldwork that should be abandoned (for example, Stacey 1988). For those who aspire to sainthood, perhaps it is. As psychologist Urie Bronfenbrenner commented more than forty years ago, "The only safe way to avoid violating principles of professional [and, we would add, personal] ethics is to refrain from doing social research altogether" (1952, p. 453).

IV. Postscript: Personal Accounts of the Field Experience

These necessarily abstracted and perhaps too ordered statements on "getting along" cannot really convey the full flavor of the field experience. For this, we recommend reading one or more personal accounts, such as in any of the following:

> Nigel Barley, *The Innocent Anthropologist: Notes From a Mud Hut* (1986).
>
> Manda Cesara, *Reflections of a Woman Anthropologist: No Hiding Place* (1982).
>
> Peggy Golde (ed.), *Women in the Field: Anthropological Experiences,* second edition (1986).
>
> John M. Johnson, *Doing Field Research* (1975).
>
> Nita Kumar, *Friends, Brothers, and Informants: Fieldwork Memoirs of Banaras* (1992).
>
> Annette Lareau, appendix on "Common Problems in Field Work: A Personal Essay" in her *Home Advantage: Social Class and Parental Intervention in Elementary Education* (1989).
>
> Bronislaw Malinowski, *A Diary in the Strict Sense of the Term* (1967).
>
> Hortense Powdermaker, *Stranger and Friend: The Way of an Anthropologist* (1966).
>
> William B. Shaffir and Robert A. Stebbins (eds.), *Experiencing Fieldwork: An Inside View of Qualitative Research* (1991).
>
> Carolyn D. Smith and William Kornblum (eds.), *In the Field: Readings on the Field Research Experience* (1989).
>
> Rosalie H. Wax, *Doing Fieldwork: Warnings and Advice* (1971).
>
> William F. Whyte, appendices to the fourth edition of his *Street Corner Society* (1993).

This chapter, combined with the preceding one, may have led you to view fieldwork as "adventure." It is certainly that, as almost any veteran will testify (endlessly). But it is something else as well, or it is nothing at all. It is *hard work*—hard, disciplined, and sometimes tedious work.

We now turn to the most essential aspect of field research—*data logging*. Data logging is the reason we try to get in and get along in the field in the first place. If it is omitted, fieldwork is indeed relegated to mere personal adventure.

CHAPTER 5

LOGGING DATA

Throughout the research, a process of **data logging** (that is, of careful recording) is carried out in various forms. Fieldnotes and interview write-ups are the most basic of these, but logging may also include mapping, census taking, photographing, sound recording, document collection, and so forth.

The model is that of *logging,* very much in the way our naturalist counterparts in biology have long been accustomed carefully to record observations on the actions and noises of the animals they research. The logging model is especially appropriate because it suggests a receptive, almost passive, approach to amassing data. The task of naturalistic researchers is not so much to "procure" data for recording as it is to *register* the social events unfolding or the words being spoken before them. The researcher does not simply wait for "significant" (sociologically or otherwise) events to occur or words to be said and then write them down. An enormous amount of information about the settings under observation or the interview in process can be apprehended in apparently trivial happenings or utterances, and these are indispensable grist for the logging mill. Understandably, then, the naturalistic tradition views as either naive or arrogant both the complaint of the novice investigator that he or she "didn't make any notes because nothing important happened" and the boast of professional that he or she did not take any fieldnotes because they "get in the way. They interfere with what fieldwork is all about" (quoted in Jackson 1990, p. 18). As Rosalie Wax warns us:

> The fieldworker may also think twice about following the example of those would-be ethnographers who assert or boast that they take few fieldnotes or no notes at all. The fact is that most of the people who say that they are able to get along without taking notes do not write anything worth reading. (1971, p. 141)

In fact, Wax's warning together with published admissions of a certain cavalier attitude toward the writing of fieldnotes (Jackson 1990; Sanjek, ed., 1990) might lead one to believe that recent pronouncements by ethnographers about the "fictional" character of their narratives (discussed below) may be based on the genuinely fictional character of those narratives. That is, to paraphrase Wax, perhaps the people who say they are able to get along without taking notes are able to write something worth reading only if they "make it up."

In methodological discussions (especially relative to participant observation), data logging is frequently justified as a "memory device" for the research. It allows you to recall the extraordinarily complex range of stimuli with which you have been bombarded. Such a justification, certainly, resists contradiction. But it seems to us to miss the point: *The logging record is, in a very real sense, the data.* Stated obversely, the data are not the researcher's memories (which notes, interview write-ups, films, etc. merely assist); the data consist of whatever is *logged.*

It is for this reason that the recording task is the crucial aspect of the naturalistic analysis of social life. And it is here, perhaps more than in any other aspect of the process, that the researcher requires discipline. "Getting in" and "getting along" may involve difficult and painful ethical, personal, and professional choices; they also generate a certain excitement. Data logging, in contrast, is often simply *boring.* As we warned in Chapter 1, if the researcher lacks any personal emotional attachment to the concerns of the research, the quality (and even the completion) of the project may be jeopardized. And tenacious data logging is certainly one of the key sites of jeopardy.

In this chapter, we begin with a brief discussion of recent challenges to the "facticity" of fieldwork data, then go on to an overview of the logging task as it pertains both to intensive interviewing and to participant observation. We then consider separately the different forms the log takes in each research mode: the interview guide and write-up in intensive interviewing and fieldnotes in participant observation.

I. Data: Fact or Fiction?

Among a small number of contemporary social scientists, the assertion that fieldwork is an essentially literary enterprise has gained considerable currency. In this milieu, to proclaim the "fictitiousness of facts" has become a surefire way to "demonstrate" both one's epistemological sophistication and one's superiority to all those who believe otherwise. Norman Denzin, an articulate spokesperson for what has come to be known as the "poststructural–postmodern" approach to ethnographic work, repeatedly takes on what he sees as the "dated" and epistemologically naive viewpoint of "social realism."

> [Social realism] assumes that an obdurate social world exists and that the events, meanings, and activities in this world can be accurately recorded by a skilled interviewer–participant observer. . . . Consider some troubling

alternatives. The ethnographers' text creates the subject; subjects exist only insofar as they are brought into our written texts . . . [This] countertheory [to social realism] justifies treating each document as a separate story. *It also renders fruitless . . . debates over who got the facts right.* (1992b, pp. 124–125; emphasis added)

This challenge to "social realism" in fieldwork by Denzin (1989, 1992a) and others (for example, Clifford and Marcus, eds., 1986; Clough 1992), as well as the more general challenge to all human knowing posed by postmodernist–poststructuralist philosophy, is likely to engender many years of continuous and complex debate (recent "realist" responses include Best 1994; Charmaz 1994; Dawson and Prus 1993a, 1993b, 1994; Sanders 1994; Snow and Morrill 1993). A small "how to" guide like this one is hardly an appropriate format for any serious or substantial entrance into the debate, but because our views tend toward a social realist position, some response does seem in order. In Chapter 8, we shall offer a detailed rendering of what our position entails (and how it differs from other positions) relative to the analysis of one's data. Here we want only to deal briefly with two aspects of the question raised by the Denzin extract: are data—in this case, fieldwork data—fictional?

First, data are sometimes claimed to be fictional because fieldnotes filter rather than mirror what "actually" happens. We have said just above that researchers should register events which unfold before them and we believe this is the appropriate mindset to bring to the data logging task. At the same time, we certainly concur that all human observations of the world (whether of the social, the biological, or the physical world) are necessarily filtered. Human *perception* is always human *conception*: What we "see" is inevitably shaped by the fact that we are languaged; by our spatial, temporal, and social locations (by culture, history, status); by our occupational or other idiosyncratic concerns; and, especially relevant here, by the scholarly discipline within which our "looking" takes place. But this is the stuff of introductory philosophy and sociology courses and is hardly revolutionary material with which to blow away a generally social realist orientation to research. And to grant that the researcher is *selecting out* only certain pieces from the raw flux of the phenomena that surround her does not say that she is *creating* those pieces. Filtering is not fabricating. A filtered reality is simply a filtered reality, it is not—unless we want to enter an Orwellian "Wonderland" and insist on our right to make words mean whatever we want them to mean—a fiction.

A second basis for arguing that data are fictional is the assertion that interpretations of reality vary (they are "socially constructed"). Again, this is an unassailable point. Even highly positivistic scientists and scholars always seek truth with a small "t," provisional truth, truth that is granted the status of truth only until it is (inevitably) shown to be not-truth. But we need to understand that not all human information is interpretation (except in the sense of being filtered). In this regard, it is useful to remember the distinctions that famed semanticist S. I. Hayakawa makes among reports, inferences, and judgments. Hayakawa defines *reports* as interchanges of information that adhere to the following rules: "[F]irst, they are *capable of verification*, second, they exclude, as far as possible, *inferences* and *judgments*" (1978, p. 33; emphasis in the original). An example of a report is this fieldnote entry: "When I arrived at the meeting there were six people in the room." *Inferences,* on the other hand, Hayakawa says, are statements "about the unknown made on the basis of the known" [e.g., this group generally has a small turnout at its meetings], and judgments are expressions "of the writer's approval or disapproval" (1978, p. 36). While within the fieldwork context, judgments might better be defined as expressions of the writer's analytic decisions about the meaning of her or his reports, the overall point remains the same. When we argue about whose "inferences" and "judgments" are "right," we may be involved, as Denzin suggests, in fruitless debate. After all, neither inferences nor judgments can be definitively verified. Reports, on the other hand, are capable of definitive verification, and thus debates over them are important and meaningful. When we dismiss such debates, we do so at our peril.

If we are to creep toward even the most rudimentary understanding of ourselves as a species, it *does* matter whether and how many Jews died in European concentration camps during the 1930s and 1940s; it *does* matter whether and how many civilian deaths resulted from the bombing of Baghdad during the 1991 Gulf War; it *does* matter whether or not the infant mortality rate of the United States is higher than that of other affluent nations. And for the groundedness and fruitfulness of your research, it *does* matter whether there were six people or twelve people or six hundred people in the room when you arrived; it *does* matter whether an apartment does or does not contain a toilet (see Adler, Adler, and Johnson, eds., 1992); it *does* matter whether the people you quote said the things you claim they say when you claim they say them. We will undoubtedly never be able to get all our reports "right," but it matters very much that we try. And the data log is the critical linchpin of our attempts.

II. The Logging Task

As we have indicated, the format of data logging in exclusively interview and exclusively observation studies is rather different (although many interviewers also take fieldnotes and many observers also do interviews). Nevertheless, many aspects of the logging task are pertinent to both modes. We shall consider five: data sources, researcher roles and access to data, problems of error and bias, protecting confidentiality, and the mechanics of logging.

A. Data Sources

In the naturalistic tradition, the prime sources of data are the *words and actions* of the people you are interviewing or observing. These are recorded mainly via written notes but also, on occasion (depending on appropriateness and resources), via photographs, films, audio tapes, or video tapes. You also may tap *supplementary data sources* (documents, for example).

1. Words and Actions

In both intensive interviewing and participant observation studies, you "get at" your prime sources of data—words and actions—through a combination of *looking, listening,* and *asking.* Which activity is dominant varies from situation to situation, from one time period to another, and from one mode of research to another. If you are an unknown investigator in a public or open setting, looking and listening will probably dominate, and asking will be possible only in limited situations (for example, Karp 1980, 1973). Unknown observers in closed settings may also have to rely heavily on listening and looking, since too much asking would be out of character for their setting role. If you are involved in intensive interviewing, on the other hand, asking and listening come to the fore, although you are, of course, simultaneously (if not predominantly) observing the interview in progress.

It is probably known observers, then, who have the greatest freedom (and also the greatest necessity) to utilize all three activities. At times, they may merely watch what is going on. At other times they may both watch and listen, or combine looking and listening with asking. Known observers are expected to carry on conversations with people in the setting; this not only will serve the task of "getting along," but also (in the form of questioning) will be informational in nature. Asking may elicit information not available from mere passive looking and listening or, at least, may speed up the information-collection process. Thus, known participant observers will spend a good deal of their time in the field asking questions such as these:

Who is he?

What does he do?

What do you think she meant by that?

What are they supposed to do?

Why did she do that?

Why is that done?

What happens after _____?

What would happen if _____?

What do you think about _____?

Who is responsible if _____?

As a form of activity, such asking is certainly a normal feature of everyday life. The naturalistic investigator is simply using this fact for research purposes, although perhaps asking questions much more frequently than ordinary participants in the setting would do. Questioning of this kind is often called *casual interviewing* and it is a key part of participant observation. The observer (and the intensive interviewer) may also utilize a more indirect means of asking questions—what David Snow, Louis Zurcher and Gideon Sjoberg have called "interviewing by comment" (1982). This is an attempt to elicit information verbally by making a statement rather than by asking a direct question. And as we suggested above, participant observers may also engage in intensive interviewing with people in the setting. These interviews, however, tend not to arise out of consideration of a general topic, as in traditional intensive interviewing, but out of specific queries that have accumulated in the field.

None of these activities is esoteric. People in everyday social life carry on precisely this kind of interweaving of looking, listening and asking. Naturalistic research differs only in that these actions are more self-conscious, directed, and intentional.

2. Supplementary Data
Depending on the question or questions being asked, the character of the setting, the form of research, and so on, you also may amass data through supplementary sources. Investigators frequently collect documents that are generated by the setting or that have to do with questions or topics of interest. Census taking may be useful, as may map making where physical settings are pertinent. Materials on the historical aspects of a people, setting, issue, and so forth will help place the data in context. Relevant newspaper and magazine clippings may expand your understanding of the present. In short, conscientious naturalistic investigators not only scan the immediate data site for words and actions but also are sensitive to the possible value of a wide range of supplementary information that may come their way (see, for example, Dowdall and Golden 1989; Gould, ed., 1985; Margolis 1990; Schwartz 1989; Walker and Moulton 1989; Webb et al. 1981).

3. "Mucking About"
In talking about data collection as we have just done, we may perhaps have imparted to the process an orderliness, purposefulness, and directedness that is not fully justified. Especially in the early stages of research (but also often intermittently from start to finish) there is a considerable "mucking about" quality to data collection. The researcher becomes a kind of human vacuum cleaner, sucking up anything and everything she comes upon that might even remotely prove useful. One of the few accounts of this aspect of fieldwork can be found in Candace Clark's

later "methodological confessions" about her 1987 study of the emotion of sympathy:

> In the earliest stages of my research, I collected data greedily—and somewhat guiltily. My approaches, productive though they seemed to me and systematic as I tried to keep them, were unlike the methods described in the pages of most current journals and unlike those I had previously used. Could real research consist of reading novels to see when I felt sorry for the characters? Did it count as data to overhear, in a restaurant, a wife feeling sorry for her husband? (1989, p. 137)

In addition to reading fiction and eavesdropping, Clark's "mucking about" activity included looking at sympathy greeting cards, reviewing the qualitative research literature for instances of "people in plights that ought to get them sympathy" (p. 144), engaging in focused conversations with friends and acquaintances, and doing some experimental manipulation of people's levels of sympathy—all this before she turned to the more conventional collection technique of intensive interviewing. Interestingly enough and tellingly, because informants often had difficulty remembering or relating their sympathy experiences in the interviews, those data alone would probably not have enabled Clark to write a piece as evocative and insightful as the one she did produce. It was the mucking about data, *combined with* what she learned from the interviews, that did the trick.

B. Researcher Roles and Access to Data

As we have seen in our discussion of the earlier stages of the research process, differing researcher roles and situations engender differing problems and advantages. This is no less true with regard to data logging.

1. Unknown Investigators

In public and open settings, the unknown observer experiences few blockages to data access. In many such locations—waiting settings, parks, restaurants, coffee houses, and so forth—note taking is facilitated by the typical self-engrossed activity of lone persons within them. That is, you can simply spend your time writing (or map making or census taking or whatever) without appearing "strange." (The use of cameras, tape recorders, and so forth may be more difficult.) Of course, as we noted above, unknown observers must rely primarily on what they see and hear, since much asking activity would "blow the cover." Hopefully, however, they have correctly evaluated their data site, and the kinds of data they are logging are appropriate to their interests.

The unknown observer in a closed setting has particularly good access to insider understandings (for which the known observer, especially the outside researcher, often must rely on informants, as discussed in Chapter 4, Section II.C.4). You can become intimately familiar with the particular role you are playing simply by playing it, and you are likely to become intimate with at least some of the other participants in the setting with whom you share problems and experiences. On the other hand, limitations to data access are built into occupying an existing role. When you actually perform a role that is necessary to and already a part of the setting, you must use a good portion of your time performing that role. This reduces freedom to wander about and observe the activities of other roles. And since no one knows about your "researcher self," you must curtail actions that express that self, such as questioning and open or frequent note taking. The range of matters into which you can openly inquire is restricted. If you move beyond asking about things that are role-appropriate, you may arouse suspicion. And people may become suspicious if you jot down notes openly or withdraw too frequently for the purpose of surreptitious note taking.

2. Known Investigators

Known investigators—whether doing intensive interviewing or participant observation—enjoy the tremendous advantage of being able to move about, observe, or question in a relatively unrestricted way. Of course, known observers who are also full participants in a setting share some of the time–space restrictions of their unknown counterparts. But like known outside observers and intensive interviewers, they do not have to cover up their investigative activities. Only common standards of decorum, tact, courtesy, and circumspection—that is, only the necessity of getting along with the participants—need interfere with their "snooping" and "prying." And note taking is generally not problematic. The people being interviewed usually expect interviewers to be taking notes. In fact, a failure to do so may communicate lack of seriousness or inattention. And while it can be situationally inappropriate or strategically unwise for known observers to take notes in the immediate presence of the people being researched, known observers are also considerably freer to structure their own time so as to withdraw intermittently for note-taking purposes.

3. Teams

For data logging purposes, **team research** can be quite advantageous. Two or more observers or interviewers can simultaneously be looking, listening, or asking in different places and with different people, generating a potentially broader and richer data log in a shorter period of time. To facilitate analysis, however, all members of the team must be as familiar with the data being logged by their teammates as with their own. As the sheer quantity of data increases, this can become burdensome, if not impossible. As we mentioned briefly in Chapter 2 (Section III.B.3), teams may also intensify the problems of "getting along" simply because more people in the field can generate more errors (see, for example, Shaffir, Marshall, and Haas 1980). Nonetheless, if data quantity and familiarity problems can be solved and if social relations aspects are adequately coordinated, the logging advantages of team research certainly recommend it.

C. Problems of Error and Bias

We indicated in Chapter 2 that (postmodernist and poststructuralist critiques aside) naturalistic investigation, with its preferences for direct apprehension of the social world, has somewhat fewer problems with validity than do research traditions that rely on indirect perception. Nonetheless, it is still the case that for every piece of information received by the naturalistic researcher *a question must be raised regarding its truth,* that is, about the degree to which it is an accurate depiction of physical or verbal behavior or belief. We must be concerned with the verification of our "reports" (as we discussed in Section I). We know from our everyday experience that disagreements about the facts of an event, for example, are quite common. A good part of the work of courts of law is devoted to sorting out more or less plausible but opposing depictions of "the facts." Similarly, disputes about the facts abound in historical research and among operators of military, industrial, and other systems of intelligence. And, it would seem that everyday life, law, history, and intelligence systems teach us that there is no easy way to determine "the facts."

Therefore, you, the investigator, like people in everyday life and in more specialized areas, are constantly faced with the question, "What really is the case?" You are faced with this question at two levels. First, regarding your own perceptions: Have I seen or heard this accurately? Second, regarding other people's reports: Is this reporter providing me with an accurate account?

While there is no royal road to truth, there are some basic questions or tests that you can use to evaluate your own perception and the perceptions of other people:

- *Directness of the report.* Is this account based on direct perception, or is it second-, third-, or fourthhand? If it is not direct, is it therefore to be treated with caution *as fact,* even if it is accurate as image?

- *Spatial location of the reporter.* Even if the report is firsthand, what was my (or my reporter's) spatial location such that this perception might be accurate in some respects but still skewed or partial?

- *Social locational skewing of reported opinion.* With regard to reports of opinion, what might there be about the relation between myself and the reporter that might lead her or him to lie, distort, omit, falsely elaborate, or otherwise be less than accurate?

- *Self-serving error and bias concerning reports.* From what I know on other grounds about my own or the reporter's commitments, values, and announced biases, are there reasons to be suspicious of the content of this report? Does it fit all too conveniently with what I want to believe, or what the reporter might want to believe, about people and events? That is, is it *self-serving* and therefore to be regarded with caution?

- *Previous plain errors in reports.* From what is known about my or the reporter's previous perceptions, am I an accurate observer or listener? Is the reporter? Have I or the reporter made errors in the past, even though these are not self-serving errors?

- *Internal consistency of the report.* Is this report consistent within itself? Are there spatial–temporal facts stated at one point that contradict spatial–temporal assertions at other points? Were the events of this report possible within the time and space constraints given in the report or known about on other grounds? Do the people involved unaccountably contradict themselves within this report?

- *External consistency; agreement among independent reports.* Is this account consistent with other accounts of the same events or experiences? Have I assembled enough independent accounts, subjected them to the above questions, and then compared them for degree of agreement? On points of remaining disagreement, have I made sufficient effort to speak with more participants in the event or with people involved in the experience who are otherwise qualified reporters in order to arrive at a truthful account?

Of course, reports can pass all these tests and still be false. Against that possibility, we offer the maxim that truthful observation or listening depends heavily on the sincere good faith, open-mindedness, and thoroughness of the observer. In the end, the readers of your analysis will subject it to these same kinds of questions and thus decide what degree of trust to place in it.

Peculiarly, despite considerable professional and philosophical concern about error and bias in naturalistic studies, these topics rarely arise in connection with accomplished works (but see Adler, Adler, and Johnson, eds., 1992; Holmes 1987; Levy 1984). They rarely appear even as unpublished allegations along the grapevine of professional social science. Perhaps constant general worry about potential error and bias protects the naturalistic investigator from their actual occurrence. (For those interested in the more technical issues surrounding validity and reliability in fieldwork, see Gilmore 1991, Kirk and Miller 1986.)

D. Protecting Confidentiality

In most naturalistic investigations, the question of providing confidentiality to the people studied (discussed in Chapter 3, Section IV) does not usually arise until the write-up stage (see Chapter 10). That is, it is ordinarily only when the fruits of your research have been transformed into analysis that you become concerned to disguise identities and locations (if disguise is what you intend). However, some types of sensitive research push this concern with confidentiality backward in time, starting at the point of data logging. If you are studying people engaged in illegal or politically suspect activity, for example, or people involved in activities kept secret from their associates, or well-known figures who are speaking openly only with the assurance that it is "off the record," you may want to take considerable precaution with the data log itself. Carol Warren's handling of her research log on "closet" gay men is exemplary:

> Tape recorded interviews were stored without identifying tags (although voices could be identified), and were erased after transcription and use. Field notes were kept in unlocked storage; however, pseudonyms were used throughout the recording of field notes, and a master list of names matched to pseudonyms [kept in locked storage] was discarded following the write-up of the material. (1977, p. 96)

Warren's cautions were prompted solely by a concern for the people she was studying. Current researchers are usually guided in addition by the "consciences" of their professional associations. The sociological *Code of Ethics,* for example, is quite explicit in insisting that sociologists, "to the extent possible . . . anticipate potential threats to confidentiality. Such means as the removal of identifiers . . . should be used where appropriate" (American Sociological Association 1989, p. 3).

A final observation: As we discussed in Chapter 2 (Section III. E), the ASA code goes on to say, "Confidential information provided by research participants must be treated as such by sociologists, *even when this information enjoys no legal protection or privilege and legal force is applied*" (p. 3, emphasis added). Given such an injunction, sociologists should understand confidentiality practices in data logging as strategies not only for protecting the people they study but also for protecting themselves.

E. The Mechanics of Logging

For reasons that will become clear in Chapter 9 (having to do with manipulating data in order to generate analysis), it is absolutely essential that the data log—in the form of recorded interviews, fieldnotes, or both—be *duplicated* or *available for duplication* so that you can produce multiple copies of each page of interview transcription or fieldnotes if you want them. With the older technologies, this required carbon paper or carbon sets for the initial recording, photoduplicating, or recording on spirit masters or stencils for runoff. Now, of course, logging directly into a laptop or personal computer (PC) simplifies the task enormously. And with the proliferation of portable PCs, it seems likely that few researchers today—even in remote locations—rely primarily on pencils and notebooks. However, if you are among the many who resist modern technologies or, if you simply cannot afford or do not have access to a computer, at minimum, invest in a typewriter. Rendering the data log in typescript (with wide margins and frequent paragraphs) will greatly facilitate the analytic manipulation to come. Researchers who prepare their notes or transcribe their interviews by hand are adding another level of tedium to an already tedious task and are quite likely, as a consequence, to settle for incomplete, shallow interview write-ups and sketchy fieldnotes. Prospective fieldworkers who cannot use a keyboard (whether on a typewriter or a PC)—who cannot even "hunt and peck" with reasonable speed—should *learn* to do so before entering the field. Naturalist research relies primarily on social relations and analytic skills, but if its one requisite technological skill—typing—is absent, these skills may easily be negated. (The alternative, secretarial assistance, is a rare occurrence, but one that will be discussed below.)

While the ubiquity of the personal computer has simplified both the initial recording of the log and its duplication (but *always* remember to print out at least one hard copy of everything and to make one or two electronic copies, e.g., backup disks), the PC and its associated software have added a new and complex level of decision making to the research process. A considerable number of software programs for the manipulation and analysis of qualitative data are currently available. They become especially relevant, of course, in a later research stage than the one we are discussing here. But, because using them for analytic purposes may require special formatting of the log and may even require using them to log, you should decide whether to use one and, if so, which one before transcribing a single interview or writing up a single fieldnote entry. As we discuss in Chapter 9 (Section III.A.2), we have as yet no solid demonstration of the merits of using these programs for analytic purposes, but there seems little doubt of their value for data storage and retrieval purposes. General discussions of the uses of computers in qualitative work and comprehensive overviews of appropriate and available programs and applications can be found in Blank (ed.) 1988, Fielding and Lee (eds.) 1991, Richards and Richards 1994, Tesch 1990, and Weitzman and Miles 1995. You should review one or more of these texts to acquaint yourself with the many data-manipulation possibilities inherent in normal word-processing program capabilities (for example, word counts, multiple filings of entries, movements of copies of entries in and out of established files, and so forth) as well as to help you decide whether the more specialized analytic programs might work for you.

Our advice at this juncture is to risk moving beyond your current level of computer skills but not too much beyond. Transforming data into analysis is a difficult task by itself. Little is to be gained, we think, by compounding the difficulty of the task by adding to it the burden of achieving a high level of computer literacy. Thus, if you are already familiar and comfortable with a variety of software programs, then by all means be open to using an analytic program. (But take seriously Reneta Tesch's observation that "[e]ach programmer has her/his own way of deciding what works best. . . . [T]wo programs that perform exactly the same functions can have quite different 'architectures'" [1990, p. 174]. And, be careful to select a program whose "mind" works at least somewhat like your own.) However, if, like us, you are something of a "Luddite" and do not make use of much more than the word-processing capacities of your PC, the "cut and paste" school of data manipulation is probably the better choice. And it is this tried and true (though admittedly technologically primitive) approach to analysis that we shall describe in Chapter 9.

As we have seen, the data-logging tasks in intensive interviewing and participant observation are similar in many ways. But there are also several important differences. Therefore, we will now consider each mode separately.

III. Data Logging in Intensive Interviewing: Guides and Write-Ups

In intensive interviewing, you initially log the data via an instrument known as an "interview guide." In this section, we first discuss the preparation of such a guide, then go on to the matter of doing the interview with the guide, and finally consider the production of the actual log: the writing up of the interview.

A. Preparing the Interview Guide

The interview guide is considerably less formal or structured than the questionnaire or interview schedule used in survey research or opinion polling, but the care with which it is created is no less crucial. Its production requires serious thought.

1. Puzzlements and Jottings

Logging data by means of intensive interviewing with interview guides reasonably begins with you, the prospective investigator, taking some place, class of persons, experience, abstract topic, and so on as problematic or as a source of puzzlement. If you take this puzzlement seriously and decide to pursue it as a topic of investigation, and if you judge that interviewing is the most appropriate procedure (see Chapter 2), you then sit down in a quiet place and use what is called "common sense." You ask yourself, "Just what about this thing is puzzling to me?" Without worrying about coherence and the like, begin to jot down questions about these puzzling matters and, at various times over several days or weeks, continue to do so. Questions may occur at odd moments—while you are taking a shower, listening to conversations, driving, opening mail—so you should keep a small notebook handy at all times. In this phase, it is also useful to mention the topic to friends, acquaintances, and associates; they may suggest additional questions or stimulate new dimensions of puzzlement. Jot these down as well.

What are you doing at this stage? You are "teasing out" and recording those things defined as puzzling in the context of your own and your associates' cultural understandings. You are preparing to use what is puzzling relative to that cultural perspective as a point of departure for interviewing. A not insignificant element of this cultural perspective will, one hopes, be some knowledge of those puzzlements institutionalized in the literature of a relevant social science discipline. In addition, it is entirely proper to locate and read books and articles on the particular, concrete matter of concern. In reading, you can discover what others who have written about and studied this matter found puzzling and what kinds of questions they ask and note the kinds of answers they have offered.

At the operating level, it is wise never to put more than one puzzlement or particular kind of question on a single sheet of paper or card. The effort at this stage is to retain maximum flexibility in organizing. Listing no more than one thought per page extends your capacity to organize and reorganize at will.

2. Global Sorting and Ordering

As these puzzlements accumulate, they develop into an incoherent assembly. Hopefully, as you have been going along, you have also been thinking about the kinds of general clusters or topics into which these various puzzlements fall. You should also have recorded ideas on the overall structure or organization of the puzzlements, because eventually you must give these puzzlements or questions a global or comprehensive design. If they have been written on separate pieces of paper or cards, you can thus begin to sort them physically into separate piles of paper or cards on some flat surface. Several sortings and resortings may be necessary in order to establish the number of "piles of paper"—or, more abstractly, *topics*—that seem best to arrange your accumulated concerns. Whatever the several topics, it is not necessary to strive for any kind of sophisticated social scientific sense in formulating them. Indeed, it is preferable for the topics to be quite straightforward and commonsensical, the better to communicate with the people to be interviewed.

The following is an example of global organization, drawn from Robert Weiss's guide for the first interview (of three) for his study of the work lives of "successful" men (1990). Note that it does not, except in its lack of "elegance," differ greatly from outlines of articles, books, or structured interview schedules. Here, as elsewhere in life, straightforward, logical, orderly thought is applied:

1. A Day at Work
2. Tasks at Work
3. How R[espondent] Came to This Work
4. Gratifications and Burdens of Work
5. Recognitions and Rewards (Weiss 1994, pp. 49–50)

Like the Weiss guide, our second example of global organization, which is drawn from Lyn Lofland's (1982, 1985a) research on loss and connection, illustrates the additional point that the topics should be sequenced in a manner that your informants are likely to find reasonable—semichronologically, for example.

1. Who is lost?
2. When?
3. Tell me about the relationship prior to "loss": dyadic career.
4. Tell me about the loss itself.
5. Prior loss experience.
6. Immediate response to the loss: emotional, physical, behavioral.
7. Development/changes through time regarding feelings and actions.
8. Looking at the relationship from the current perspective.

Sometimes sorting at the global level generates a list of topics, areas, or questions that come to constitute the entire guide, as for example in Ritchie Lowry's guide for interviews with community leaders:

1. Could you indicate several major changes in Micro City [a pseudonym used by Lowry] in the last decade which you feel are particularly important?
2. In your opinion have these changes been good or bad for the community?
3. In light of these changes what do you predict for Micro City's future?
4. Will these future changes and problems be good or bad?
5. What do you think constitutes an "issue" or problem to us here in Micro City? Can you give some examples?
6. Can you indicate several leaders of the community who in your opinion have contributed most to Micro City in their concern for these changes? Can you identify the general sources of effective leadership in Micro City?
7. What role do you think community organizations, institutions (like the college, PG&E, PT&T), individuals, the mass media, and the general public have played and should play in community issues and problems?
8. What is the best way of handling issues or problems like those you have mentioned in a community like ours?
9. If you had the power to do anything you wanted for the good of this community, what would you do or suggest be done? What changes would you like to see made in the community? (Lowry 1965, pp. 235–236)

As we have suggested above, in constructing your global design, try to adopt the perspective of the people you will be interviewing and to think about what will make sense and be most acceptable to them. If some topics are of a sensitive character or potentially embarrassing to them or to you, it is often better to address these toward the end of the interview. The hope is that by treating the less sensitive material first, you will build trust and rapport during the course of the interview itself, making it easier subsequently to deal with more tension-laden topics. Sometimes it is wise to begin with relatively neutral "facesheet items" (see Section II.A.5 below) as an innocuous way of getting into the question-and-answer process.

3. Section Sorting and Ordering

Once you have tentatively established an overall design for the guide, assuming it does not constitute the entire guide, you can turn to particular piles of puzzlements within the overall design and begin to plan a reasonably commonsensical ordering of concerns and questions. For example, as we saw above, Robert Weiss's interview guide for his study of occupationally successful men contains a global section dealing with the issue of "Gratifications and Burdens of Work." Within that section, the guide then specifies that the following questions and concerns be addressed.

a. What is R[espondent] going for in his work?

b. What does R have in mind as he does his work?

c. Obtain incidents in which R was unhappy at work and when work produced distress.

d. Obtain incidents of stress. (Weiss 1994, p. 50)

Similarly, global section 6 of Lyn Lofland's interview guide on loss and connection (dealing with immediate responses) contains the following questions:

a. What exactly did you do in the first days or week following the loss? Different than normal?

b. What exactly did you feel in the first days or week following the loss? Different than normal?

c. How did others act toward you? How did you feel about their actions?

d. Did the loss seem appropriate, timely, untimely, meaningless, meaningful?

e. Did the loss in any sense seem to free you? How?

f. [If appropriate,] did you attend the funeral or other services?

4. Probes

In interview guides, the emphasis is on obtaining narratives or accounts in the person's own terms. You want the character and contour of such accounts to be set by your informants. You might have a general idea of the kinds of things that will comprise the account but still be interested in what they provide on their own and the terms in which they do it. As the informants speak, you should be attentive to what is mentioned and also to what is *not mentioned* but which you feel might be important. If something has been mentioned about which you want to know more, you can ask, "You mentioned _____; could you tell me more about that?" For things not mentioned, you might ask, "Did _____ happen?" or "Was _____ a consideration?"

Such questions are called **probes.** In interview guides, a series of probes are often connected to a specific question in order to remind the interviewer to probe for items that might not be mentioned spontaneously. Robert Weiss's question "What is R going for in his work?" contained the following probes:

> Obtain incidents in which R's work was gratifying to him.
>
> What were the gratifications?
>
> If noted, ask about challenge, achievements, contributions. (1994, p. 50)

And in exploring "relational career," Lyn Lofland's guide for her study (1982) contains a reminder to probe for the following:

> How did relationship develop?
>
> What sorts of things done together?
>
> What sorts of things talked about together?
>
> Intensity—time together in a typical week/year.
>
> Changes in intensity through time.
>
> Emotional tone.
>
> Changes in emotional tone.
>
> Importance placed by you on the relationship.
>
> Changes in importance.

This is not to say that every question must be outfitted with one or more prepared probes. It may happen that you do not, at a given time, have much idea of what to probe for. Many on-the-spot probes are likely to be used spontaneously in order to amplify or clarify an account. And many kinds of questions may not especially require probes (although they can doubtless be invented for any question).

5. Facesheets and Fieldnotes

For purposes of identification, bookkeeping, and generally keeping track of the interviews and social characteristics of interviewees, interview guides commonly devote a page or so to gross factual data. Such a page is often the first sheet of the guide and is therefore called the **facesheet.** The following are among the items typically appearing on the facesheet:

- interviewee's name (or a code number, if the topic is a sensitive one and names keyed to code numbers are to be kept in a separate place)
- the number of the interview (if you choose to keep track of interviews by number rather than name)
- date of interview
- place of interview
- sex
- age
- education
- ethnicity
- place of residence
- place of birth
- occupation or other position
- religion

(Any given facesheet may, of course, omit particular items if they are not relevant to the study.)

Beyond information of this sort, additional social items will probably be cast according to the purposes of the interview and will therefore vary a good deal from one study to another. Even though the facesheet is typically the first sheet, facesheet questions are not necessarily the first questions you ask. Depending on the topic, the degree of trust, and so forth, it may sometimes be preferable to go directly into the interview itself after giving the introduction. In that case, the facesheet questions are sometimes treated almost like a formal afterthought, a minor duty that you have to perform in interviewing. Whether you fill it out first or last, you will probably want the facesheet to be the first sheet of the guide so that you can later easily identify the guide itself.

In addition, interviewers sometimes find it useful to append a postinterview comment sheet to the guide. This is not material that is shared with the informant. Rather, it is simply a space for you to jot down **fieldnotes** on the interview itself after you and the informant have parted. You may include time of day of the interview, a description of the setting (if it is new to you) and the informant (beyond that noted on the facesheet), the emotional tone of the interview, any particular difficulties (methodological or personal) that were encountered, your own feelings during and about the experience, insights and reflections, and so on. The jotted notes on such sheets are later incorporated (perhaps in expanded form) into the interview write-up and become a portion of the data log. Remember also that intensive interviewing may involve you in relationships with your informants that transcend the interview encounter or encounters. If that is the case, fieldnotes recording extra-interview observations and conversations may be appropriate; you can add such notes to the relevant interview write-ups so that they become part of the data log.

In "deconstructing" interview guides into their constituent elements as we have done above, we have necessarily foregone reproducing any but the single-level Lowry guide in its entirety. For those who might find them useful, complete examples of more complex guides are reproduced in the following research reports:

> Mihaly Csikszentmihalyi and Eugene Rochberg-Halton, *The Meaning of Things: Domestic Symbols and the Self* (1981).
>
> David Hummon, *Commonplaces: Community Ideology and Identity in American Culture* (1990).
>
> Meredith B. McGuire (with the assistance of Debra Kantor), *Ritual Healing in Suburban America* (1988).
>
> Laurel Richardson, *The New Other Woman: Contemporary Single Women in Affairs With Married Men* (1985).
>
> Eve Spangler, *Lawyers for Hire: Salaried Professionals at Work* (1986).
>
> Jacqueline Wiseman, *The Other Half: Wives of Alcoholics and Their Social–Psychological Situation* (1991).

B. Doing the Interview

We have already discussed much about the social relational aspects of interviewing (Chapter 4). Here we shall deal with the more technical matters of introduction, format, leading questions, interviewer activity during the interview, and the use of separate guides.

1. Introduction

Recall from Chapter 3 (Section II.B.2) that the "getting in" phase of intensive interviewing requires an "account"—an introduction, as it were, to the potential informant. This account indicates the topic or topics to be covered, the probable length of time required, promises of confidentiality if appropriate, and so forth. At the time of actually sitting down to the interview, you should repeat much of this material and, if called for, provide additional information. The point at both stages is to acquaint the person honestly and clearly with what you are asking her or him to do. The more than thirty-year-old list of self-instructions in Fred Davis's guide for interviewing handicapped people still provides a stellar example of proper introductory material:

- Explain purpose and nature of the study to the respondent, telling how or through whom he came to be selected.

- Give assurance that respondent will remain anonymous in any written reports growing out of the study, and that his responses will be treated in strictest confidence.

- Indicate that he may find some of the questions farfetched, silly or difficult to answer, the reason being that questions that are appropriate for one person are not always appropriate for another. Since there are no right or wrong answers, he is not to worry about these and do as best he can with them. We are only interested in his opinions and personal experiences.

- He is to feel perfectly free to interrupt, ask clarification of the interviewer, criticize a line of questioning, etc.

- Interviewer will tell respondent something about himself—his background, training, and interest in the area of inquiry.

- Interviewer is to ask permission to tape record the interview, explaining why he wishes to do this. (1960; see also McCracken 1988, pp. 67–69)

Such lists should be read as providing a set of points to cover, some when asking for the interview and all when beginning to interview. But it should not be interpreted mechanically as a set order of items to be run through in rote fashion. You will probably want to vary the style and order of coverage according to the dictates of the circumstances. The important point is that these are matters of common politeness and involve information that the informant has a right to know.

2. Flexible Format

As you can see from the wording and layout of the interview guide examples provided above, a guide is *not* a tightly structured set of questions to be asked verbatim as written, accompanied by an associated range of preworded likely answers. Rather, *it is a list of things to be sure to ask about when talking to the person being interviewed*. For this reason, the interview instrument is called a *guide* rather than a schedule or questionnaire. You want interviewees to speak freely in their own terms about a set of concerns you bring to the interaction, plus whatever else they might introduce. Thus, interviews might more accurately be termed *guided conversations*.

It happens that people vary a good deal as to how freely they speak or how chatty they are. When you encounter less verbal interviewees, it is likely that you will go through the interview guide in the order that you have set up the questions. The interviewee may provide little in response to each question, giving you little place to go except on the next question.

Fortunately, however, many people are verbal, chatty types. In response to a given question they will raise all manner of leads and puzzlements that may merit pursuit, either at that point or reasonably soon thereafter. (Ideally, you should pursue such a lead at a moment when it is also of concern to the interviewee.) Also, in the course of talking about things the interviewee cares about, he or she may inadvertently answer some of the questions in other parts of the guide. The interview guide in such cases provides a checklist of sorts, a kind of inventory of things you want to talk about during the interview. You can check them off as they are accomplished.

3. Leading Questions

A word of caution about wording questions: Avoid posing questions in such a way that they communicate what you believe to be a preferable answer. Questions so posed are known as *leading questions*. Thus, instead of starting off with "Don't you think that . . . ?", begin with something like "What do you think about . . . ?" Instead of "Is it not likely that . . . ?", use something like "How likely would you say it is that . . . ?"

The following is an interview extract from Mihaly Csikszentmihalyi's and Eugene Rochberg-Halton's study of the transactions between people and their "things." It nicely illustrates not only neutrality in the wording of questions but also something of the free-flowing and probing character of intensive interviewing.

One of the things that we bought most recently is a chest downstairs that's done by North American Indians. And we fell in love with that when we were in Canada this summer, and we brought it home, and I just love having it in the living room.

Why?

Well, because we have made somewhat of an effort this year to study Indian art. We went to many shows, and we did some reading, and when we went to Canada we saw this piece in a gallery and we had seen many things like it at the shows and it is a thing we could afford, and so we bought it. And since then we have seen this Indian show at the Art Institute. They had a day where they had the Indian chief of the tribe come in and it was the same tribe that made this chest. And so we spoke to the people. The symbols and the things that they showed us and some of the other things that they had to sell, are so very similar, because this particular tribe are part of the Whale People, and only this tribe can use certain symbols and they used it for centuries in their art. So that's kind of a nice thing and we value it.

And what would it mean to you not to have this chest?

I would feel that the surrounding part, the living part would be pretty empty. I would hate to have to start collecting knicknacks and mementos.

So you're speaking of all of your art as a group?

I would group all of the atmosphere, the feel that you get. . . . (Csikszentmihalyi and Rochberg-Halton, 1981, pp. 182–183)

4. Attending, Thinking, Taking Notes, Taping

In our view, it is imperative that you tape-record the interview itself. Since there is no strict order of questioning and since probing is an important part of the process, you must be alert to what the informant is saying. If you have to write everything down at the same time, you are unlikely to be able to give him or her adequate attention. Your full attention *must* be focused on the informant. You must be thinking about probing for further explication or clarification of what is now being said, formulating probes that link current talk with what has already been said, thinking ahead to asking a *new* question that has now arisen and was not accounted for in the guide (plus making a note so you will not forget the question), and attending to the informant in a manner that communicates to her or him that you are indeed listening. All of this is hard enough in itself. Add to that the problem of writing it down—even if you take shorthand in an expert fashion—and you can see that the process of note taking in the interview decreases your interviewing capacity. Therefore, if conceivably possible, *tape-record.* Then you can interview. (In group interviews, or their variant, focus-group interviews, taping with adequate equipment becomes even more crucial; see Morgan 1988, p. 60.)

But there are dangers in tape-recording, too. Some people have found themselves not listening to the interviewee because they assume they have it all down on tape. The best way to fight against this tendency is to take sparse notes—key sentences, key words, key names, and so forth—in the course of the interview and to keep close account of what has already been talked about and what remains to be talked about. This is note taking in its best sense: for the purpose of staying on top of what is going on in the interview. You take notes on what has already gone on and on what has come up that you should ask about before the interview is over. (You also have a basis for reconstructing the interview should— terrible of terribles—the tape recording fails!)

5. **Separate Guides**
Because the interview guide provides a checklist and a memory device (a place for taking small notes during the interview), it is wise to use a fresh copy of the guide for each interview. For most researchers, located in settings where reproduction is easy and inexpensive, this should not prove burdensome. And the advantage is that the annotated guide for each separate interview becomes a recording and memory device at the time of writing up the interview and during full analysis. For jotting purposes, too, you should be careful not to cram the questions and probes together on a page, but rather space them out, leaving ample room for notes.

C. Writing Up the Interview

Having completed the interview, you can, if you are affluent or have extraordinarily indulgent associates, simply have the tape transcribed verbatim. You can then study the transcript and begin to analyze it. However, a strong caution should be given about such transcriptions: *Do not let the transcripts pile up without studying them as they become available.* You should spend, at minimum, as much time *immediately* studying and analyzing the interview material as you spent in the interview itself.

Ideas for analysis should be set down in the form of memos. Possible requests for a reinterview of the same person on particular topics should be considered. As we will explain in Chapter 9, you should perform "coding" and "memoing"—the heart of the process of developing analysis—as you go along, rather than after all the interviews are done. (See Chapter 9 for the rationale behind these admonitions and for explanations of the specific procedures involved.)

So much for the affluent. More numerous are the do-it-yourself transcribers. Transcribing tapes is a chore. But it also has an enormous virtue. It *requires* you to study each interview. Listening to the tape piece by piece forces you to consider, piece by piece, whether you have accomplished anything in the interview. It stimulates *analysis* (or at least this is the proper frame of mind to adopt while doing it). When a distinction, a concept, or an idea occurs to you (a **code**), write it into the transcription as an analytic note. For out of these bits and pieces of analysis—codes and memos—you will build the larger analysis that will become your research report.

Since you are following this guide and are therefore unlikely to be aiming for what is known as "conversation analysis" (Atkinson and Heritage, eds., 1984; Boden and Zimmerman, eds., 1991; Heritage 1985), it is generally not necessary for you to transcribe every word, exclamation, or pause that occurs in an interview. Indeed, there may be entire answers or descriptions given by the interviewee that you will feel need only to be summarized or recorded as *having occurred*. You do not necessarily need a verbatim transcription of everything the interviewee said, as the written record will indicate where to look for it on the tape. If you later want to have a verbatim version of a particular part of the interview, you can easily locate and transcribe it.

The written record of the interview, then, is an amalgam of the following:

1. summaries and notes of what the informant said generally at some point,
2. verbatim transcription of responses that seem important at the point of the write-up,
3. fieldnotes of relevant extra-interview encounters with the informant,
4. personal emotional experiences,
5. methodological difficulties or successes, and
6. ideas—little, tentative pieces of analysis (matters discussed as *codes* and *memos* in Chapter 9).

The process of writing up is a crucial one in this kind of research enterprise. You should expect to spend about *twice* as long writing up the interview in this fashion as you spent in conducting it.

One other point: In the course of writing up the interview, new questions and puzzlements are likely to occur. These should be recorded and later considered for incorporation into future interviews as questions or probes. If there are a great many new questions, you should consider reinterviews.

Interviews of this kind tend to produce a rather large amount of rich material. Before long, you have assembled a significant data log that you need somehow to manage. Indeed, the management problem is such that researchers who conduct studies utilizing qualitative interviewing tend to employ rather few interviews. While a few studies may be based on a hundred or more interviews (Vaughan 1990 involved 104, and Hamilton and Biggart 1984 involved 110), it is our impression that most are based only on approximately 30–50 interviews. Given the material management problem, numbers in that range seem quite reasonable. The researcher legitimately sacrifices breadth for depth.

IV. Data Logging in Observation: Fieldnotes

What the write-up is to intensive interviewing, fieldnotes are to participant observation: the crucial data log out of which the analysis will emerge.

For better or worse, the human mind tends to forget much that has occurred and to do so rather quickly. Thus, you need some means to overcome this tendency in yourself. Writing is such a means. In the form of continued notes by which the past is retained in the present, writing is an absolutely necessary, although not sufficient, condition for comprehending the objects of observation. Aside from getting along in the setting, the fundamental concrete task of the observer is the taking of fieldnotes. If you are not doing so, you might as well not be in the setting. Observers in many public settings are often able to take notes on the spot and to do so continuously during their entire time in the field. They will need later to transform their handwritten scrawls into typed copy, certainly, but the recording process itself is relatively unproblematic for them. For the majority of naturalistic investigators, however, the process involves a more complex sequence: mental notes, jotted notes, and then full fieldnotes in our formulation; scratch notes, fieldnotes proper, and fieldnote records in Roger Sanjek's rendering of the process (1990b, pp. 95–103; see also Bernard 1994, Ch. 9).

A. Mental Notes

Let us assume you are meeting with people or attending an event. The first step in taking fieldnotes is to evoke your culturally commonsensical and shared notion of what constitutes a descriptive report. From reading newspapers, magazines, and the like, you are already familiar with the character of "sheer reportage." It concerns such matters as who and how many were there, the physical character of the place, who said what to whom, who moved about in what way, and a general characterization of an order of events.

The first step in the process of writing fieldnotes is to orient your consciousness to the task of remembering items of these and, as the research develops, other kinds. This act of directing your mind to remember things at a later point may be called making *mental notes*. You are preparing yourself to be able later to put down on paper what you are now seeing.

B. Jotted Notes

If you are writing actual fieldnotes only at the end of a period of observation or at the end of a day (a relatively typical practice), you should preserve these mental notes as more than electrical traces in the brain. Such traces have a very high rate of decay. One way to preserve them provisionally is with *jotted notes*. Jotted notes are constituted of all the little phrases, quotes, key words, and the like that you put down during the observation and at inconspicuous moments. They have the function of jogging your memory at the time of writing fieldnotes.

Many fieldworkers carry small, pocket-sized tablets or notebooks precisely for the purpose of jotting down notes. Any surface will do, however: the cover of a book, a napkin, the back of a pamphlet, and so forth.

1. Memories

In the field, a current observation often brings back a memory of something that happened on a previous occasion that you forgot to put in your fieldnotes. Include these memories—identified as such—in your jotted notes.

2. Jotting Inconspicuously

As mentioned above, whether you are a known or an unknown observer, the general rule of thumb is, "Don't jot conspicuously." Of course, you may also be doing interviewing in the field while observing. In that case, to seem competent, you should take notes of the kind described for intensive interviewing. Indeed, the interviewees will *expect* you to take some kind of notes to indicate that you are indeed seriously interviewing them! And there may be other occasions when someone expects you to write something down on the spot. There also may be occasions when note taking in the setting is not only appropriate for you but also for all the other participants. But in ordinary day-to-day observation it seems wisest not to flaunt the fact that you are recording. If you are a known observer, the observed are already well aware of being observed. You need not increase any existing anxieties by continuously and openly writing down what you see and hear. Rather, jot notes at moments of withdrawal and when shielded.

3. Fuller Jottings

In addition, before getting to the full fieldnotes, you might make more elaborate jottings on the way home or while waiting for a bus or before going to bed. But one word of warning regarding both jotted notes and fuller jottings: Never write them on both sides of anything! We quote Jacques Barzun and Henry F. Graff:

> There is in research one absolute rule that suffers no exception. NEVER WRITE ON BOTH SIDES OF ANYTHING. If you violate the rule and do it once, you will do it again; and if you do it from time to time you can never remember when you have done it; you thereby condemn yourself to a frequent frustrating hunt for "that note," which may be on the other side of some unidentifiable slip or card or page. You will go by it a dozen times without seeing it, turn over hundreds of pieces of paper to recover it. (1977, p. 23)

C. Full Fieldnotes

At the end of the day (or of a shorter observation period), you should cloister yourself for the purpose of making *full fieldnotes*. All those mental notes and jottings are *not* fieldnotes until you have converted them to a running log of observations.

1. Mechanics

Before we discuss the typical contents of fieldnotes, some "mechanical" aspects need to be described.

As a general rule, *write promptly*. Full fieldnotes should be written no later than the morning after an observation day. If you observed only in the morning, then write them up that afternoon. If you observed only in the afternoon, do the notes that evening. The underlying rule is to minimize the time period between observation and writing.

Psychologists have found that forgetting is very slight in the first few hours after a learning experience but accelerates geometrically as time passes. To wait a day or more is to forget a massive amount of material. Happily, it has also been found that memory decays very little during sleep. That is, forgetting has more to do with the acquisition of new experience than with the sheer passage of time. Therefore, it is reasonably safe to sleep on a day's or evening's observations and to write them up the first thing the next morning, thus avoiding the necessity of staying up half the night. But if you wait for days, you are likely to remember only the barest outlines of the observation period. And even if you can remember more than the barest outlines, the chances are excellent that what will be erased from memory are those small phenomena that are omnipresent in social life but which rarely make their way into our accounts. Long delays between observation and fieldnote entry increases the likelihood that your notes will contain, for example, no information on your own fleeting emotions, much less the expressed fleeting emotions of others. Nor, as another example, are your notes likely to contain much description of small gestures, facial expressions, body movements—those important ephemera that we so easily forget.

As we have previously emphasized, writing fieldnotes takes *personal discipline* and *time*. It is all too easy to put it off for a day or so, especially since actually writing the notes may take as long or longer than the observation. Indeed, as a rule of thumb you should plan to spend as much time writing as you spent observing. This, of course, is not invariant. Some observers spend considerably less time on notes and are still able to perform good analysis. Many others have been known to spend considerably more than equal time in writing up their notes. How much time you personally spend depends, too, on the demands of the setting you are observing and the proportion of your total time being devoted to the study.

But one point is inescapable. All the fun of actually being out and about mucking around in some setting must be matched by cloistered rigor in committing to paper (and therefore to future usefulness) what has taken place.

Some observers have access to the luxury of dictating machines and secretaries. And, of course, "talking" your fieldnotes takes much less time than writing them. Such affluents need the same advice as we gave for intensive interviewers: Get the transcriptions as soon as possible and review them thoroughly, making further notes in the process. While dictation saves time, it also keeps you from really having to think about what has happened and from searching out analytic themes. Writing, on the other hand, stimulates thought, or at least so it seems for a great number of people.

But the opportunity to dictate one's fieldnotes into a machine is not limited to the affluents. Inexpensive and compact tape recorders make this a possibility for almost all researchers. And there are certainly a number of advantages to the practice. One can, for example, "talk into the tape" instead of making written jotted notes and, since most of us can speak faster than we can write, the accumulation of the day's oral jottings will often be detailed enough to constitute full fieldnotes. Similarly, while one cannot usually write while walking or driving, one certainly can talk during such periods, thus putting otherwise "wasted" time to productive use. Unfortunately, for every advantage, there always seems to be an equal disadvantage. In this instance, the problem is that, as with interviews, recordings on tape are not directly available for analysis. To be useful, they have to be transcribed. And as we discussed above, transcription is a tedious, time-consuming process. It will probably take you longer to transcribe your dictated full fieldnotes than it would have taken to record them in written form in the first place. The temptation will be great to put the job off until "later" when you "will feel more like doing it." Some researchers have reported starting out by dictating their notes but having to give up the practice because "later" simply never came. If you are extremely disciplined and compulsive about your work, you may find the tape recorder a faithful assistant. But if you have even the slightest tendency toward procrastination, stick to your keyboard.

2. Contents

Of what do fieldnotes consist? Basically, they are a more or less chronological log of what is happening to and in the setting and to and in the observer. More specifically, the types of material described below typically and properly appear in fieldnotes.

- For the most part, fieldnotes are a running description of events, people, things heard and overheard, conversations among people, conversations with people. Each new physical setting and person encountered merits a description. You should also record changes in the physical setting or people. Since you are likely to encounter the same settings and people again and again, you need not repeat such descriptions, but only augment them as changes occur.

Observers often draw maps into their fieldnotes, indicating approximate layouts and the physical placement of people in scenes, as well as their gross movements through a period of observation. Since the notes will be chronologically arranged, you should also keep records of the approximate times at which various events occur.

The writing of running descriptions is guided by at least two rules of thumb: (1) Be concrete, and (2) distinguish verbatim accounts from those that are paraphrased or based on general recall.

Rather than summarizing or employing abstract adjectives and adverbs, attempt to be behavioristic and *concrete*. Attempt to stay at the lowest possible level of inference. Avoid, as much as possible, employing the participants' descriptive and interpretive terms as your own. If Person A thought Person B was happy, joyous, depressed, or whatever, report this as an imputation of Person A. Try to capture Person B's raw behavior, leaving aside for that moment any final judgment as to B's actual state of mind or the "true meaning" of his or her behavior. The participants' beliefs as to the "true meaning" of objects, events, and people are thus recorded as being just that—beliefs.

Novelist and social observer Truman Capote claimed to be able to recall verbatim several hours of conversation. Such an ability is strikingly unusual. More typically, people recall some things word for word and many other things only in general. Whether you are giving a verbatim account should be indicated in your fieldnotes. You might consider adopting notations such as those employed by Anselm Strauss et al. in their study of a mental hospital: "Verbal material recorded within quotations signified exact recall; verbal material within apostrophes indicated a lesser degree of certainty or paraphrasing; and verbal material with no markings meant reasonable recall but not quotation" (Strauss, Schatzman, Bucher, Erlich, and Sabshin 1964, p. 29).

- As observation periods mount up, you may find yourself recalling—often at odd moments—items of information you have not previously entered into the fieldnotes. An occurrence you previously saw as insignificant or simply forgot now presents itself as meriting record. Summoning it up as best you can, enter the item's date, content, the context, and so forth into the current day's notes.

- If you are working at it at all, analytic ideas and inferences will begin to occur to you; for example, how things are patterned in the setting, how present occurrences are examples of some sociological or other concept, or how things "really seem to work around here." Some of these ideas may seem obvious and trivial; some may seem farfetched and wild; and many may seem in between. *Put all of them into the fieldnotes.* The only proviso is to be sure to mark them as analytic ideas or inferences. (A good way to do this is to enclose them in brackets.)

When you eventually withdraw from the setting and concentrate on your analysis, you should thus have more than raw field material. The period of concerted analysis is greatly facilitated if during the fieldwork itself you are also logging conceptual material, creating a foundation of possible lines of analysis and interpretation. Such material may range from minute pieces of analysis to broad ideas about the master theme or themes of the study. In Chapter 9, we will discuss these aspects of fieldnotes more fully as the processes of *coding* and *memoing*.

You are likely to have more of these codes and memos on analytic directions in your notes than you will ever include in the final report. But, by building a foundation of tentative pieces of directions for analysis, the analytic period will be much less traumatic. Analysis will become a matter of selecting from and working out analytic themes that already exist.

- In addition to providing a record of the setting and of analytic ideas, fieldnotes are used for recording your impressions and feelings. You have personal opinions of people, emotional responses to being an observer and to the setting itself. You can feel discouraged, joyous, rejected, loved, and so forth. To provide some degree of distance, you should also record whatever aspects of your emotional life are involved in the setting. If you feel embarrassed, put down, looked upon with particular favor, or if you fall in love, hate someone, have an affair, or whatever, this private diary should keep track of such facts. This can serve at least three important functions. First, in being (at least privately) honest with yourself about your feelings toward objects, events, and people, you may find that some of the participants *also* feel quite similar things and that your private emotional response was more widespread, thus providing a clue for analysis. In feeling, for instance, that some person in the setting is getting unjustly treated by a turn of events, and getting privately angry over it, you may also discover later that many other people privately felt the same way. And a fact of this kind may lead to important analytic trails. Second, your emotional experience, even if not shared by others in the setting, may still suggest important analytic leads. For example, repeated experiences of anxiety or disquiet when talking with informants *may* simply mean that you are finding the fieldworker role a difficult one. But it *may* indicate that the worldview of the people you are studying is far more distant from your own than you have yet appreciated. Third, you will periodically review your fieldnotes, and during analysis you will work with them intensively. A concurrent record of your emotional state at various past times can later, away from the setting and in a cooler frame of mind, allow you to scrutinize your notes for obvious biases. You become more able to give the benefit of the doubt in cases where you were perhaps too involved or uninvolved in some incident. This running record of your opinions, impressions, emotions, and the like should, of course, be labeled as such in the notes. (For a detailed discussion of the "use and abuse" of emotions in fieldwork, see Kleinman and Copp 1993.)

- Any given day's observations are likely to be incomplete. An account of an incident may lack an adequate description of a given person's behavior or conscious intentions. The incident may only be sketchily known. A well-described incident may lead you to look for further occurrences of events of that kind. In other words, a given day's notes raise a series of observational questions and call for notes for further information. It is reasonable to make these notes as you are writing up your full fieldnotes. You can then review and assemble them as reminders of unobtrusive questions to ask particular people or of things to look for.

3. Style

Several additional stylistic aspects of fieldnotes relate to both the mechanical and content matters we have discussed.

For one thing, there is the inevitable question of how long and full the notes should be. How many pages should notes run for a given observation period? It happens that observers differ enormously in the detail and length of the fieldnotes they keep. Some seem to be frustrated novelists and have been known to write 40 or more single-spaced pages on a three-hour period of observation. Other observers might write only a few pages. Here there are no set rules. Settings differ enormously, as do observers' verbal compulsions. The kinds of phenomena to which observers are sensitive vary quite widely. At minimum, though, you ought to write up at least a couple of single-spaced typed pages for every hour of observation. It is quite likely that you will want to write much more.

Fieldnotes are typically quite private documents, or at least accessible only to your trusted friends, as in most team observer situations. So, *let them flow.* You need not attempt to employ totally correct grammar, punctuate with propriety, hit the right keys, say only publicly polite things, be guarded about your feelings, or use any of the other niceties most people affect for strangers. The object in fieldnotes, rather, is to get information down as correctly as you can and be as honest with yourself as possible. Unless you choose to make them so, your notes will *never* be public documents, so *write on*. Let all those mental and jotted notes flow out, typing like the "compulsive" you are hopefully becoming. Field-notes are, after all, behind the scenes. It is at the next stage—concerted analysis—that all of this is processed for propriety.

We have perhaps made fieldnotes sound intimate and revealing and therefore fascinating reading. To a degree they are. But the overwhelm-ing portion consists of running descriptions that are mundane, unevent-ful, and dull. Indeed, if they were otherwise, people would simply publish their fieldnotes. It is precisely because they are little in and of themselves that it is necessary to do analysis. Therefore, do not start out believing that the fieldwork venture, and fieldnotes in particular, will be an exciting affair. Patience, persistence, drudgery, and dullness occur here, as everywhere else in social life. Still, fieldnote writing can be punctuated by periods of elation and joy over events and over the occurrence of insights, ideas, and understandings.

4. Samples

Among the more serious barriers to the creation of a richly detailed data log is the conception, frequently held by beginning researchers, that fieldnotes constitute a kind of literary product. We have attempted to "scotch" that idea in our preceding discussion of style, but perhaps more convincing evidence is needed. To that end, here are three brief extracts from the notes of three different fieldworkers. Although, as you can see, the style of each is quite different, the three extracts are alike in laying no claim to "literary" value. These researchers are recording what they see as straightforwardly and as quickly as they can; they are not con-cerned with prose style or even with rendering their descriptions in a manner that readers might find interesting.

> An approximately four-year-old boy is sitting between two women, the older of which is apparently his mother, on molded plastic chairs in the mall facing the closed entrance of a pizza place. The boy is moving a miniature replica of a car over the connecting arms of the chairs. He holds up the toy car to his mother and announces: "It's a jeep." The boy's mother replies: "No, it's a car from a long time ago." The boy begins to move the toy car over the arms of the chairs once again but it falls down into the seat of the other woman's chair. The boy's mother looks at him and says: "That's a bad boy." The other woman picks up the car and hands it to the boy. The boy's mother instructs him to "say thank you." The boy turns to the woman and says "thank you," and the woman responds "you're welcome." The boy then turns to this mother and asks

"When's the pizza open?" (Spencer Cahill, research published as "Childhood and Public Life: Reaffirming Biographical Divisions" 1990)

By way of illustrating how she (T.) needed help in dealing with parents, she told me the following case of sexual behavior among the children. X (the sister of D., now in program) was on top of a little boy, his penis was erect. T. was conflicted as to how to handle this. "I knew I couldn't go directly to the mother, because she would beat the little girl and give her a thing about sex." But I didn't know how to talk to her. So I made an appointment for myself with XX (preg. [pregnancy] counselor, consultant on sexual behavior, consultant for ECE); I spoke to her about it, asked her to speak to my parents about sexual behavior among children. A couple of years later I was able to speak to D's mother. (Note: I was not able to get the full story of this incident because at this moment the two new student teachers walked in. I will follow it up at a later date.) (Carole Joffe, research published as *Friendly Intruders: Childcare Professionals and Family Life* 1977)

Six men alone, most reading, holding briefcases or just staring. All in business suits. Two men together, talking. All men within vision sitting with legs crossed. Young middle class girl, long hair, late teens, early 20's, reading. Woman, possibly lower middle class with preschool age child, staring or looking after him. Bus boy passes behind me, drops glass, everyone looks this way, but casually, in a disinterested fashion. Young middle class woman, mid 20's reading, posed, book held high. Two elderly ladies sitting together. Except for one side where there are two men together and then a space and then another man, people are pretty far apart. There is only one line of chairs where both males and females are sitting and there are two women together and one male. Both women who are reading are sitting straight in their chairs, books held high, not slouching whereas several men have slid down in chairs or more generally positioned themselves more comfortably. (Lyn Lofland, research published as *A World of Strangers: Order and Action in Urban Public Space* 1985b)

Because here we have necessarily corrected the typographical errors that appear in the originals, even these extracts provide a less than fully realistic picture of fieldnotes. For those who desire more authenticity, facsimiles of actual "fieldnotes in the raw" are provided on pages 122–135 of Roger Sanjek's *Fieldnotes: The Makings of Anthropology* (1990).

V. Interview Write-Ups and Fieldnotes as Compulsion

If all the above advice about writing up interviews and keeping detailed fieldnotes sounds unbearably tedious, take heart. Once you have established a regimen of transcribing and note taking relative to interviews and of jotting regularly and then making disciplined, full notes relative to observation, these tasks can come to have a demand and a logic of their own. You can come to feel that unless something your informant said is not only on the tape but also transcribed or summarized, or that unless something you observed appears in your full notes, you are in peril of losing the words or the actions. That is, you can come to experience a *compulsion* to write up everything lest it be lost forever. Upon reaching that level of felt responsibility for logging data, you are fully engaged in fieldwork.

The preceding chapters describe only the first part of the story of doing naturalistic research. The whole point of starting where you are, of getting in and getting along, and, most especially, of logging data, is the performance of social science analysis. We now turn to that challenge.

PART TWO

FOCUSING DATA

While *gathering* data in the ways described in Part One, the researcher also begins a second major line of activity, that of *focusing* those data. By "focusing," we mean that the investigator begins to envision:

• possible *topics* on which to concentrate,

• *questions* to ask about those topics, and

• treatment of them that will *arouse interest*.

Discussed in Chapters 6, 7, and 8, respectively, each is a form of consciousness that, when applied to data, begins to turn those raw materials into social science analysis. We say "begin" because a third activity—that of analysis (described in Part Three)—is also necessary.

Prior to analysis, though, the researcher needs to understand the nature of social science *topics*, *questions*, and *interests*, which we cover in the following three chapters.

CHAPTER 6

THINKING TOPICS

T he title concept of this guide—"social settings"—points to a domain of study, but taken alone is too abstract to be of great help in detailed inquiry. For purposes of detailed inquiry we need more elaborated or refined ideas about social settings, ideas relating to their *units* of social organizational scale and to their substantive *aspects*. When combined, units and aspects form *topics*.

I. Units and Aspects Combine into Topics

By *unit* of social organizational scale, we mean the magnitude or size of social setting at which we elect to conceptualize our data. Three basic dimensions of scale are (1) the number of people involved, (2) the period of time on which we focus, and (3) the physical size of the territory the setting occupies. At a lower level on these three dimensions, the analyst might, for example, focus on a unit involving only two people interacting over a period of only a few seconds in the physical space of only a few square feet. Even more microscopically, one might focus on the tiny "speech acts" of a single person. At much higher levels of social organizational scale, the unit might contain thousands of people considered in the perspective of decades as they interact over hundreds of square miles. Prototypical units at this scale include the urban neighborhood, the small city, and the rural town.

By *aspects* of social settings we mean forms of their social content or substance, irrespective of their scale. Below, we address three aspects on which researchers frequently focus: cognitions, emotions, and hierarchy.

As mentioned, specific units and aspects taken together provide guiding *topics* in the task of focusing data. After more fully explaining what we mean by units, we will show how they combine with aspects to form topics.

II. The Contexts of Topics: The Substantive Domains of Society

However, before undertaking those discussions, we need to relate units, aspects, and topics to the broad canvas of "society" as the larger and encompassing context within which (or on which) analysis is conducted.

The holistic entity termed *society* is, in the industrial democracies at least, conceived by its members as divided into a range of substantive domains or areas focusing on distinctively different concerns and utilizing varying principles of organization. Although people do not necessarily agree on the exact nature and number of these substantive domains, there is a fair consensus on thirteen that can be grouped into four categories.

1. The first category of substantive domains focuses on the production and distribution of the basics of life itself: the *economy,* which produces sustenance, and the *polity* and *religion,* which deal with organizing and legitimizing the distribution of economic and other valued goods.

2. The second category of domains pertains to major ways that humans stratify themselves. These are the dimensions of *social class, sex, ethnicity,* and *age.*

3. The third category of domains addresses basic situations of human life that are unavoidably problematic: the reproduction of the species in the *family* (or, conceived more generically, in intimate relations), the socialization of the young in *education,* coping with crime and other deviance in *criminal justice,* and addressing illness in medicine and *health care.*

4. Last, two domains are concerned with the physical container of society itself: the relation of humans to the *natural environment* (as in resource destruction and depletion), and their relation to the physical environment they have constructed for themselves—the *built environment* (as in low-density "sprawl" or homelessness).

We sketch this canvas of domains making up society for the purpose of pointing out that the units and aspects we are about to explain can (and should) be studied in any and all of these substantive domains. What we outline in this chapter (and in every other chapter, for that matter) is an omnibus tool kit of focusing ideas that can be brought to bear on any social thing in any substantive domain (including some not on the above list, such as the military, culture, sports, and media).

We feel it is important to stress this point to forestall the possible concern that we have not addressed one or another substantive matter that is of key interest to particular people. Our answer to this concern is that *any* substantive social matter in *any* domain can be analyzed insightfully when guided by the focusing concepts explained in this chapter (and combined with the guidance provided in other chapters).

III. Units

Although there are some commonly employed units of social settings, there is no definitive and agreed-upon set of them. Therefore, what we present here as units is a set of tendencies one can see in fieldwork reports rather than a definitive depiction of *the* units of social science. The practical meaning of this for you as a researcher is that you should feel free to adapt and innovate in thinking about the scale or scales of social organization at which you are going to organize your analysis (or analyses).

The units are arranged roughly from the microscopic to the macroscopic in terms of increasing duration, space, and human population. Put differently, the scale of social organization is increasing as we move from unit to unit. It is important to recognize, therefore, that each new unit introduced *contains* units discussed prior to it rather than being separate from them.

A. Practices

Among the smallest units of a social setting or of social organization are social **practices**, recurrent categories of talk or action on which the observer focuses as having analytic significance. The activity is, by definition, one the participants regard as unremarkable and as a normal and undramatic feature of ongoing life. It is only the analyst who, by collecting instances of it and dwelling on it, singles it out as something remarkable.

Stan Bernstein's timeless study of student "fritters" provides an apt example of such inventive "dwelling." A "fritter" is "a justification a student gives to her or himself for not doing student work in response to felt pressures to work" (1978, pp. 17–34). Bernstein developed this concept in the course of interviewing students who were coping with the open-ended, never-finished task of studying. He discerned four main classes of fritters:

1. *person-based,* including "biological necessity" and "rest on your laurels";
2. *social-relations based,* including group discussion and group work fritters;
3. *valuative-based,* including fritters of "the Higher Good," "experience broadens," and "existential moods"; and
4. *task-based,* including work scheduling (e.g., "time symmetry" and "great divide" fritters), preparation and creativity fritters (e.g., "the first step is the hardest").

Other kinds of practices on which fieldworkers have focused include rituals and taboos in uncertain situations (Gmelch 1971) and verbal "ploys" for aligning discrepant behavior with self-image (Kalab 1987, Pestello 1991).

B. Episodes

In contrast to practices, **episodes** are by definition *remarkable* and *dramatic* to the participants and therefore to the analyst as well. Precisely because of this, researchers frequently study the ordinary varieties of episodes: divorce, sudden and catastrophic illness, being a victim of a crime, committing a crime, social and natural disasters, crowd disorders, and so forth. Indeed, a significant portion of several social-analytic specialties is devoted to the analysis of episodes. We have in mind, especially, the study of the family, deviance, crime, crowd behavior, and social movements.

Episodes differ in the number of people and the length of time they involve. Many criminal acts, for example, tend to the relatively brief and individualistic side. Episodes that involve a few more people and extend over months or years were the focus of Fred Davis's classic study of families with a child stricken by polio (1972). He reports that such small groups must cope with problems the child has with (1) *appearance,* with regard to usual assumptions about people's physical attractiveness, wholeness, and symmetry of body parts; (2) *participation* in usual childhood activities; and (3) *association* with peers.

Since the stigma of polio is visible, the families cannot employ the strategy of "passing." Instead, they use strategies of "normalization" or "disassociation":

1. Normalization is the effort to make light of the handicap or to deny that it has any importance.

2. Disassociation involves efforts to insulate the child and family as a whole from events and involvements that might force recognition of the handicap as a "difference." Disassociation frequently involves the following:

   a. Resentment and anger towards "normals" accompanied by feelings of self-hatred deriving from the child's inability to live up to the prized normal standards.

   b. Passive acceptance of the child's exclusion from the world of "normals" punctuated periodically by attempts to ingratiate him or herself.

   c. Retreat to a more or less privatized sphere of hopes and fantasies in which the harsh impress of the normal standard is tenuously kept at bay.

   d. An attempt to recast and reformulate personal values, activities, and associations so as to avoid or remove the sting from the often negative, condescending, and depreciating attitudes of "normals." (F. Davis 1972, pp. 103–130)

Episodes can involve hundreds, thousands, or even millions of people, as they do in "revolutionary" situations (Walton 1984), crowd disorders (N. Johnson 1987, 1988; McPhail 1995), joyous public occasions (J. Lofland 1985), or even community decision crises (Maines and Bridger 1992, Zablocki 1980).

C. Encounters

An **encounter** is a tiny social system formed when two or more persons are in one another's immediate physical presence and strive to maintain a single (ordinarily spoken) focus of mutual involvement. The life span of an encounter is only as long as the people remain together. Thus, most encounters endure only a few minutes and at most a few hours. Copresence in public restrooms (Cahill et al. 1985), sidewalk verbal exchanges (Anderson 1990), requests for minor aid in public settings (Gardner 1986), and committee meetings, job interviews, and individual meetings of college classes are all prosaic illustrations of encounters.

Encounters differ from the units discussed above (and from some that follow) in that they tend to be bounded *social systems,* that is, fields of forces set up and maintained by the *relations* among the people who are present. In this same sense, though, encounters are similar to some of the units we will discuss below, especially small groups, relationships, and formal organizations. These units are also bounded fields of forces (although the fields must generally be maintained for a longer period of time).

D. Roles

In their clearest form, **roles** are consciously articulated and abstracted categories of social "types of persons." In this sense, a role is both a label that people use to organize their own activity and one that they apply to others as a way of making sense of their activity.

1. Ascribed and Formal Roles

The most socially "obvious" instances of roles are, of course, those that are "ascribed," meaning imputed to a person because of particular physical characteristics, such as sex, ethnicity, and age. Formal roles are linked to such notions as "position," "office," and "occupation"; they are commonsensically understood in societies with an abundance of formal organizations and "organizational charts."

2. Informal Organizational and Occupational Roles

Within formal roles of an organizational or occupational sort, there commonly exist informal *supplements* to the formal role structure, as in the widespread tendency to distinguish among people with whom one works in terms of how strict or loose they are in conforming to the "official" rules of an organization.

Settings involving captivity commonly generate what are known as *argot roles,* roles characterized by the use of labels produced by and reflecting the problems of the setting. Prisons, for example, are lush gardens for argot roles. In men's prisons of some decades ago, analysts thus recorded such slang labels as "the right guy," "wolf," "tough," "gorilla," "hipster," and "ball buster" (Giallombardo 1966, p. 285).

3. Social Types
Social life and people are highly fluid and ambiguous objects of perception. Formal and informal organizational and occupational roles, therefore, are often insufficient guides to action. The upshot is yet further devices for "coding" people that Orrin Klapp has termed *social types*. These are "concepts of roles that have not been fully codified and rationalized . . . [that are] a chart to role-structures otherwise largely invisible and submerged" (1958, p. 674). Social types are constructs that fall, conceptually, somewhere between individual, idiosyncratic behavior on the one side and formal or informal role behavior on the other. "Between knowing a person's formal status only and knowing him intimately, there is a kind of knowledge that 'fills in'" (1958, p. 674). Social types make possible a "finer discrimination than the formal . . . structure recognizes" (1958, p. 674). Consider, for example, the following types:

Underdog	Two-timer
Bigshot	Uncle Tom
Smart operator	Dragon lady
Dude	Crackpot
Good guy	Fanatic
Bully	Simpleton
Liar	Sissy
Fool	Sad sack
Cheat	(Klapp 1971, p. 12)

4. Social Psychological Types
Pushing the concept of role to its extreme, some investigators have conceived what are usually thought of as personality traits or types as types of roles. One of the most ambitious efforts of this nature is the work of Murray Davis and Catherine Schmidt, who distinguish between "obnoxious" and "nice" people in terms of differing *interaction roles* (1977).

E. Relationships

Two parties who interact with some regularity over a relatively extended period of time and who view themselves as "connected" to one another form a **social relationship**. Such pairings vary in myriad ways: the positive or negative character of the emotions prevailing, the degree of interdependence, the amount of trust, the parties' relative amounts of power, the amount each knows about the other, and so forth. Terms used to describe relations that capture certain of these variations include *friend, intimate, bargaining, marital, cultivated, stranger, adversary, tyrannical, impersonal,* and *bureaucratic.*

No relationship is stable; all have histories of change. An analytic study by Fred Davis focuses on such changes. By observing the relationships developed by people who are physically handicapped in a visible way, he sought to "delineate in transactional terms, the stages through which a sociable relationship" between a "normal" and a visibly handicapped person may typically pass. He found three such stages:

1. *Fictional Acceptance.* Unlike earlier societies . . . in which a visible handicap automatically relegates the person to a caste-like, inferior status . . . in our society the visibly handicapped are customarily accorded . . . the surface acceptance that democratic manners guarantee to nearly all.

2. *"Breaking Through"—Facilitating Normalized Role-Taking.* In moving beyond fictional acceptance, what takes place essentially is a redefinitional process in which the handicapped person projects images, attitudes and concepts of self which encourage the normal to . . . take his role . . . in terms other than those associated with imputations of deviance. . . . As the handicapped person expands the interactional nexus, he simultaneously disavows the deviance latent in his status; concurrently, to the degree to which the normal is led reciprocally to assume the redefining . . . self-attitudes, he comes to . . . view as more like himself . . . those aspects of the other which at first connoted deviance for him.

3. *Institutionalization of the Normalized Relationship.* Having disavowed deviance and induced the other to respond to him as he would to a normal, the problem then becomes one of sustaining the normalized definition in the face of the many small amendments and qualifications that must frequently be made to it. . . . This third, "normal but" . . . stage of the relationship, if it endures, is institutionalized mainly in either one of two ways. In the first, the normal normalizes his perceptions to such an extent as to suppress his effective awareness of many of the areas in which the handicapped person's behavior unavoidably deviates from the normal standards. . . . [The second way] is for the normal to surrender some of his normalcy by joining the handicapped person in a marginal, half-alienated, half-tolerant, outsiders' orientation to "the Philistine world of normals." (F. Davis 1972, pp. 120–132)

F. Groups

A few (up to a dozen or so) people who interact with some regularity over an extended period of time and who conceive of themselves as a social entity (a "we") form a social **group**. Informal leisure and work groups, cliques, networks, and families are prime examples.

1. Cliques

Some types of informal groups weave their way through larger, more formal organizations; they bind their members in invisible but powerful ways. Such groups are commonly called *cliques*. In observing executives in several commercial and industrial firms, Melville Dalton noticed that the webs of informal ties among them assumed different forms, which he classified in terms of their relation to the formal structure of the encompassing organization:

1. *Vertical Cliques* usually occur in a single department . . . between a top officer and some of his subordinates. They are vertical in the sense that they are up-and-down alliances between formal unequals.

   a. *Vertical Symbiotic Cliques.* The top officer is concerned to aid and protect his subordinates. . . . The subordinates fully advise him of real or rumored threats to his position. . . . There is a satisfying exchange of services.

   b. *Vertical Parasitic Cliques.* The exchange of services between the lower and higher clique members is unequal. The lower ranked person or persons receive more than they give and may greatly damage the higher officer.

2. *Horizontal Cliques* . . . cut across more than one department and embrace formal equals for the most part.

   a. *Horizontal Defensive Cliques.* It is usually brought on by what its members regard as crises . . . [and] is strong for only the limited time necessary to defeat or adjust to a threat.

   b. *Horizontal Aggressive Cliques.* Their action is a cross-departmental drive to effect changes rather than to resist them, to redefine responsibility, or even directly to shift it.

3. *Random Clique.* As compared with the more functional cliques, this one is random in the sense that its members may come from any part of the personnel, managers and managed, and that they do not anticipate important consequences of their association. (Dalton 1959, pp. 57–65)

2. Adaptive Significance

Groups have *adaptive significance,* that is, they provide ways for people collectively to cope with their circumstances. Among industrial workers with extraordinarily monotonous jobs, for example, Donald Roy observed group efforts to relieve the pressures of highly repetitive work. Himself employed in such a job (one that involved stamping leather or plastic parts all day), Roy (1976) observed that his work group was structured around the adaptive activities of "times" and "themes."

1. Times consisted of almost hourly group breaks or interruptions that served to punctuate the monotony. Roy enumerated a variety of times in the daily series: "peach time" (group sharing of a peach), "banana time," "window time," "lunchtime," "picking-up time" (someone coming for their latest output), occasional talk, "fish time," "Coke time," and so on.

2. Themes consisted of a range of sometimes nonsensical, sometimes serious talk in which the group members engaged. There were a variety of kidding themes, sexual themes, themes about people's problems, and simple "chatter themes."

G. Organizations

Organizations are consciously formed collectivities with formal goals that are pursued in a more or less articulately planned fashion. Some major aspects of the analysis of organizations include the circumstances of their formation, how they recruit and control members, the types and causes of the goal-pursuit strategies they adopt, and the causes of their growth, change, or demise. Analyses of organizations as goal-pursuing entities often focus on their formal and informal strategies. Nicole Biggart's discussion of "obscuring the economic in the social" in direct selling organizations (DSOs) is an example of a formal strategy:

> [S]ome network DSOs effectively obscure the financial transaction that, in fact, is taking place: they present themselves as direct selling companies that paradoxically do not sell. For example, Mary Kay beauty consultants profess that they do not sell cosmetics. Rather, they "teach skin care" and the skillful use of cosmetics. Shaklee distributors do not sell vitamins and soap, they "share products" that enhance good health. . . . By transforming selling into a nurturing function such as "teaching" and "sharing," many distributors come to see their economic activities as primarily acts of caring. (1989, pp. 116–117)

In contrast, Philip Selznick's principle of "cooptation" provides an example of an informal strategy. He defined *cooptation* as "the process of absorbing new elements into the leadership or policy-defining structure of an organization as a means of averting threats to its stability or existence" (1953). This idea evolved out of Selznick's immersing himself in the day-to-day operations of the Tennessee Valley Authority. He discovered that it was useful to conceive of

> this general mechanism . . . [as assuming] two basic forms: formal cooptation, when there is a need to establish the legitimacy of authority or the administrative necessity of the relevant public; and informal cooptation, when there is a need for adjustment to the pressure of specific centers of power within the community. (1953, p. 259)

From this viewpoint, an infinite variety of acts could be understood as instances of one or another of the two basic types of cooptation, and cooptation itself thus became the major organizing principle in his analysis.

Among efforts to depict generic *types* of organizations, we may refer to Erving Goffman's concept of the "total institution." Observing a mental hospital, Goffman began to contemplate ways in which that establishment resembled organizations not usually thought of as similar to it. As he thought about other organizations, such as tuberculosis sanitariums, monasteries, boarding schools, and so forth, he began to see his own research setting as an instance of a more general type of setting:

When we review the different institutions in our Western society, we find some that are encompassing to a degree discontinuously greater than the ones next in line. Their encompassing or total character is symbolized by the barrier to social intercourse with the outside and to departure that is often built right into the physical plant, such as locked doors, high walls, barbed wire, cliffs, water, forest, or moors. These establishments I am calling *total institutions.* . . .

A basic social arrangement in modern society is that the individual tends to sleep, play, and work in different places, with different coparticipants under different authorities, and without an overall rational plan. The central feature of total institutions can be described as breakdown of the barriers ordinarily separating these spheres of life. (Goffman 1961, pp. 4–6)

Having formulated and explored the general characteristics of this abstract concept, Goffman then went on to trace out and explicate the consequences and corollaries of these characteristics. In so doing, he made the minute aspects of social life in the mental hospital he studied take on more general meaning and relevance.

H. Settlements

Complexly interrelated sets of encounters, roles, groups, and organizations, existing within a socially defined territory and performing a range of life-sustaining functions, are often labeled **settlements.** Very large settlements—cities of many thousands or even millions—are considerably beyond the grasp of the naturalistic researcher. But the study of smaller settlements—villages, towns, ghettos, neighborhoods, blocks— is richly represented in naturalist fieldstudy literature. The classic anthropological study, for example, is a descriptive account of an entire "simpler" society; these societies are generally comprised of a single village or cluster of villages. Thus, the analytic unit for a good deal of work in anthropology is, in fact, the settlement (e.g., Heider 1991, Levy 1973, Lutz 1988, Scheper-Hughes 1992). Within sociology, a number of studies that are considered classics of fieldwork are also studies of settlements. Four of these, interestingly enough, focus on Italian (or mixed-Italian) neighborhoods in large cities: William F. Whyte's *Street Corner Society: The Social Structure of an Italian Slum* (1993), in Boston's North End; Herbert Gans's *The Urban Villagers: Group and Class in the Life of Italian-Americans* (1962), in Boston's West End; Gerald Suttles's *The Social Order of the Slum: Ethnicity and Territory in the Inner City* (1968), in Chicago; and Jonathan Rieder's *Canarsie: The Jews and Italians of Brooklyn Against Liberalism* (1985), in New York.

As in most naturalistic research, the settlement study is normally conducted by a lone investigator, or at most by a two-person team. As long as the unit is not too large—that is, no larger than a contained neighborhood or a small town—this has proved a satisfactory arrangement. (See, for example, Baumgartner 1988, Gans 1967, Horowitz 1983, Kornblum 1974, Merry 1981, J. West 1945.)

However, the study of larger settlements—medium-sized towns or small cities—requires the use of research teams, sometimes of considerable size. Robert Lynd's and Helen Lynd's pioneer study of Muncie, Indiana (1929), for example, was made possible by a research team composed of the authors, two additional investigators, and a staff secretary; the restudy performed by Caplow et al. (1982) was enormously more elaborate. The data for Arthur Vidich's and Joseph Bensman's study of a rural community (1968) was produced by a larger project, the "Cornell Studies in Social Growth," which involved a substantial research team. And the classic "Yankee City" series—five volumes recording several years of study of Newburyport, Massachusetts—was the work of W. Lloyd Warner, a number of other major investigators, and a host of students, mostly undergraduates, from Harvard and Radcliffe. (The series includes Warner and Lunt 1941, 1942; Warner and Srole 1945; Warner and Low 1947; and Warner 1959.)

Historically, at least within sociology, when the unit of investigation has been at the level of the settlement, researchers have rarely moved beyond detailed description in their reports. The written production might contain small pieces of analysis of less encompassing units (see, for example, William F. Whyte's depiction of streetcorner group hierarchy in Section IV below), but analysis of the settlement as a unit has been largely ignored. At most, investigators have contented themselves with establishing the presence or absence of "community," that is, whether or not the territorial area under study was meaningful to the inhabitants.

More recent work, however, has begun to consider the settlement unit in more complex terms. Gerald Suttles's study of an inner-city Chicago neighborhood, for example, attempted to articulate the particular form of social organization exhibited by what he called the "Addams Area." In so doing, he went far beyond the question of presence or absence of community:

> The overall pattern is one where age, sex, ethnic and territorial units are fitted together like building blocks to create a larger structure. I have termed this pattern "ordered segmentation" to indicate the two related features: (1) the orderly relationship between groups and (2) the sequential order in which groups combine in instances of conflict and opposition. (1968, p. 10)

I. Social Worlds

Modern means of transportation and communication provide the basis for the rise and proliferation of a nebulous type of social unit that contains most if not all of the units described above but which is not reducible to any of them. The term **social world** is often used to capture these sprawling, shapeless entities, examples of which include the sports world, the California political world, the worlds of sociology, stamp collecting, and Wall Street.

Drawing on the work of David Unruh, a social world may be said (1) to encompass a large but indefinitely known population, (2) to have vague boundaries that can be crossed simply by choosing to stay abreast of events in that world (through the relevant communications media), (3) to have no or weak central authority, (4) to have a high rate of social change, and (5) to contain predominantly informal social roles—although in some instances, roles may be quite formal (Unruh 1983).

One important method of analyzing social worlds is in terms of the social roles that seem most dominant. Unruh, for example, has compared the prevalence of stranger, tourist, regular, and insider roles in various social worlds (1979, 1980).

J. Lifestyles or Subcultures

Last, some social scientists have conceptualized **lifestyles** or **subcultures**, terms that refer to global adjustments to life by large numbers of similarly situated persons. Benjamin Zablocki and Rosabeth Kanter have distinguished among lifestyles in terms of those that are dominated by a person's location in an economic system and those that are not. Economically dominated lifestyles can, in turn, be divided into three types:

1. *property-dominated,* as in the "elite ranks of the upper class";
2. *occupation-dominated,* as in those occupational pursuits that virtually absorb their practitioners; and
3. *poverty-dominated,* as in American urban ghettos (Zablocki and Kanter 1976).

Probably due to greater ease of access, the third type has been perhaps the most studied. Elliot Liebow's analysis of his interviews with homeless women, for example, is organized around the six main areas of the women's lives, expressed in the chapter titles as:

1. Day by Day
2. Work and Jobs
3. Family
4. The Servers and the Served
5. My Friends, My God, Myself
6. Making It Together (Liebow 1993)

Similarly, David Snow and Leon Anderson (1993) importantly organize the report of their "Study of Homeless Street People" around what they identify as the major constraints and elements of the homeless subculture, including: Wage, Labor and Institutionalized Assistance; Shadow Work; Tenuous Ties; and Salvaging the Self.

But, as Zablocki and Kanter have argued, lifestyle is not always reducible to economic status (1976, pp. 271–294). Values and tastes, among other factors, enter in and stimulate a vast number of diverse lifestyles: neocounterculturalists (Epstein 1991), taxi-dancers (Cressey 1932), lesbians (Krieger 1983), tattoo artists (Sanders 1989), surfers (Irwin 1973), nudists (Douglas and Rasmussen 1977), and hoboes (N. Anderson 1923) to name but a few drawn from varied historical periods.

IV. Aspects and Topics

Few researchers attempt to capture the full sociological substance or content of the unit or units on which they are focused. Rather, as we have noted above, they zero in on one or more "pieces" of that substance. We refer to these "pieces" as **aspects** and to the combinations of unit(s) and aspect(s) as **topics**. To enumerate all aspects of all the units that qualitative researchers have written about—that is, to be encyclopedic about topics—would necessitate many volumes. But since our goal here is to be illustrative rather than exhaustive, we limit ourselves to a small sample of studies concerned only with **cognitive, emotional,** or **hierarchical** aspects of one or another unit. (Possible combinations of units and aspects and the "locations" of our example studies are shown in Figure 6.1 on the following page.)

A. Cognitive Aspects or Meanings

The most fundamental and ubiquitous aspects of any unit are cognitive ones—the meanings embedded in or associated with it. Meanings are the linguistic categories that make up the participants' views of reality and which define their own and others' actions. Other frequently used words for meanings are norms, understandings, interpretations, definitions of the situation, typifications, ideology, beliefs, frames, worldviews, perspectives, and stereotypes. All these terms share a common focus on a humanly constructed set of concepts that participants consciously single out as important aspects of reality. Meanings are *transbehavioral* in the sense that they do more than describe behavior—they define, justify, and otherwise *interpret* behavior as well.

1. Variations in Scope

Meanings vary in terms of the breadth or range of situations to which they apply. At the broader level are meaning "packages" that are life-encompassing, that lay claim to relevance for virtually any topic that might be discussed. Such packages are often called ideologies, worldviews, *weltanschauungs*, or philosophies. While meanings of this

	Aspects		
Units	Cognitive	Emotional	Hierarchical
Practices		Clark 1987	
Episodes			
Encounters	L. Lofland 1985b		E. Anderson 1990
Roles	Sudnow 1979	Smith and Kleinman 1989	
Relationships			Glaser and Strauss 1965
Groups	J. Lofland 1977		Whyte 1993
Organizations		Biggart 1989	
Settlements			
Social Worlds			
Lifestyles			

Figure 6.1   Units and Aspects Combine into Topics: Matrix with Example Studies. *Note:* The studies referenced in the matrix cells are described in the present section of this chapter.

sort may be of relevance in an analysis of smaller-level units such as practices or encounters, they are usually treated as aspects of units at the level of group or above. Thus, in studies of groups or organizations, for example, a significant section of the research report is often devoted to "ideology," with attention paid both to its latent and more obvious themes and its delimited as well as more general applications.

Analyses of the complex cognitive schemes or "worldviews" of groups and organizations often center on the question of how participants bring the scheme into play in defining some problematic topic. For example, in John Lofland's report concerning a religious group with a "world-saving" ideology, members believed that they were destined to make thousands of new converts, worked hard to achieve that goal, but failed to do so. How then, Lofland asks, did the group "define" or explain this chronic gap between aim and actuality? His answer is that it drew upon its ideology to fashion three basic explanations for its repeated failures.

First, the American group was an offshoot of the Korean founding body, which had gone for years without success before beginning to make large numbers of converts. They would remind themselves that they were perhaps only following "the Korean pattern."

Second, they would apply their general "principle of restitution" which held that God and Satan alternated in their influence. Current failure was due to Satan's dominant influence, which would later be counter-balanced by God's good influence on prospects in the making of converts.

Third, members believed that God would deliberately withhold his help from them in order to see how well they could do on their own. Current failure was testing for strength. (1977, pp. 244–245)

2. Rules as Meanings

Rules (or norms) differ from other meanings mainly in the degree of positive moral preference attached to them and in the clarity of their formulation. Specific units may be analyzed, then, in terms of the rules that participants use to guide their conduct. Sometimes rules are so fully codified and articulated by the participants that the analyst has little to do beyond writing them down. More frequently, the analyst is faced with the task of *discerning* them from the regularities of actors' behavior. In Lyn Lofland's study of stranger encounters, for example, she outlined six principles or rules that people seemed to be using to maintain their privacy and social distance during these encounters.

First Principle: Minimize Expressivity. Keep one's facial expression impassive. . . .

Second Principle: Minimize Body Contact. Keep oneself to oneself. . . .

Third Principle: Look Before You Sit. Keep oneself apart. . . .

Fourth Principle: Minimize Eye Contact. Keep one's eyes to oneself. . . .

Fifth Principle: When in Doubt, Flee. Keep oneself protected. . . .

Sixth Principle: When in Doubt, Disattend. Keep oneself aloof. . . . (1985b, pp. 153–155)

3. Latent Meanings

Rules are not the only sorts of meanings that may be unarticulated. And some meanings may not only be unarticulated, but also unrecognized. A key job of the analyst in such a situation, then, is to give form to these latent meanings (sometimes also called typifications). David Sudnow's study of the occupational role of public defender (P.D.) provides a particularly incisive illustration of this sort of analytic work. Sudnow identified a meaning complex in the world of the public defender that he labeled "normal crimes."

I shall call *normal crimes* those occurrences whose typical features, e.g., the ways they usually occur and the characteristics of persons who commit them (as well as the typical victims and typical scenes) are known and attended by the P.D. For any of a series of offense types, the P.D. can provide some form of proverbial characterization. For example, *burglary* is seen as involving regular violators, no weapons, low-priced items, little property damage, lower class establishments, largely Negro defendants, independent operators, and a non-professional orientation to the crime. (1979, p. 478)

"Normal crimes," then, is a typification built out of a large range of categories, such as the personality, class, race, and age of the defendants; the scenes; the victims' characteristics; and the criminal acts themselves. These categories cohere into batches of "usual" or "routine" kinds of criminal events (as distinct from narrowly construed, statutorily defined criminal acts).

While the term *normal crime* is not in the vocabulary of public defenders, they do use more narrow working terms. P.D.s often refer to "such cases," "crimes such as this," "the same kind of case as the others," as well as to "burglars," "petty thieves," "narcos," and so on. Sudnow invented the term *normal crimes* as a more encompassing designation of this class of meanings. In addition, characterizing "clients" in the ways just indicated is particularly common in circumstances where a small number of "servicers" process or otherwise deal with a large number of people. Such situations give rise to simplified typifications or "client typologies" (see Mennerick 1974).

4. **Reality Constructionist Stance Toward Meanings**
You will find that meanings are more easily "seen" and analyzed if you assume what is called the "reality constructionist" stance. This stance is composed of several themes, among which are these presumptions:

1. Meanings are not inherent in reality but are imputed to it by humans.
2. Meanings are fragile and precarious and therefore treated gingerly by most people and defended when attacked.
3. Meanings are devices by means of which advantaged people defend and legitimate their privileged circumstances and the less advantaged accommodate themselves to their disadvantaged positions—that is, meanings are self-serving.
4. Because the situations of living are constantly changing, new and often novel meanings are constantly being generated to cope with new contingencies.

B. Emotional Aspects or Feelings

To separate cognitive and emotional aspects of units—to separate meanings from feelings—is, of course, to distort the experienced world. As we will see in the examples below, cognitions are an integral part of feelings just as emotions are an integral part of meanings. But we separate them here for two reasons: one, because to do so simplifies our expository task; and two, because to do so gives well-deserved and long-ignored emphasis to the role of emotion in human social life. Historically, social scientists have been guilty of a strong cognitive bias in their analyses (Hochschild 1979, 1983); only in the last several decades, especially in the last several years, have researchers begun both to appreciate the fact that humans ubiquitously, routinely, and simultaneously *feel as well as think* (S. Gordon 1981, 1985; Lutz and White 1986; Stearns and Stearns 1985; Stearns and Stearns, eds., 1988) and to incorporate the fruits of that appreciation into their published reports.

1. Emotion and Practices
It is perhaps easiest to recognize the possible importance of feeling to one's analysis if one is concentrating on a lower-level unit. After all, the bond of many relationships is love or affection (Bell 1981; Marston, Hecht, and Robers 1987; Wiseman 1986), the substance of many encounters is angry recriminations (Denzin 1984) or jealous tirades (Ellis and Weinstein 1986), and the content of some episodes is panicky flight (N. Johnson 1988) or ecstatic revelry (J. Lofland 1985, Ch. 2).

At the level of practices, Candace Clark's study of the exchange of sympathy in everyday life provides an enumeration of normatively prescribed and routinely performed verbal conventions that help maintain a reasonable flow of sympathy between and among persons. These are:

1. using genuine and serious situations and events as the justification for claiming sympathy;
2. claiming sympathy at reasonable and legitimate intervals;
3. actually making the claim to sympathy when the justification is real and the interval is within the acceptable levels; and
4. repaying the gift of sympathy with gratitude, deference, esteem, or sympathy itself (summarized from Clark 1987).

2. Emotion and Roles
Many roles generate emotional problems or experiences that are unique to or uniquely configured in them. Allen Smith and Sherryl Kleinman report, for example, that in their encounters with the human body, medical students "often experience a variety of uncomfortable feelings including embarrassment, disgust, and arousal" (1989, p. 58) that formal training, per se, does little to alleviate. The authors were interested in how students managed these "uncomfortable" and "inappropriate feelings," and their analysis outlines five widely used strategies for coping with, if not eliminating, the problems.

1. *Transforming the contact.* Students redefined their encounters with cadavers or patients as involving not an interaction with a person but as a mechanical or analytic problem of scientific medicine.

2. *Accentuating the positive.* Having defined their encounters as primarily involving problems of science, students generate excitement and other positive feelings over the fact that they are practicing "real medicine."

3. *Using the patient.* Students are sometimes able to control their uncomfortable feelings by focusing on the feelings of patients—either empathizing with patients or blaming them for having inappropriate emotions.

4. *Laughing about it.* Students can transform situations that provoke discomfort in them by making jokes about them.

5. *Avoiding the contact.* By controlling their visual fields or by skipping or abbreviating certain examination procedures, students are sometimes able to avoid the kinds of contact that give rise to unwanted emotions (summarized from Smith and Kleinman 1989, pp. 60–65).

3. Emotion and Organizations

We suggested just above that the relevance of emotions to one's analysis may be more apparent at the level of smaller units such as practices and roles. But recent work has demonstrated that a focus on the emotional aspects of organizations may offer a key point of entry to an understanding of that unit. Here we provide only a single illustration of research on this topic, but many others may be found in Fineman (ed.) 1993 and Van Maanen and Kunda 1989. Our example is Nicole Biggart's study of two direct selling organizations, Mary Kay Cosmetics and Amway Corporation (1989; discussed above in Section III.G). She identified both as "charismatic" capitalist enterprises in which the emotions of "awe" and "loyalty" bind employees to their employers. By "teasing out" and listing the ways in which these emotion-suffused enterprises differ from the traditional rationalist bureaucracy, Biggart is able to see them as a distinct "type" of organization. The features of this type are enumerated in Figure 6.2.

C. Hierarchical Aspects or Inequalities

It is probably not exaggerating too much to suggest that a concern with the hierarchical aspects of social life has consumed more working hours and generated a greater volume of publications than any other issue in social science. This is as true among fieldworkers focusing on the more micro levels as it is among macro-oriented analysts focusing on economic and political "systems." Although we have an overabundance of relevant examples from which to draw, we must here limit ourselves to a few studies dealing only with encounters, relationships, and groups.

1. Hierarchy in Encounters

The encounter is certainly one of the most micro-level units one can study. Yet oddly enough, it is also a location that allows one to observe

Figure 6.2 Example of an Organizational Emotions Topic: Biggart on
Bureaucratic and Direct Selling Types of Organization

	Bureaucratic Organization	Direct Selling Organization
Legitimation	Universal rules, laws	Mission: substantive philosophy of founder and belief in moral values of entrepreneurialism
Membership	Bureaucratic officials	Followers
Differentiation	Horizontal differentiation by function; vertical differentiation by expertise	Minimal differentiation of sales work; administration separated and may be differentiated by function
Stratification	Hierarchical distribution of authority, rewards, status	Undifferentiated authority structure joined to status hierarchy; administration may be hierarchical
Recruitment	Universalist appointment based on expertise and experience	Particularist recruitment for commitment potential, affective bonds
Compensation	Financial rewards, especially salary	Combination of material, purposive, and solidary incentives
Character of tenure	Career	Way of life

Source: Biggart, *Charismatic Capitalism*, 1989, p. 130, Table 4, "Bureaucratic and Direct
Selling Types of Organization," footnote deleted. Reprinted by permission of the
University of Chicago Press. © 1989 by The University of Chicago Press.

both the *operation of macro systems of inequality* (based on class, race, or
sex, for example) in the lives of human actors and the *creation and
re-creation of those systems* by individual human actors. Analyses of
encounters reveal, for example, that stratification arrangements may be
communicated and enacted through diverse practices. Elijah Anderson's
dissection of the elements of the "street etiquette" practiced in encounters between individuals separated by both class and race include (1)
ballet-like sequences for street passing, (2) the use of dogs as walking
companions, (3) rituals guiding the carrying of cash, and, as illustrated
in the following passage, (4) elaborate eye- and face-work.

> Many people, particularly those who see themselves as more economically
> privileged than others in the community, are careful not to let their eyes
> stray, in order to avoid an uncomfortable situation. As they walk down the
> street, they pretend not to see other pedestrians, or they look right at them
> without speaking, a behavior many blacks find offensive. . . .

[W]hites of the Village often scowl to keep young blacks at a social and personal distance. As they venture out on the streets of the Village . . . they may plant this look on their faces to ward off others who might mean them harm. Scowling by whites may be compared to gritting by blacks as a coping strategy. (1990, pp. 220–221)

2. **Hierarchy in Relationships**
The relationships between unequals are fertile ground for understanding hierarchy, and the modern workplace is a fertile field. Studies of service workers and their customers, for example, emphasize the interactional dominance of the customer. Such studies often analyze the meanings that workers apply *to* their customers (e.g., F. Davis 1959) or the strategies they use *on* their customers (Rafaeli 1989) as they attempt to cope with the demeaning aspects of the relationship. Studies of professionals and their clients, in contrast, depict a situation in which the relational "edge" is reversed. Barney Glaser and Anselm Strauss, for example, in their study of interactions between medical personnel (especially physicians) and hospitalized dying patients, outline the varying practices that the former can use to keep the latter unaware of their dying status (or to maintain a "closed awareness context" in Glaser's and Strauss's terms).

> They will comment favorably on his daily appearance, hoping he will interpret their comments optimistically. . . . They also practice sleight of hand, like magicians, drawing the patient's attention away from a dangerous cue by focusing his attention on an innocent one. . . . The physician may even put on diagnostic dramas for him, sending him for irrelevant tests. (1965, p. 36)

3. **Hierarchy in Groups**
Members of groups generally rank one another and possess different degrees of influence over one another. Collectively considered, these personal differences in power, influence, and centrality form a group hierarchy or system of status inequality. There may be struggles over placement in the hierarchy, over the hierarchy itself, or between two or more hierarchies in the same setting; nonetheless, a ranking system tends to exist, even if it is fluid and changing. Figure 6.3 shows such a system among a streetcorner group that William F. Whyte (1993) called "the Nortons." Note that while it is composed of separate individuals, the system requires simultaneous specification of the relative positions of several individuals. And being based on a principle of hierarchy, it illustrates the most fundamental and primitive structural meaning of the concept of a group.

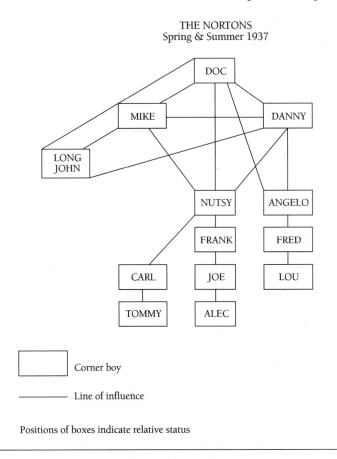

THE NORTONS
Spring & Summer 1937

☐ Corner boy

──── Line of influence

Positions of boxes indicate relative status

Figure 6.3 Example of a Group Hierarchy Topic: Whyte Diagram of a Streetcorner Group. *Source:* Whyte, *Street Corner Society,* 1993, p. 13. Reprinted by Permission of The University of Chicago Press. © 1943, 1955, 1981, 1993 by The University of Chicago Press.

V. Two or More Units or Aspects as Topics

The dominant imagery of the foregoing description of units and aspects combined into topics is that of *one* unit combined with *one* aspect. This is fine as a way to start and can work well as the guiding image of a study if it fits satisfactorily with the data at hand and with one's more specific substantive concerns. In fact, one-unit-combined-with-one-aspect is a commonly employed generic formula in fieldstudies.

But this is also *only one* image or formula. Possible additional images or generic formulae include conjoint or simultaneous focus on (1) one aspect of *two* or more interacting units at the *same scale* of social organization, (2) one aspect of two or more interacting units at *different scales* of social organization, and (3) *two or more aspects* of units at the same scale or at different scales of unit organization.

Among these more complex possibilities, we draw special attention to the simplest form of the first possibility just listed: focus on one aspect of two units at the same scale. The image here is that of two relatively equal units in interaction. In a derivative way, the interaction between them becomes, conceptually, the *unit* of analysis. Some *aspect* (or form) of *that interaction* between the units becomes the focus (the topic) of the analysis. Conflict, cooperation, competition, and negotiation are among the aspects or forms of interaction between two (or among more) units to which social analysts have attended most intensively (e.g., Kriesberg 1982).

The suggestion, then, is that one can conceive social reality as "units" and "aspects" of units *and also as* fields of interactive relations between or among two or more units and aspects.

VI. Units, Aspects, and Topics Form a Mindset for Coding

The *ideas* of units and aspects and their combination into topics should be thought of as providing you a *mindset* to bring to the task of making analytic sense of the data you are logging. Specifically, units and aspects forming topics make up the mindset you bring to the activity of *coding* your data, a major activity you carry on in developing analysis, which we discuss in Chapter 9.

Bringing a mindset to your data is to be distinguished from mechanically applying specific units and aspects to your data. We emphatically urge the former rather than the latter. While you want to be mindful of units and aspects, you want to remain *flexible* about exactly what units–aspects–topics you will pursue in coding and in evolving analysis. This chapter should provide you a general orientation to the *kinds of things* for which to look in coding data, *not* a preformed schemata of things for which to code. But, on the other hand, you should also feel free to use any specific units, aspects, or topics described above if they help in coding your data. You should also be open to drawing on units, aspects, and topics we do not mention in this chapter. (On the question of preformed versus emergent codes, see Miles and Huberman 1994, pp. 56–63, who contrast "a priori" and "inductive" approaches to coding.)

Units and aspects combined into topics provide the first of the three lines along which you want emergently to focus your data. The second line of focusing is to ask *questions* about those topics, the task to which we now turn.

CHAPTER 7

ASKING QUESTIONS

Units and aspects—*topics*, as treated in the last chapter—are entities about which one asks *questions*. Whatever your topic, in the beginning is the question. Social analysts commonly pose *eight* basic questions about social topics. These are presented in schematic overview and in their relations to each other in Figure 7.1 (page 124). To assist in grasping all eight as we discuss them in this chapter, think of the middle six in Figure 7.1 (numbers 2 through 7) as forming three sets of two questions each as follows:

Questions 2 and 3, **Frequencies and Magnitudes**, ask how often we observe something and its strength or size.

Questions 4 and 5, **Structures and Processes**, ask how, in detail, something is organized (structured) and how it operates over time (processes).

Questions 6 and 7, **Causes and Consequences**, ask what factors bring something into existence (causes) and what effects something has (consequences).

These six questions are flanked on the "front side," so to speak, by the question of what the "something" *is* in the first place—the question of its *type* or types, a depiction of its defining features.

The six middle questions are flanked on the other side by an eighth question, that of human *agency*, which brackets the foregoing seven and asks how people strategize their actions in and toward situations and settings.

We have physically arranged the elements of Figure 7.1 to highlight how questions are commonly coupled and also how they are different from one another. Thus:

Questions 1, 2, and 3 (types, frequencies, and magnitudes) are shown external to the box that represents the topic under study in order to display them as matters we observe from the outside.

Questions 4 and 5 (structures and processes) are shown inside the box symbolizing the topic in order to indicate that structures and processes are internal properties of the object of study. (Also, the phrase "structure and process" is a common social science coupling.)

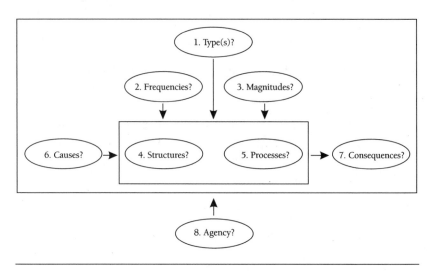

Figure 7.1   Eight Questions

Questions 6 and 7 (causes and consequences) are shown to the left and right of the box, symbolizing the topic in order physically to represent causes as coming *before* the topic of study in time and in order physically to represent consequences as coming *after* the object of study in time. (The phrase "causes and consequences" is also a common coupling in social science language.)

Question 8 is shown outside the large box around the first seven questions in order to represent it as an entirely different kind of question, that of active human agency.

We hope that referring back to Figure 7.1 and the overview given here will assist you in understanding the eight questions that we will now discuss in some detail.

I. What Are the Topic's Types?

One of the most creative and important but often unappreciated moments in social analysis is the act of posing and answering the question, "What *is* this thing (or things) I see before me?" You might, indeed, ask this question at the very basic level of discerning new kinds of units or aspects of social settings to add to the lists we gave in Chapter 6. Much more likely, though, you will ask the more delimited question, "What type of some already identified unit or aspect is it?" Or, worded differently, "What specific *type* of encounter, organization, emotion, hierarchy—or whatever—is it?"

A. Single Types

Many important advances in social analysis are simply artful depictions of a single type of practice, relationship, meaning, hierarchy, or other unit or aspect. Consider, for example, Erving Goffman's isolation of the concept of the "total institution" (see Chapter 6, Section III.G). As we saw, he developed this organizational type after considering the features of the particular organization he was studying (a mental hospital). By asking himself what were the *general* features of that hospital, he evolved the idea of the "total institution."

Philip Selznick's scrutiny of the Communist party and his characterization of it as a "combat party" displays the same logic. Selznick observes that, analytically,

> the major concern is to identify the system, to state what the "nature of the beast" is. The task is to construct a conceptual model of a functioning institutional system. But this is also an exercise in typology. We view the structure we are studying as an instance of a class of objects whose general features are to be explored. The class may have only one member but it is the kind of thing we are dealing with that interests us. We ask, What kind of a social system is the Communist party? We answer by developing a model of the "combat party," including its strategies. (1960, p. xiv)

B. Multiple Types

This logic is, of course, easily extended to conceiving numerous types that are variations on some more abstract type. Especially if you are observing more than one concrete setting, the variance that naturally exists among the units you encounter is likely to make multiple "typing" not only a possibility but also a necessity. Looking back through Chapter 6, we see multiple types used in several examples, including:

- types of cliques in organizations, as reported by Melville Dalton (1959) (Section III.F.1);
- types of lifestyles, as propounded by Ben Zablocki and Rosabeth Kanter (1976) (Section III.J); and
- types of medical student role strategies, as depicted by Allen Smith and Sherryl Kleinman (1989) (Section IV.B.1).

C. Rules of Typing

Classification or type schemes are guided by two basic rules of procedure and outcome:

> First, you should choose the content of the classification or type in such a way that you can place each case into only one category thereof. This is called the **rule of mutual exclusiveness** of categories.

Second, the categories you devise should make it possible to classify all (or almost all) of the relevant cases. This is called the **rule of exhaustiveness.**

As a practical matter, however, in most research there will be at least a few cases that defy categorization. These residual cases you can simply put to one side and label "other" or "mixed."

D. Typologizing

On occasion, the topics under study seem to possess some complex but systematic interrelation. In such a case, you can often discover what that interrelation is by specifying a small number of relevant variables whose *conjoint* variations accurately incorporate the patterns you have already discerned (and point out others you have not yet fully contemplated). This process of charting the possibilities that result from the conjunction of two or more variables is variously called substructing (Miles and Huberman 1994, p. 184), dimensionalizing, cross-classifying, and, our preference, *typologizing*.

For example, in examining the diverse environments in which American nonprofit organizations operate, Kirsten Grønbjerg (1993) found that the complexity of the diversity of their environments was fruitfully reducible to and articulated by a conjunction between just two underlying and dichotomized variables. As Figure 7.2 shows, these variables are the degree to which a nonprofit's environment is dominated by private sector providers of the same kind of service (treated as yes or no) and the degree to which the public sector is dependent on a nonprofit organization for the service it provides (also treated as yes or no). Thus "substructed" or "typologized," the myriad of variations in the environments of nonprofits is simplified into the four basic patterns shown in Figure 7.2—the patterns of cooperation, accommodation, competition, and symbiosis.

Substructing or typologizing thus helps to make an analysis more systematically coherent, and, by showing the logical possibilities, it can sometimes call attention to existing but unnoticed patterns or to the empirical absence of a logically possible pattern (thus raising the question of why it is absent).

We must caution, however, that typology construction can easily become a sterile exercise. Unless performed within the context of full and extensive knowledge of and sensitivity to the actual setting, it will reveal little or nothing. Arbitrary box building is not a substitute for a close feel for the actual circumstances.

Environment dominated by private-sector
providers of the nonprofit's service?

		No	Yes
Public dependent on the nonprofit for the service it provides?	Yes	Cooperation (e.g., social service nonprofits)	Accommodation (e.g., health nonprofits)
	No	Competition (e.g., education nonprofits)	Symbiosis (e.g., community development nonprofits)

Figure 7.2 Example of Typologizing: Grønbjerg on Environments of Nonprofit Organizations. *Source:* Adapted from Grønbjerg 1993, p. 20, Table 1.1, "Nonprofit Institutional Environments." Copyright 1993 by Jossey-Bass Inc., Publishers.

II. What Are the Topic's Frequencies?

It is sometimes useful and important to count how often something occurs and to develop summarizing statistics in such forms as percentages and means. There are, in fact, some quite elaborate procedures for counting and analyzing many kinds of social phenomena. These are codified under such rubrics as "descriptive and inferential statistics," "sampling," "survey research," and "systematic observation techniques."

The more elaborate forms of answering frequency questions are outside the scope of this manual. Happily, as we have indicated in Chapter 2, many other guides provide instruction on them, including Babbie 1995 and Baker 1994, and we refer you to them rather than duplicate that work here.

In this context, though, we want to remark that devotees of determining frequencies—of counting and statistics—have given counting a fearful name by promoting very complex and often arcane forms of it. In fact, there are many important but still *very simple* counts that can and should be done in fieldstudies. We have in mind, for example, such extremely simple but telling counting activities as:

- the average number of times a group meets over several months,
- the number of pages devoted to given topics in a set of group publications, and
- the numbers of people at various gatherings.

Such countings are so simple that no special instruction in them is required. And, all fieldstudies should apply simple arithmetic operations to key aspects of the accumulating field data. (See further Miles and Huberman 1994, pp. 252ff, on "counting.")

III. What Are the Topic's Magnitudes?

The question of frequencies refers to occasions of something occurring, whereas the question of magnitude refers to the strength, intensity, or size of instances of an occurrence. As with the determination of frequencies, determining magnitude is a quantitative question that, in more sophisticated forms, involves very complicated measurement procedures that we do not treat in this guide. The same works referred to just above, however, provide appropriate instruction. Nonetheless, one should not shy away from thinking about and establishing magnitudes should this question loom as central in one's data.

IV. What Are the Topic's Structures?

The question of structures can be viewed as a more elaborated and detailed version of question 1, the question of types. Aside from the single feature or the few features that differentiate a topic from other topics, what are its more intricate and precise characteristics? Of what more complicated and exhaustive properties and traits is it comprised? Metaphorically, the difference between a "type" and a "structure" is the difference between a rough, simple sketch of a building and the detailed architectural drawings for constructing that building. The former provides only the general idea or concept, while the latter furnish the details of its actual composition.

Ideal typing is both a prominent procedure for answering and a form of answer to the question of structure. As a procedure, the analyst starts to identify the components of a structure and begins to notice that the case or cases at hand display many tendencies that move toward, but do not fully display, their logical extremes. The pattern actually seen in the case or cases at hand is partial, attenuated, or weak in some fashion. But the cases at hand *tend* toward some logical structural pattern that you, as analyst, can envision. Such a realization makes it possible to use the cases under study to define a potential "pure" or "ideal" type or types. Max Weber, an important user of this practice in social science, stated it thus:

> [An ideal type] . . . is not a description of reality but it aims to give unambiguous means of expression to such a description. We construct the concept "city economy" [for example] not as an average of the economic structures actually existing in all the cities observed but as an ideal-type . . . formed by the one-sided accentuation of . . . a great many diffuse, discrete, more or less present and occasionally absent concrete individual phenomena. . . . In its conceptual purity, this mental construct . . . cannot be found empirically anywhere in reality. . . . Research faces the task of determining, in each individual case, the extent to which this ideal-construct approximates to or diverges from reality. (1949, pp. 90–93)

Put differently, an ideal type is a logical extreme, an ideal form, a hypo-thetical case, a pure case, or an ideal construct (Lopreato and Alston 1970, p. 95).

Joyce Rothschild-Whitt's formulation of contrasts between bureau-cratic and collectivist-democratic organizations (1979) is an especially clear use of ideal type logic. Observing six collectivist work organiza-tions in a Southern California city, she was struck by their tendency toward structuring themselves quite differently from more "ordinary" work organizations. Drawing on existing theories of formal organiza-tions, she specified eight areas or dimensions of organizational function-ing (as shown in the left-hand column of Figure 7.3 on pages 130–131). Then, she contrasted the already existing ideal type formulation of features of bureaucratic organizations with the ideal features she derived for collectivist-democratic organizations. These contrasts are shown in the middle and right-hand columns of Figure 7.3.

As a practical strategy, it is helpful to develop ideal types in pairs of *polar* (that is, logically or theoretically opposed) extremes. Rothschild-Whitt's counterposing of bureaucratic and collectivist-democratic or-ganizations illustrates this well. Such a pairing makes it clear that practically all empirical instances range along the continuum between the given extremes.

Let us briefly describe one common ideal-typing procedure. The first step is simply to list all conceivably distinctive and relevant features of the topic at hand. Then scrutinize this long and disjointed list with an eye toward trimming it down and determining which elements are logi-cally related to which others. Group those features that appear interre-lated. To put it another way, the unit or units and the aspect under study present themselves as incoherent aggregations of infinite aspects. The task of the analyst is to "disaggregate" them to achieve a coherent identification and ordering.

The aim, of course, is to expand the range of ordered experience and enhance our understanding by providing new concepts and their compo-nents (for example, the idea of the "collectivist-democratic organiza-tion" and its eight specific features).

V. What Are the Topic's Processes?

The second half of the structure–process couplet is of course *process*. Dictionaries commonly define this word as "the action of continuously going along through each of a succession of acts, events or developmen-tal stages," and as a "continuing operation or development marked by a series of gradual changes that succeed one another in a relatively fixed way."

Figure 7.3 Example of Ideal Typing: Rothschild-Whitt on Two Ideal Types of Organization

Dimensions	Bureaucratic Organization	Collectivist-Democratic Organization
1. Authority	1. Authority resides in individuals by virtue of incumbency in office and/or expertise; hierarchical organization of offices. Compliance is to universal fixed rules as these are implemented by office incumbents.	1. Authority resides in the collectivity as a whole; delegated, if at all, only temporarily and subject to recall. Compliance is to the consensus of the collective which is always fluid and open to negotiation.
2. Rules	2. Formalization of fixed and universal rules; calculability and appeal of decisions on the basis of correspondence to the formal, written law.	2. Minimal stipulated rules; primacy of ad hoc, individual decisions; some calculability possible on the basis of knowing the substantive ethics involved in the situation.
3. Social Control	3. Organizational behavior is subject to social control primarily through direct supervision or standardized rules and sanctions, tertiarily through the selection of homogeneous personnel especially at top levels.	3. Social controls are primarily based on personalistic or moralistic appeals and the selection of homogeneous personnel.
4. Social Relations	4. Ideal of impersonality. Relations are to be role-based, segmental and instrumental.	4. Ideal of community. Relations are to be wholistic, personal, of value in themselves.

Source: Rothschild-Whitt 1979, p. 519, Table 1, "Comparison of Two Ideal Types of Organization." Reprinted by permission of the author and the American Sociological Association.

Four related concepts are helpful in thinking about processes:

A *stage* is "a period or step in a process, activity, or development" or "one of several periods whose beginning and end are usually marked by some important change of structure" in "development and growth."

A *step* is "a stage in a gradual, regular, or orderly process."

Figure 7.3 (continued)   Example of Ideal Typing: Rothschild-Whitt on Two
Ideal Types of Organization

Dimensions	Bureaucratic Organization	Collectivist-Democratic Organization
5. Recruitment and Advancement	5.a. Employment based on specialized training and formal certification.	5.a. Employment based on friends, social-political values, personality attributes, and informally assessed knowledge and skills.
	5.b. Employment constitutes a career; advancement based on seniority or achievement.	5.b. Concept of career advancement not meaningful; no hierarchy of promotion.
6. Incentive Structure	6. Remunerative incentives are primary.	6. Normative and solidarity incentives are primary; material incentives are secondary.
7. Social Stratification	7. Isomorphic distribution of prestige, privilege, and power; i.e., differential rewards by office; hierarchy justifies inequality.	7. Egalitarian; reward differentials, if any, are strictly limited by the collectivity.
8. Differentiation	8.a. Maximal division of labor; dichotomy between intellectual work and manual work and between administrative tasks and performance tasks.	8.a. Minimal division of labor; administration is combined with performance tasks; division between intellectual and manual work is reduced.
	8.b. Maximal specialization of jobs and functions; segmental roles. Technical expertise is exclusively held; ideal of the specialist-expert.	8.b. Generalization of job functions: wholistic roles. Demystification of expertise: ideal of the amateur factotum.

A *period* is a "time often of indefinite length but of distinctive or specified character" or "a division of time in which something is completed and ready to commence and go on in the same order."

A *phase* is a "stage or interval in a development or cycle: a particular appearance or stage of a regularly recurring cycle of changes."

For the purposes of this guide, these four terms are synonyms. We have listed and defined each in order to clarify the idea of processes by highlighting the variety of words with which you can describe their elements.

Researchers seek to observe and analyze three basic forms of process: cycles, spirals, and sequences.

A. Cycles

A **cycle** is a "recurrent sequence of events which occur in such order that the last precedes the recurrence of the first in a new series." It is a "course of operations or events returning upon itself and restoring the original state" or a "series of changes leading back to the starting point."

Social settings, of course, tend to be explicitly organized in terms of cycles based upon the calendar: seasons, months, days, and so forth. Often such cycles are so well known—so commonsensical to an author's projected audiences—that they are not even reported. In the long run, however, we may find the neglect of such reporting to have been a serious omission. Future audiences with quite different cycles may puzzle over how we, in this period of history, did in fact break up our time and cycle it. Indeed, with the impending extinction of so many ways of life, a description of how cycles are set is already becoming indispensable. The people and settings on which many researchers have reported can often no longer be directly observed. (See, for example, Horace Miner's description of the "yearly round" in St. Denis, a French-Canadian parish [1939, pp. 141–168].)

In addition to standard calendar-based cycles, there are revolving regularities of a less planned, recognized, and scheduled nature. Thus, in analyzing several years in the history of a small, "end-of-the-world" religion, John Lofland (1977) observed that the group went through four cycles of collective hope and despair over the problem of making converts. The group was committed to the goal of making many thousands of converts. In stark contrast to this goal was the fact that the group could interest, much less convert, very few people. Each of the four observed cycles of hope and despair over three years had the following characteristics:

1. Some event occurred, or some plan was devised, that provided a collective sense of hope that many converts would soon be made.
2. Action was organized around the event or plan.
3. This action eventually failed, in the group's own estimation.
4. The failure led to a collective sense of despair of ever attaining the goal.
5. The group then came full circle back to a new event or plan.

Such analyses can be further combined with an effort to specify generally the practices, episodes, meanings, and so forth upon which the cycles are predicated. Thus, in this example, four kinds of activities and definitions provided the impetus necessary to initiate the first stage of a new cycle.

New hope was generated when the entire believership decamped and migrated en masse (a rather common strategy in religious history).

New hope was generated by announcing to the believers the imminent but unspecified arrival on the scene of their messiah.

New hope was generated by defining the present time as one for preparatory planning; thus missionizing was put off to a later time when, aided by the things done now, goals could really be achieved.

New hope was generated by geographical dispersion of believers on missionary quests. A sense of expansion and potency was derived from new places and people, if not from larger membership. (Adapted from J. Lofland 1977.)

B. Spirals

Some processes do not show the degree of relative stability seen in cycles. Instead, they display a **spiral** pattern, a "continuously spreading and accelerating increase or decrease." One of the more familiar forms of this phenomenon is seen in the tension or conflict between social units that are hostile to one another. It is especially visible in large units, such as settlements, tribes, neighborhoods, and total societies. There are even special terms for this type of spiral: *escalation* and *deescalation*.

Edwin Lemert's analysis of a spiraling interaction process that can lead to a person being labeled and hospitalized as "paranoid" provides a classic illustration of the spiraling process within a smaller social unit. In his "Paranoia and the Dynamics of Exclusion," Lemert describes these stages of the spiral:

1. The person ("X") who is disposed to participate in subsequent stages already displays one or another kind of interpersonal difficulty with his work associates, in particular a tendency to disregard primary group loyalties, to violate confidences, and to assume privileges not accorded him or her.

2. X's associates tend for a time to perceive X as a variant normal, but one or more events cause a reorganization of the associates' views; they now see X as "unreliable," "untrustworthy," "dangerous," or someone with whom others "do not wish to be involved."

3. Associates begin to engage in patronizing, evasive, and spurious interaction with the person; X is avoided and excluded from interaction.

4. X perceives the associates' new attitudes; this strengthens X's initial tendencies to disregard confidences and so forth (Step 1) and promotes X's demands to know what is happening.

5. The associates deal with the increasing difficulties posed by X by strengthening their own patronizing, avoidance, and exclusion (Step 2). They begin, moreover, to *conspire* among themselves in developing means to deal with X.

6. X senses this conspiracy, but it, and all other difficulties, tend to be *denied* by the associates. The flow of information to X declines more and more, and the discrepancy between expressed ideas and true feelings among the associates widens, thereby increasing X's ambiguity as to the nature of situations and of the associates.

7. Steps 4–6 repeat themselves, creating greater and greater tension. X and the associates each respond to the difficulties posed by the other, in a process that spirals and feeds upon itself, a process that is *mutually* constructed.

8. Finally, if all the associates' efforts to discharge or transfer X fail, they will attempt to force X to undergo an extended sick leave, psychiatric treatment, or, in the extreme case, commitment to a mental hospital (summarized from Lemert 1972, pp. 246–264; see also on "synergy" in spirals, J. Lofland 1993, Part III).

C. Sequences

The most common rendering of process is as a time-ordered series of steps or phases, which is different from cycles or spirals. In **sequences**, the first and last steps are not "connected" as in cycles, nor is there an accelerated movement to a "stronger" or "weaker" level of operation as in spirals.

Investigators tend to trace sequence processes from one of three different starting points.

1. Tracing Back

Perhaps the most common starting point is an outcome. For example, a person has embezzled money, used a certain drug, or converted to a strange religion; a crowd has rioted; an organization has disbanded; a community has adopted a growth-limit law. All of these occurrences can be seen as outcomes.

If you ask, "What are its causes?," you have posed a quantitative question and must proceed accordingly (as in Section VI below). If, on the other hand, you ask, "How did this build up?" or "How did it happen?" and begin to trace back through the histories of various cases of that outcome, you are pursuing the qualitative analysis of sequence. Your aim is, inductively, to scrutinize relevant cases in order to glean a process or processes from them. In a trace-back analysis, the researcher attempts to discern any typical stages through which the actors or action pass in a process that culminates (or does not culminate) in a particular outcome.

2. Tracing Forward

Alternatively, you may be concerned with what happens *after* a decisive event, as in, for example, veterans returning from wars, people being told they are dying, newlyweds adapting to marriage, or communities being hit by a disaster and faced with problems of recovery. An example is Bradley J. Fisher's analysis of the three phases of "career descent" among the institutionalized elderly confronting their own declining levels of health and physical ability (1987):

1. Resistance to Staff Evaluation: The Cognitive Dissonance Phase

2. Acceptance and Tarnished Self-Image: The Cognitive Consonance Phase

3. Revised Opinion and Adjustment: The Enhanced Self-Image Phase

3. Tracing Through

A third starting point is to consider the history of the process as a whole. This method has obvious advantages in situations lacking a dramatic episode from which to trace forward or backward. The most well-known trace-through models are the various depictions of the early stages of human development and the stages of development in adulthood.

We conclude our discussion of qualitative process analysis by indicating that its special contribution is its power to report the details of social change. It enables us to observe "through what play of forces, in what sequences of stages and with what existential consequences for the persons involved" social life moves (F. Davis 1972, p. ix). Julius Roth describes this power nicely in a review of a quantitative survey analysis of consumer defaults on loans:

> A one-shot interview survey of a population sample provides one with measures of variables to be correlated. At best, it provides frequencies or proportions of cases with given characteristics or in which given things happen. . . . But surely what a consumer protection advocate is most interested in is not so much the percentage of "types of harassment" used by each type of creditor, but rather, the step by step process by which creditors enforce payment and the kinds of counteraction available to consumers to protect their interests. And for the student of some branches of sociology, the most interesting issues are not the percentage breakdowns, but the interrelated actions of creditors and consumers in a context of laws and administrative and legal agencies. For such an analysis, the most relevant data come from detailed studies of appropriate cases. (1977, p. 115)

We also want to point out that qualitative process questions and quantitative causal questions *supplement* and *complement* one another. Or, as Mirra Komarovsky put it, a qualitative study

> is often directed to the following problem: assuming phenomena A and B to be associated, can we discern the sequences of stages, the network of links which connects the two? By contrast, [a causal account] poses the problem: why B rather than not-B? Under what conditions, that is, will B appear or fail to appear? For example, [Williard] Waller [1938] criticized

the usual [causal] analysis. He traced alienation in marriage as a process moving "in a cyclical fashion to its denouement in divorce." In so doing, Waller does throw a new light on the way in which some marriages come to divorce but he does not face the problem of why others remain stable. On the other hand, the early correlation studies demonstrated the differential associations between regions, size of family, or economic conditions and divorce, but they failed to specify the links involved in these associations. (1957, pp. 12–13)

VI. What Are the Topic's Causes?

"What are the causes of X?" is perhaps the most frequently asked question in social science. It may be phrased in a variety of ways, such as:

What are the conditions under which it appears?

What facilitates its occurrence?

What are circumstances in which it is likely to occur?

In the presence of what conditions is it likely to be an outcome?

Upon what factors does variation in it depend?

Under what conditions is it present and under what conditions is it absent?

A. Requirements of Causal Inference

In the same way that they cannot answer complex questions of frequency and magnitude, qualitative fieldstudies are not designed to provide definitive answers to causal questions. This fact is best understood by briefly outlining what is required in order to say "A causes B" with any reasonable degree of confidence.

First, for whatever you want to find the causes of, you must have instances not only of its occurrence but also of its nonoccurrence (or absence or attenuation). That is, you must begin with a *variation* in the "dependent variable." This is what we have referred to above, in question 3, as the determination of *magnitudes*—the size, intensity, or scale of something. The variation need not necessarily be as strong as that between occurrence and nonoccurrence; it can be something on the order of "more present/less present" or "stronger/weaker." In a naturalistic study, this range of necessary variation simply may not occur. There may be instances, say, of "present" or "stronger" but no instances of "absent" or "weaker." And without such variation, obviously, there is nothing to compare.

Second, you must have some reliable and consistent way to determine or *measure* presence versus absence, stronger versus weaker, over a set of units that display the variation. But, in fieldstudies, devising and per-

Independent Variable

		Present (or stronger, etc.)	Absent (or weaker, etc.)
Dependent Variable	Present (or stronger, etc.)	1 100%	2 0%
	Absent (or weaker, etc.)	3 0%	4 100%

Figure 7.4 Perfect Covariation of Two Variables

forming the necessary quantification procedures is likely to be very time-consuming, and these procedures are likely to be quite obtrusive. (The inappropriateness of performing paper and pencil tests, systematic checklists, or other such procedures may be a sufficient reason not to attempt them. See, however, Webb et al. 1981.)

Third, you must consider this measured variation in the dependent variable *conjointly* with some other measured variation that you provisionally think causes it in some sense. The simplest possibility is depicted in Figure 7.4, which shows a dependent and an independent variable considered in perfect covariation. In order to show that the independent variable is a cause of the dependent variable, the measured instances of both must tend to fall into Cells 1 and 4, or Cells 2 and 3, rather than be distributed evenly across all four cells.

Fourth, the presumed cause *precedes* the effect in time.

But there is a fifth complication. There is always the question of whether, despite covariation and proper time order, you can ever be really *certain* a particular independent variable is the cause (or is among the important causes) of the dependent variable. This is the classic problem of "correlation not proving causation." Some other unknown factor, or some known but unmeasured factor, may be the cause or among the causes.

Very elaborate procedures have been developed to meet these requirements of establishing causality—procedures that are often quite difficult to implement in field situations. Also, there are procedures designed to meet a number of other requirements that we have not mentioned. Collectively, these procedures are often termed "quantitative social research," and many manuals on how to "do" them are available. Among others, we would refer you again to Babbie (1995) and Baker (1994), plus the readings they cite.

B. The Moral

The moral is this: The techniques and technology of qualitative studies are not the same as those of quantitative studies. Using the procedures in this guide alone, you will not acquire measured and controlled variations in dependent and independent variables and you will therefore not have the systematic quantitative data necessary to determine causation.

Beyond questions of technique and technology is, however, the *frame of mind* associated with each. If you get into a strongly quantitative frame of mind, you are likely to have your attention drawn away from the major qualitative features of the setting itself. You can easily trap yourself into exclusive concern with very small problems simply because these problems are amenable to quantification. Erving Goffman puts this point well in describing his fieldwork in a mental hospital:

> Desiring to obtain ethnographic detail regarding selected aspects of pa-
> tient social life, I did not employ usual kinds of measurements and
> controls. I assumed that the role and time required to gather statistical
> evidence for a few statements would preclude my gathering data on the
> tissue and fabric of patient life. (1961, p. x)

C. Causation and Conjecture

We do not, however, wish to rule out discussion of causes. Even if the search for them is not your definitive task, it can still be an appropriately qualified pursuit. You will be continually confronted with many variations that present themselves as simultaneously occurring contrasts (in which two or more elements coexist at more or less the same time), as serial contrasts (in which the same element changes over time), or in other ways. You may thus be prompted to ask what brings about these variations.

It is perfectly appropriate to be curious about causes, as long as you recognize that whatever account or explanation you devise is *conjecture*. (More formally, such conjectures are called *hypotheses* or *theories*.) You can certainly focus your analysis on conjectured causes of variations. But be certain to label them as such. And since you will probably simply state such causes and leave them untested, you should not allow the causal conjecture portions of the report to become too large or too dominant a part of the total study. Numerous of the studies mentioned in Chapter 6, for example, contain sections devoted to causal theories, but they do not stand or fall on these auxiliary causal accounts. Whatever eventually might be found to account for the variations and patterns they document, the variations and patterns themselves are likely to stand as findings.

For the above reasons, also, phrase your conjectures in a *qualified* way. Because you are, in fact, unlikely to have systematic knowledge on correlated variations, it is wise to present your conjectures in a way that indicates humility. This necessitates the appropriate use of qualifying phrases such as:

"It is possible that. . . ."

"It seems to be the case that. . . ."

"Although the data are not systematic, it appears that. . . ."

In other words, be honest about the factual standing of your causal assertions.

D. The Importance of Auxiliary Causal Accounts

Auxiliary conjectures in a qualitative report not only are permissible, but also play important and indispensable roles in social science. There are three reasons for this. First, because quantitative researchers and theorists are typically at a distance from and ignorant of the phenomena they study, they often turn to qualitative studies to gain a sense of what the phenomena are like and of what variables they ought to look for. In order to find substance for quantitative technology, the more astute of such researchers study qualitative reports. This is as it should be. The qualitative researcher has gotten close to people somewhere in the world. Although he or she may not have developed a fully correct and definitive depiction of causal accounts, the conjectures raised by the variations and patterns recorded provide a foundation for quantitative research.

Second, researchers who do not comprehend participants' own causal theories are apt to make profound errors not only in ascribing causes but also in characterization. This is especially likely where there is great social distance (because of differences in age, sex, ethnicity, geography, and so forth) between the analyst and the participants. Specifically, there is a pronounced tendency to define ill-understood behavior as bizarre, sick, or irrational when on closer inspection such definitions turn out to be quite unwarranted.

It ought, moreover, to be obvious that the researcher is not the only person who notices variations and puzzles over their causes. Members of social settings—at least the more verbal, intelligent, and sophisticated of them—do so as well. They develop their own hypotheses or theories to account for variations. Often these are quite perceptive and persuasive, perhaps to the point of rendering much further study—and especially quantitative study—a waste of everyone's time and money.

Third, under many circumstances of limited time, money, and topic importance, the causal theories that the qualitative analyst presents may be sufficient to the task. Elaborate quantitative research may contribute only small increments of precision to a thorough qualitative analysis. A sense of proportion or perspective is required in applying social research technology. Often it is unjustifiable to send out a quantitative battleship to answer questions that can be dealt with quite adequately by qualitative gunboats.

E. Forms of Causal Accounts

Causal accounts vary in their structure and complexity. We will here describe three forms (with a preference expressed for the third).

1. Single Cause

The most rudimentary account is that which refers to a single factor or cause as explaining some variation. The problem with such an account is not so much that the single factor referred to is unlikely to be associated with the variation, but that there are bound to be others. Almost a century of quantitative social research has yet to turn up any very strong associations between a variation and only one factor. You can take this fact as a safe guide in developing your own conjectures.

2. List of Causes

You are likely to achieve greater accuracy by developing a series of independent variables that account for a variation. However, even though such lists may prove "accurate" (if at some point subjected to quantitative tests), you need not be satisfied with them.

3. Cumulating Causes

Rather, you can attempt to specify the manner in which factors must accumulate through time and in what certain sequence in order to cause a particular variation. That is, a more sophisticated causal account focuses upon *process* in the eventuation of outcomes, rather than providing simple, *static* depictions. The concern is with successions of dependencies through time or ways in which prior conditions may or may not develop into succeeding conditions of a given outcome. This type of account focuses on ways in which alternatives may or may not be present—ways in which, and the degree to which, action may be constrained. It orients thought to the accumulation of factors: Each factor is a condition of an outcome but not sufficient for it; each factor makes an outcome possible or more probable but not yet determined (cf. Miles and Huberman 1994, pp. 147ff, on "the power of qualitative causal analysis").

F. Situational Versus Dispositional Causes

To a social analyst, the appropriate content of variables to stress in causal accounts is *situational* or *social organizational*. This seemingly obvious point is actually quite difficult to grasp. Beginning social analysts, especially, tend to have a culturally endowed penchant for inter-

preting individual and organizational behavior as a consequence of supernatural, physical, chemical, or—especially—*psychological* factors.

The pioneering work in the social and situational realm of causes was
Emile Durkheim's *Suicide* (1951; originally published in 1897). At the
time of his research, suicide was not viewed as something that could be
socially caused. It was Durkheim's genius to establish decisively that it
could be and is. Since then, a legion of researchers have documented the
fruitfulness of looking first (if not foremost and only) to *current* arrangements, social circumstances, or situations in accounting for practices,
meanings, or whatever. The social situationalist approach is thus *now*-
oriented. Holding aside "personality" or whatever remote and disposi-
tional notions, you ask yourself what combination of current arrangements
would conduce almost anyone to act in the particular ways observed.
Consider such applications of the situational emphasis as these:

- Waitresses' expressions of distress, such as crying, can be a function
  of how work is organized rather than of a "waitress" or "female"
  personality (Whyte 1948).
- The structure of power in organizations, rather than inherent gender
  characteristics, determines women's conduct in large organizations
  (Kanter 1977).
- Class consciousness, rather than being a characteristic that individual
  workers must possess in order to engage in collective action, actually
  arises during the course of such action (Fantasia 1988).
- Disoriented behavior and heavy drinking, rather than being precipi-
  tants of homelessness, are responses to homelessness (Snow and
  Anderson 1993).

Stated more broadly, the social researcher seeks the explanation of
variations in behavior in situations and social organization rather than
in physics, biology, psychology, or other nonsocial realms.

VII. What Are the Topic's Consequences?

The question of consequences can be seen as the second half of the
causal question. That is, we now view the dependent variable as an
independent variable and attempt to look at *its* dependent variable
consequences.

A. Requirements of Inferring Consequences

Because the question of consequences is simply the question of causes
"pushed forward," the five requirements of causal inference (Section
VI.A just above) also apply here. That is, you must have (1) a variation
that you can (2) measure (3) in covariation with another relevant

variable, and in (4) the appropriate time order, and (5) you must control for spurious associations. As we have noted, these conditions are hard to meet in qualitative fieldstudies. But, like causal conjectures, consequential conjectures are still legitimate, as long as they are made with qualification and humility (Sections VI.B and C).

B. Consequences of What, for What?

Consequential accounts typically depict relationships between a given, central topic and one or several other affected topics. One procedure for tracing or specifying consequences is to decide on a specific topic and then survey other topics (units and aspects) you have identified in terms of the effect that the central topic has on them, as we have schematized in Figure 7.5.

This is not to suggest, however, that an analysis of consequences should be a mechanical listing of effects. Your actual analysis (if you elect to deal with effects at all) must take into account such constraints as the amount of relevant data you have (see Chapter 5) and how interesting the things you have to say about them are (see Chapter 8).

The consequences of "deviant" roles have been of particular interest to social scientists, and this interest has taken an ironic twist. In conventional wisdom, deviant roles—roles performed by group members who act in deviant ways and who are labeled as deviant—are seen as having only destructive and unwanted effects. Several social analysts, however, have argued the reverse. One such study identified deviant informal or social roles among policemen. These were the "doorman" (or "asskisser," a person excessively concerned to impress superiors), the "mouth man" (a person given to indiscreet gossip and "being in the know"), and the "wheel man" (an officer given to reckless driving of a patrol car). In many respects, there was general disapproval of all three roles and of those performing them. The researchers noted, however, that these role players also performed certain necessary and unpleasant tasks in the department. Had these deviants not already been available, others would have had to do this "dirty work." Specifically, the mouth man was also maneuvered into tasks of carrying bad news to superiors; the doorman was used strategically to spread information others wanted put abroad; the wheel man was deployed to take risks in situations others quite rationally avoided (Reed, Burnette, and Troiden 1977).

These authors generalized that "deviants make it possible for others to maintain a personal and collective image of moral righteousness in spite of the normative limitations which they face. . . . [Thus] it is for . . . quite concrete, practical purposes that groups often need their deviants" (1977, p. 574). Indeed, many have argued that because of several "functional needs" of social organization, all groups *induce* people to play deviant roles.

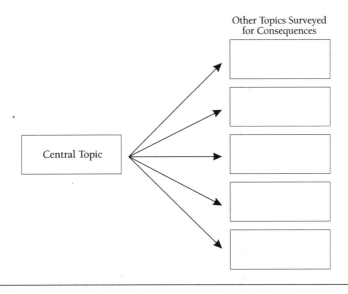

Figure 7.5 Surveying for Possible Consequences of a Central Topic

Consequences analyses have been performed on many other aspects of units at diverse scales of social organization. One example is Robert Merton's well-known argument that corrupt political machines in American cities have functioned to provide additional routes of social mobility for talented persons in disadvantaged ethnic minorities. Political machines thereby make a contribution to the political and social stability of the entire society by keeping down the level of minority dissatisfaction (1968, pp.126–136). And, asking why poverty persists in spite of widespread condemnation, Herbert Gans has delineated fifteen "functions" or benefits the affluent derive from poverty that help to explain why it does not go away. Among these functions are: The poor do dirty work no one else will do; they subsidize a variety of activities for the affluent; they create many jobs for servicing and controlling them; they are a dumping ground for damaged goods, preventing total loss (1972, pp. 275–289).

C. Consequences and System Needs: Functionalism

One special form of consequential analysis assumes that the unit of analysis is a social system, an integrated whole that is striving to maintain itself in its current state. Analysts, therefore, look for the contribution that various parts of the system make to maintaining the larger whole. One classic formulation puts it this way:

The *function* of any recurrent activity, such as the punishment of a crime or a funeral ceremony, is the part it plays in the social life as a whole and therefore the contribution it makes to the maintenance of the structural continuity.

By the definition here offered "function" is the contribution which a partial activity makes to the total activity of which it is a part. The function of a particular social usage is the contribution it makes to the total social life as the functioning of the total social system. (Radcliffe-Brown 1935, pp. 396, 397, emphasis in the original)

Thus, in the study of deviant roles among policemen summarized above, the specifically functional aspect is that the performance of certain unpleasant tasks is necessary for the maintenance of the police department. The deviant roles documented (or their equivalents, if these particular ones had not developed in the department) are therefore *functionally necessary* roles.

As an analyst, you may or may not feel you are justified in adopting this strong a form of consequences analysis. Often, you can do analyses of consequences without positing the existence of a social system with "functional needs." Moreover, consequences analysis need not focus only on effects that *maintain* a social arrangement. You can as easily focus on consequences that *bring change* in the arrangement.

D. Other Wordings of the Consequences Question

In order to encourage playfulness of mind, we want to report several other ways of asking the question of consequences. Here are two variations on the functionalist approach:

What *functions* are served by the existence of this practice that would not be served in its absence?

What *role* does this practice, pattern, or variation play in the maintenance of this setting in its present form?

And here are three nonfunctionalist wordings:

What are the typical *results* of this phenomenon in this setting?

What *ends* are served by the existence of this pattern?

What are the *products* of this variation in the standing pattern?

E. Consequences Distinguished from Intentions

Because a social activity has certain consequences or functions does not necessarily mean that such consequences or functions are *intended* by the participants. Intention—conscious or unconscious—may or may not be involved. For example, Thomas Kochman has described various verbal practices among some African-American males and has suggested these functions or consequences of those practices:

Through rapping, sounding and running it down, the black in the ghetto establishes his personality; through shucking, gripping, and copping a plea, he shows his respect for power; through jiving and signifying he stirs up excitement. With all of the above, he hopes to manipulate and control people and situations to give himself a winning edge. (1969, p. 34)

Kochman here attributes intention to the participants. He may or may not be correct in doing so. What is more important is that the functions he asserts can be evaluated independently of whether or not the participants *intended* their interactional practices to have these consequences.

VIII. What Is Human Agency?

We have discussed seven questions that the analyst asks about social *topics,* be these *units, aspects,* or some combination of them. Taken as a set these questions may be seen as variations on a single point of view. Here we will identify this viewpoint and contrast it with a different approach to the analysis of social life.

A. Passivist Versus Activist Images

We may label the point of view that the seven foregoing questions illustrate the *passivist* conception of humans and social life. In this approach, as Herbert Blumer has put it, humans are treated as more or less neutral media through which social forces operate and out of which social forms and organizations are composed (1969). Types, frequencies and magnitudes, structures and processes, and causes and consequences all have their own reality in which humans are incidental features or ciphers in the workings of social organizational units and their aspects.

There is nothing wrong with this passivist image of humans in and of itself. Social life and organization *do* have their own reality. But these seven questions of the passivist approach, taken collectively, are incomplete. There is another side, an additional reality to which we must attend. This is the *activist* viewpoint, in which we view humans as creative and probing creatures who are coping, dealing, designating, dodging, maneuvering, scheming, striving, struggling, and so forth— that is, as creatures who are actively influencing their social settings. In the activist view, the focus is on how people construct their actions in various situations, on how their activity is pieced together, thought about, tried out, and worked out.

The logical relationship between the passivist and activist views of human life may be likened to the familiar perceptual puzzles in which a drawing "looked at" in two different ways appears to represent two different objects. (See Figure 7.6 [page 146], which may be seen as either a vase or two human heads in profile facing one another.) The

Figure 7.6 A Perceptual Analogy to the Activist–Passivist Contrast

contrast may also be thought of as the difference between regarding a human being as a *product* or as a *source* of social forces. In both examples, whether the drawing or person "is" one or the other is not the appropriate question. Each is *both*. Whether each is seen as one or the other depends on how you attend.

B. Activist Questions

Once you understand this passivist–activist contrast, the procedural question for doing actual research then becomes how to develop an analysis that implements the activist image.

Just as you use the seven questions above to focus your data, in the activist approach, the central question you use is "What is human agency?," or, more specifically, "What are people's strategies?" And, as with the previous questions, this one needs some elaboration to be used well. As an approach to the data, it can be divided into *two* questions:

1. What is the *situation* being dealt with?
2. What *strategies* are being employed in dealing with that situation?

People do not just act blindly; often, instead, they *construct* their actions to deal with situations—with circumstances involving people, opportunities, and constraints as these are defined by the actors in them. The activist analyst is therefore concerned with deciphering and depicting exactly what sort of situation the participants are facing.

Reports answering the agency question tend, in fact, to be organized into two main sections, one of which analyzes the situation and the other of which reports strategies. Several of the studies we summarized in the preceding chapter exemplify such a situation-strategy analysis.

- Section III.A, on practices: Students cope with the *situation* of the open-ended task by means of "fritter" *strategies* (Bernstein 1978).
- Section III.B, on episodes: Parents handle the problematic *situation* of having a polio-stricken child by *strategies* of normalization and disassociation (F. Davis 1972).
- Section IV.A.1, on meanings: Members of a religious group, unable to make many converts, cope with the *situation* of their failure by means of three linguistic *strategies* that "explain" and "justify" that failure to them (J. Lofland 1977).
- Section IV.B.2, on emotion and roles: Medical students find that the *situation* of intimate encounters with human bodies generates discomforting feelings and use the *strategies* of transforming the contact, accentuating the positive, using the patient, laughing about it, and avoiding the contact to control or contain their discomfort (Smith and Kleinman 1989).

These examples highlight the constructed character of relatively microscopic situations and strategies, but more large-scale ones also deserve attention. For example, Nicole Biggart's discussion of the way in which the direct selling organizations she studied "obscured the economic in the social" (summarized in Chapter 6, Section III.G) depicts an organizational strategy for recruiting and maintaining employees. As another example, Gerald Suttles's portrayal of "ordered segmentation" in a Chicago slum (summarized in Chapter 6, Section III.H) is a report on a "large" strategy (1968). That is, obscuring the economic in the social and ordered segmentation are strategies evolved by many people over relatively long periods of time. Particularly in the case of ordered segmentation, because it is a shared, long-term way of coping, it is easy to lose sight of the fact that it is a *constructed* strategy, as are all other large-scale social arrangements.

We tend to lose appreciation of the fact that structures are constructions because of the peculiar human propensity for *objectivation,* as Berger and Luckman have termed it (1967, pp. 60ff). Humans themselves devise strategic social arrangements but then lose sight of that fact over time because the "structure" presents itself as an "object" (thus the term *objectivation*). The human agency, or strategy, question is one way to "deobjectify" social arrangements (and, as we will explain further in the next chapter, *demystify* them). In deobjectivation we come to realize that no social arrangement simply "is." Rather, arrangements are incessantly *fabricated* and this can be seen by decomposing them into their strategic components.

Moreover, by asking "What are people's strategies?," you can achieve a better *causal* understanding of many social events. For example, in some social organizations people "speak in tongues" and display "otherworldly," "saved," or "sanctified" behavior that is seen by some insiders as supernaturally caused and by some analysts as psychologically pathological in origin. In contrast to both of these perspectives, the activist-questioner asks if the tongue-speakers and their associates engage in activity designed to *produce* such behavior. We find, in fact, that they do so act—that tongue-speakers and their coaches engage in an enormously complex, detailed, and subtle process designed socially and normatively to evoke speaking in tongues (Harrison 1974). The supernatural and pathological causal accounts are not ruled out, of course. But they are placed in a context of *construction,* of strategic accomplishment.

In conclusion, by pursuing people's strategies, the activist vantage point makes the social realm human again by focusing on human intention and authorship.

Topics (described in Chapter 6) and questions (discussed in this chapter) provide two of the three major lines along which one focuses one's data. To these we need now to add a third consideration, that of *arousing audience interest* in the particular topics and questions you select for analysis. We address this third matter in the next chapter.

CHAPTER 8

AROUSING INTEREST

Asking a *question* (Chapter 7) about a social science *topic* (Chapter 6) achieves two of the three ways in which researchers seek to focus their data. The third way of focusing data addresses the issue of: *Which* question about *which* topic treated in *which* way will *arouse the interest* of social science audiences? Readers of reports respond to them with varying levels of enthusiasm. They hail some as of major importance, regard others as trivial, and perhaps view most somewhere in between. It must be recognized, also, that readers disagree among themselves on the degree to which a report is interesting. One reader's major advance can be another's minor exercise. Nonetheless there does seem to be a reasonable amount of agreement on features that make a report more interesting and whose absence makes them less interesting.

There are three classic and well recognized categories of these features. Formulated as questions that readers ask about reports, they are:

1. Is the report *true*; that is, is it correct in the sense of being empirically accurate?

2. Is the report *new* in the sense that it does not simply repeat observations that have already been made or answer questions about topics that have already been published?

3. Is the report *important* in one or another of several senses we explain below?

We want in this chapter to suggest procedures and strategies that maximize the likelihood that social science readers will respond to your report as true, new, and important. Taking the three together, positive responses to each question form an overall assessment that your report is *interesting*—that it is meaningful, exciting, and consequential.

We are going to discuss trueness, newness, and importance as understood within *social science* framing or focusing; that is, within a social science way of collecting and ordering data. In labeling our treatment of trueness, newness, and importance as distinctively *social scientific,* we seek to establish a contrast between the statement that follows and *other* ways to frame fieldwork or qualitative data that have *different* views of trueness, newness, and importance.

Because what we are calling "social scientific" and these other forms of framing are sometimes confused with one another, after we explain the former (and its value commitments), we will discuss some alternatives. Against the background of our explication of social science framing, we will suggest that while alternatively framed reports may have humanistic or other merit, they are not "social scientific" in the sense we develop in this chapter.

I. Social Science Framing

The concepts of trueness, newness, and importance are quite abstract and their exact meanings therefore vary as a function of the contexts in which they are given specific application. Such is the case here. The meanings of trueness, newness, and importance we elaborate are specific to the collection and analysis of qualitative social science data in the fieldstudy genre.

A. True

Trueness as a dimension of arousing interest is primarily a threshold test. A report is not of any special interest simply because it is true, but it needs to be true in order to be of interest for other reasons. Even though limited in this way, trueness is obviously also of key importance.

Following the procedures for collecting data outlined in other chapters of this guide is one's best insurance of empirical accuracy or trueness. Among those procedures, we should call particular attention to these previously discussed methodological practices:

- avoid error and bias in observations (Chapter 5, Section II.C)
- exercise caution in estimating frequencies and magnitudes (Chapter 7, Sections II and III) and in making assertions of causes and consequences (Chapter 7, Sections VI and VII, respectively).

In the end, readers have only the report of your research and they are therefore especially attentive to how its particulars do or do not give them confidence that the factual materials asserted are accurate. We agree with Roger Sanjek's (1990a) argument that readers of field reports look, specifically, for three kinds of validating discussions and practices that he calls "canons of ethnographic validity." Methodologically careful researchers are, therefore, well advised to provide discussions and practices that implement these canons in their reports and to have previously engaged in the activities that give rise to them. Borrowing Sanjek's captions, these criteria are as follows.

1. Theoretical Candor
The facts asserted and that are now subject to a trueness assessment are organized and analyzed in some substantive fashion. The reader's faith in

the accuracy of the empirical details is enhanced if the researcher provides a truthful explanation of how he or she came to employ the particular form of analysis that organizes the facts. Unavoidably, only some facts from among a vast number of other available facts are actually reported and this reporting is structured by one's analytic or theoretical apparatus. "Candid exposition of when and why" such schemes were developed "enhances ethnographic validity" (Sanjek 1990a, p. 396).

2. The Ethnographer's Path

The criterion of "theoretical candor" reports one's view of the sources of one's analysis. An account of the ethnographer's path, in contrast, reports with whom one interacted, in what sequence, and how. In some studies, this is a "description of the path connecting the ethnographer and informants" (Sanjek 1990a, p. 400). A report should contain such an account and in Chapter 10, Section II.B we provide a detailed guide to appropriate topics in this account.

3. Fieldnote Evidence

The third canon of ethnographic validity, that of fieldnote evidence, involves reporting (1) one's procedures of assembling and processing data and (2) practices of presenting data in the report. Regarding procedures, how one recorded data and worked with them should be described along with the processes of developing analysis. Sufficient amounts of the empirical materials themselves should be presented. In Section I.C.4 of this chapter, we will address the question of what constitutes a "sufficient amount" of data and the form of their presentation.

These three kinds of discussions and practices do not, of course, absolutely insure that one's report will be true, or that readers will assess it as factually accurate. These three do, however, provide a mindset with which to approach the data and that serves to heighten your concern with empirical trueness. Fully executed and reported, these practices at least move one well along the road to fulfilling the evaluative standard of trueness—and, therefore, toward being of interest to an audience. (Additional aspects of these three canons are addressed in Altheide and Johnson 1994 and J. Johnson and Altheide 1993.)

The theme running through these three practices is that of exercising and exhibiting *methodological concern and caution* in one's treatment of data throughout the report. Indeed, in addition to the three practices just enumerated, at every appropriate place in the report, one should acknowledge and call attention to possible difficulties and shortcomings in one's data (cf. Miles and Huberman 1994, pp. 277ff on "standards for the quality of conclusions").

B. New

The dimension of newness as an element of arousing audience interest is founded on the reasonable desire not to waste resources assembling facts that are already well established or repeating ideas that are already developed and widely known. In research instruction contexts, neither of these possible liabilities is necessarily a problem since the aim is instruction rather than discovery of new facts or crafting new analysis. Nonetheless, strategies of newness are still of interest even to novices in training courses.

1. Relating to Existing Work

An obvious and rather easy first strategy is to use library resources to discover the degree to which one's field setting, group, or other situation has already been studied. Even if it has, the exact settings or populations already investigated are likely not identical to the one you are studying and any differences become points of newness that you are exploring.

Likewise, you can check on concepts, analyses, and theories you are thinking of using or developing. As with settings and populations, you may see that your approach differs in some way that becomes a form of newness.

Beyond and in addition to direct library checking, one highly efficient strategy of checking on existing work is to identify and locate specific people who are known to have done work that is similar to what you propose. Face-to-face, telephone, mail, or electronic contact with as many such people as is practical is very much in order and, indeed, makes your project much more interesting and informed than using library sources alone.

There is a wide range of ways in which newness can be pursued within the context of already well established analyses. In his penetrating work on the "that's interesting" response to research (as contrasted with the "that's obvious" and "that's absurd" responses), Murray Davis points to these, among other, forms of newness crafting:

- What seems to be an . . . unstructured phenomenon is in reality a . . . structured phenomenon [and vice versa].
- What seem to be assorted heterogeneous phenomena are in reality composed of a single element [and vice versa].
- What seems a stable and unchanging phenomenon is in reality an unstable and changing phenomenon [and vice versa].
- What seem to be similar (nearly identical) phenomena are in reality opposite phenomena [and vice versa] (M. Davis 1971, pp. 313–325).

2. First Report

Current societies are continually churning up new social formations and practices, especially among youth. This sheer newness stimulates interest and the evaluative responses "that's new" or "that's interesting." Therefore, a researcher who is alert to new churnings can solve the problem of being new simply by documenting a new formation or practice.

3. Unusual Setting

Social situations and settings differ in the degree to which they are socially defined as strange, ideologically or behaviorally exotic, prurient, violent, and so on. Such unusual settings also tend not to be well or often documented. As a consequence of this (and other factors), there is more interest in such settings than in many others. Therefore, one way almost to guarantee a "that's new" response is to study an unusual setting or practice. Indeed, the more unusual features a setting has, the greater is the likely sense of newness to various audiences.

Some few researchers, we might note, have been able to use the strategies of the first report and the unusual setting at the same time. For example, in the early 1970s, Laud Humphreys (1975) did the first sustained observation of homosexual encounters in public toilets—a report that aroused a great deal of interest.

C. Important

The interest-arousing dimension of "importance" is broader, vaguer, and more difficult to assess than are the dimensions of trueness and newness, and its assessment is more contentious even among social science audiences. Nonetheless, it is possible to point to a number of framing practices that, if used, tend to prompt the response "that's important." In our assessment, there are five of these. The more of them used in a report, the more important social scientists evaluating qualitative field-studies deem it to be. Not all social scientists think that all five need be present in a single report, and few reports strongly exhibit all five simultaneously. Even so, the five form a package, so to speak, of desirable framing features and provide a set of evaluative standards relating to importance.

These five framing practices differ in degree of concreteness and specificity—in the degree, that is, to which they involve concrete operations on, and features of, a research report. The first and the fifth of them—the questioning mindset and resonant content—are the most diffuse and elusive in terms of exact concrete operations and features of reports. The middle three—proposition formation, generic abstraction, and developed treatment—are more operationally specific. Therefore, if the first and fifth framing practices seem difficult to grasp, take heart— your perception is accurate!

1. Questioning Mindset

The hard-won and continually precarious hallmark of the modern mind-set that is applied in social science framing is the assiduous application of the proposition that *there is no final word* (Rauch 1993). Instead, *all* representations of reality of whatever kind must always be taken as mere claims, as likely in error, and as in need of searching examination. In historical perspective, the unremitting application of *questioning* or *skepticism* to all claims is likely the key cultural element in the rise and advance of market economies, political democracies, and liberal science, including social science.

In all these areas, questioning in the form of unceasing skeptical investigation has been, to one or another degree, institutionalized. The opposite mindset of *absolutism* also continually asserts itself and seeks to hold one or another representation of reality beyond questioning or skeptical inquiry. In the absolutist view, there *is* a final word on claimed reality, and these claims must be taken on authority, fiat, revelation, or whatever source claims to end the process of questioning. But the questioning counterview is that there is nothing that should not be doubted. Everything must be unceasingly examined. The central assertion of the questioning mindset is therefore: "Do not block the way of inquiry" (Charles Sanders Peirce, frontispiece epigraph to Rauch 1993, p. vii).

In social science research, the difference between the questioning and absolutist mindset is displayed most clearly in how researchers treat the realities asserted by the people they are studying. In absolutist treatments, these realities are assumed to be either true or false, either good or bad, but neither the judgments nor the realities being judged are themselves topics of examination. In contrast, the questioning mindset makes its own assessments problematic and also brackets the realities of the people studied as proper topics of inquiry. Using what is often also called "critical intelligence," nothing is "of course." Even one's own most passionate commitments are properly the subjects of searching inspection and critique. *All* claims require inspection in terms of factual adequacy, comfortable self-serving myths, hidden vested interests, and other forms of mystification or mere intellectual laziness.

At the level of even the most mundane data claims, the questioning mindset constantly examines the veracity of claims encountered and claims that the researcher is devising. For example, group spokespersons report a membership of 100,000. How do they know that? What do they mean by a "member"? Could they be wrong or have reasons to inflate the number or to mislead outsiders? Or person X is thought to be a fantastic (or scurrilous) human being. Do you take this belief as a fact or as a perception? Whatever the "real truth" of the matter, how do you best understand this item? Or you may think that variables A and B are linked in a given way. What is the evidence for that? Could you be wrong? Could the evidence on which you make an assertion itself be faulty?

In being so relentlessly skeptical, the questioning mindset is often at odds with the mindsets of a great many audiences that are more prone to absolutism. In particular, the *members* of virtually all social groupings do not want their realities questioned or treated skeptically. Instead, members *believe* and they want others to believe—to *not* use a questioning mindset as regards them. But, as a social scientist, the researcher is bound to doubt and to check and to hold *all* claims as simply claims.

This creates an unavoidable tension between social scientists, group members, and any champions of those members.

What we are here terming the "questioning mindset" has been referred to with a variety of other labels. We have already employed two of them: *skepticism* and *critical intelligence*. Other labels include *bracketing*, *humanistic*, *transcendent*, and *critical*. Any of these is serviceable, but each also has connotations—implied meanings—that we have wanted to avoid and we have therefore not adopted any as our identifying term. "Critical," for example, refers to a questioning orientation but also refers to politically left—Marxist, in particular—critiques of capitalist societies, the frequent referent of the terms "critical sociology," "critical theory," and "critical social science" (Fay 1987). The problem with these latter meanings of critical is that none of these bodies of thought is critical enough. Each comes to rest in its own respective absolutism. The questioning mindset is abandoned or suspended in order to "privilege" selected points of critique, while disallowing other possible critiques, especially of themselves (as discussed by, for example, Fay 1987). This is unfortunate because the term critical is otherwise quite accurate.

Because the term critical is so often associated with the political left, the questioning mindset is sometimes alleged to be merely a form of "leftist" or "radical" politics. This is an erroneous belief arising from inaccurate sampling. When sampled and reviewed more accurately, we find that the questioning mindset is not inherently either conservative or radical in its political meaning. It is, however, inherently subversive of *all* established patterns of thought, be these established patterns of right, left, or *whatever* thought. As Peter Berger has pithily expressed it: "Fomenters of revolution have as good reason to be suspicious of [the questioning mindset] as policemen have" (1971, p. 13). Indeed, some of the most hard-eyed and enthusiastic enemies of the questioning mindset are found in the radical left. Such folks differ from arch conservatives in terms of aims and perspectives rather than in terms of mindset. To quote Berger again: "My principal objection to most of my radicalized colleagues is not that they are engaged in the business of 'bringing to consciousness' [using the questioning mindset] but that they are not doing enough of it" (1971, p. 5). Rather than being easily classifiable as "left-wing" or "right-wing," the questioning mindset engages in a "consistent, unswerving application of critical intelligence—to the status quo, yes, and to any challengers of the status quo" (Berger 1971, p. 5).

Viewing Berger's observation more broadly, the commitment to exempt nothing from doubt means that the questioning mindset subjects itself to its own skepticism or critical intelligence. As Alvin Gouldner puts it,

> there is nothing that speakers . . . refuse to discuss or make problematic. [This reflexivity is] the obligation to examine what had hitherto been taken for granted, to transform "givens" into "problems," resources into

topics. . . . It is therefore not only the present but also the anti-present, the *critique* of the present and the assumptions it uses, that the . . . [questioning mindset] must also challenge. In other words: [It] must put its hands around its own throat, and see how long it can squeeze. . . . [It] always moves on to auto-critique, and the critique of *that* auto-critique. There is an unending regress in it. (1979, pp. 28, 59–60)

The questioning mindset is not as exotic or strange as it may at first blush appear to some readers. Instead, unending reflexive, autocritique is routinely practiced day in and day out by hundreds of thousands of physical and biological scientists, among other organized inquirers. The questioning mindset, that is, is the essence of liberal science and the fundamental basis of liberal society—a moral and ethical aspect to which we will come shortly.

As mentioned, as a framing practice the questioning mindset is not easily codified as an exact set of operations one performs on one's data and in one's analysis. Instead, it suffuses one's approach to both data and analysis and it is manifest in the kinds of matters the researcher is prepared to make problematic.

2. Propositional Framing
The second framing practice that contributes to a positive assessment of importance is much more concretely operational in character than the questioning mindset.

The purpose of asking *questions* (Chapter 7) about *topics* (Chapter 6) is to develop social science *answers*. Conceived most abstractly, such answers may be thought of as *propositions* about social situations or settings. Other words and phrasings that have this same meaning include:

stating a *hypothesis*
developing a *thesis*
formulating a *concept*
making an *assertion*
putting forth an *idea*
propounding a broad, unifying *theme*
addressing or solving a *problem*
specifying a *story line*
telling a *story*
framing the data
constructing general *principles*
providing a *general interpretation*

The eight questions explained in Chapter 7 provide eight basic forms of propositions that are answers to the eight questions. Stated in the starkly generic or immaculately abstract, these are:

1. Type: *X exists (or X-1, X-2, X-3, X-n exist).*
2. Frequencies: *X occurs in Y units in places 1, 2, 3, n over Z periods of time.*
3. Magnitudes: *X is of Y size, strength, or intensity.*
4. Structures: *X is structured in terms of 1, 2, 3, n.*
5. Processes: *X exhibits a process with the phases or cycles of 1, 2, 3, n.*
6. Causes: *X is caused by factors 1, 2, 3, n.*
7. Consequences: *X has consequences 1, 2, 3, n.*
8. Agency: *In X, people use strategies and tactics 1, 2, 3, n.*

Article-length reports are commonly organized in terms of only one of these eight propositional forms, with one or two others perhaps receiving secondary attention. Even book-length reports may be organized in terms of only one, although books are more likely to feature two, three, or four (but rarely all) of them.

Let us try to sharpen this depiction of propositional answers to questions about topics by showing how it is a specialized application of a broader distinction. In the broader domain of writing per se a distinction is commonly drawn between *subject* writing that describes a topic or area and *idea* writing that propounds a thesis or makes an assertion.

> Some people use the word *idea* to mean something like "topic" or "subject," phrases that indicate an *area* of potential interest, such as "economics" or "a cure for cancer". . . . These phrases might be said to be "broad" or "narrow" subjects, but they are not yet ideas because they do not say anything about economics, or a cancer cure. . . . The noun *economics* is not an idea. . . . "Economics is bull" *is* an idea. . . . The difference between noun phrases that are not ideas and statements that are ideas lies in the predication: Ideas are sentences; they complete a thought by connecting a verb to the noun phrase. Saying something about a subject requires making some kind of connection between it and something else. (Gage 1987, pp. 48–49; emphasis in the original)

In parallel, social science propositions are "idea" writing rather than "subject" writing. Propositions are assertions about topics. Notice that each of the abstract formulations of the eight propositions given just above contains a *verb* that serves to transform the subject into an idea, that is, a topic into a proposition. Specifically these verbs are: exists, occurs, is, exhibits, has, use. Cast in such a fashion, a social science report becomes more than a compilation of facts one has gathered. It is, instead, an assertion of something—a proposition.

3. Generic Concepts

The propositional framing sought in social science research is, moreover, generic rather than historically particular. By "historically particular" we

Figure 8.1   Historically Particular Versus Generic Propositional Framing:
Examples from Social Movement Studies

Example Topics and the Heirich Books	Historically Particular	Generic Propositional
social movement organization	specific named organization	type or form of organization: e.g., vanguard party, democratic-collectivist
beliefs	specific philosophy, point of view, ideology: e.g., Mormonism, National Socialism	type of point of view: e.g., totalitarianism, sectarianism, millenarianism
leaders	specific named individuals	type of leader: e.g., charismatic
strategy	description of particular events and activities	type of strategy: e.g., direct benefit, public education, strike, boycott
Max Heirich's study of movement activity at UC Berkeley in 1964–65, published as two books, one of each type	book published: *The Beginning: Berkeley 1964* (1970), 16 chapters running 317 pages	book published: *The Spiral of Conflict: Berkeley 1964* (1971), 21 chapters running 502 pages

mean primarily reporting the chronological activities observed in a situation or setting and organizing the report in chronological terms. Generic framing, in contrast, seeks to specify abstract propositions of which the historical particulars are instances.

In order to display this contrast more clearly, we have assembled several examples of the historically particular study of social movements in the middle column of Figure 8.1. While these examples are diverse, their common focus is that of a specific location in historical time.

The generic, propositional quest is, in contrast, for abstract concepts and propositions of which the historical particulars are instances. Examples of these are shown in the right-hand column of Figure 8.1 and they are juxtaposed to the historically particular versions of the same example given in the middle column.

Max Heirich's two published studies of social movement activity on the Berkeley campus of the University of California in 1964–65, shown in the bottom row of Figure 8.1, provide excellent examples of the contrast between historically particular and generic framing or abstraction. Knowing that different audiences are attuned to different kinds of accounts, Heirich's publisher arranged for Heirich to publish two books on exactly the same events! One is titled *The Beginning: Berkeley 1964* (1970). Its 317 pages are divided into sixteen chapters and report the sheer history. The second—the generically framed book—contains the same historical account, but is also much longer—502 pages divided into twenty-one chapters. It is longer and more complicated because it employs generic concepts that propositionally structure the data. Appropriately, it bears a title signaling the presence of that generic propositional analysis, which is: *The Spiral of Conflict: Berkeley 1964 (1971)*.

Here are examples of studies summarized in previous chapters that illustrate this process of "upward categorization":

- The stages through which the relationship between a physically handicapped and "normal" person may move framed as an instance of *deviance disavowal* (F. Davis 1972).

- The amount of sympathy available to persons framed as an instance of *sympathy margin* (Clark 1987).

- The body language and movement practices that occur in public encounters between persons of different racial and class groupings framed as instances of *street etiquette* (E. Anderson 1990).

In each of these studies, the analyst has asked: "Of what more abstract and social analytic category are these data an instance?" The goal is to translate the specific materials under study into instances of widely relevant and basic social types, processes, or whatever. In its *upward categorization* generic framing finds fundamental human themes and concerns in obscure and sometimes seemingly trivial social doings. The situation under study is lifted out of its historically unique details and placed among the array of matters of interest to broad audiences. In one sense, generic framing is an effort to see the universe in a grain of sand. Or, as Louis Coser has written:

> Though there is but little concrete similarity between the behavior displayed at the court of Louis XIV and that displayed in the main offices of an American corporation, a study of the forms of subordination and superordination in each may reveal underlying patterns common to both. On a concrete and descriptive level, there would seem little connection between, say, the early psychoanalytic movement in Vienna and the Trotskyist movement, but attention to typical forms of interaction among the members of these groups reveals that both are importantly shaped by the fact that they have the structural features of the sect. (Coser 1965, p. 7)

In generically abstracting, social scientists do not deny the uniqueness or historical context of events, but they do search for trans-setting patterns of types, structures, causes, functions, processes, strategies, and so forth:

> If one looks at history through the peculiar lenses of the [social scientist], one need not be concern[ed] with the uniqueness of these events but, rather, with their underlying uniformities. The [social scientist] does not contribute to knowledge about the individual actions of a King

John, or a King Louis, or a King Henry. But [he or she] can illuminate the ways in which all of them were constrained in their actions by the institution of kingship. The [social scientist] is not concerned with King *John,* but rather, with *King* John. (Coser 1965, p. 7)

There are at least three "tricks of the trade," so to speak, that social scientists sometimes use to stimulate their imaginations when they seek to develop generic conceptualizations. These are the use of *metaphor,* the utilization of *irony,* and the specification of *new forms.*

a. Dictionaries commonly define the word *metaphor* as "a figure of speech in which one kind of object or phrase literally denoting one kind of object or idea is used in place of another to suggest a likeness or analogy between them (as in, the ship plows the sea)." More broadly, metaphor involves "seeing something from the viewpoint of something else" (Brown 1977, p. 78). In social science framing, the simplest formula is "X *as* Y," as in Murray Melbin's creative analysis of *Night as Frontier* (1987), a study in which features of the literal concept of "frontier" are applied to "the night." Melbin argues that "time, like space, can be occupied and is treated so by humans. . . . Nighttime social life in urban areas resembles social life in former land frontiers" (Melbin 1987, p. 3). One of the most creative social scientists of the twentieth century, Erving Goffman, frequently employed metaphors in generating generic propositional framings, as in viewing:

    • the problem of failure in social life in terms of the classic confidence game, in which everyone is a mark, operator, or cooler (Goffman 1962).

    • contact among strangers as a theatrical situation of "performers" and "impression management" (Goffman 1959).

    • mental patients as having careers (Goffman 1961).

    • psychiatry as an instance of the "tinkering trades," or as a mere service occupation subject to the same venal tendencies (Goffman 1961).

    The point of metaphor is not simply and mechanically to translate one realm into another, but rather to "provide a new way to understand that which we already know [and to reconstitute] . . . new domains of perception" (Brown 1977, p. 98). As a guide, then, the device of metaphor counsels a playful turn of mind, as in these examples:

    The Catholic Church is the General Motors of religion.

    Heart surgeons run a boutique practice.

    Hilton Hotels are factories for sleep (Brown 1977).

b. The term *irony* is ordinarily defined as "a state of affairs or events that is the reverse of what was or was to be expected: a result opposite to and as if in mockery of the appropriate result." One applies it as a social science frame by being attentive to causes, consequences, and other aspects of social topics that are paradoxical, unintended, or unrecognized by participants.

Irony is often used with regard to questions of function or consequence (Chapter 7, Section VII). In such cases, one distinguishes between *manifest* and *latent* functions, that is, looks beyond the recognized and intended (or manifest) functions to the unrecognized and unintended (or latent) functions. The champion practitioner of sociological irony, Robert Merton, has claimed that "it is precisely at the point where the research attention of sociologists has shifted from the plane of manifest to the plane of latent functions that they have made their distinctive and major contribution" (1968, p. 120). Merton has provided many powerful examples of this precept. As summarized by Arthur Stinchcombe:

> Merton clearly loves irony. He is most pleased to find motives of advancing knowledge creating priority conflicts among scientists and hardly interested in the fact that such motives also advance knowledge. He likes to find political bosses helping people while good government types turn a cold shoulder. He likes to find Sorokin offering statistics on ideas to attack the empiricist bent of modern culture and to urge an idealistic logico-meaningful analysis of ideas. He likes to range Engels and functionalists down parallel columns to show them to be really the same. The immediate subjective feeling that one has learned something from reading Merton is probably mainly due to the taste for irony. (1975, p. 28)

Merton has been outstanding, but he has hardly been alone. What is known as the "functionalist perspective" is suffused with irony. Historically, functionalists have propounded, among other things, the notions that "increased prostitution may reduce the sexual irregularities of respectable women" (Kingsley Davis, quoted in Schneider 1975, p. 325) and that incompetent group members may help their groups more than harm them (Chapter 7, Section VII.B; Brown 1977, Chapter 5).

Conceived more broadly, irony involves documenting a contrast between a surface or official understanding of a social arrangement and additional, *also real*, but muted or hidden social facts. Because social life is replete with discrepancies between formal plans and actual conduct, between the official, visible, and public and the unofficial, invisible, and private, social researchers are obviously able to make such contrasts the objects of analysis. Peter Berger has referred to this broader use of irony as the "debunking motif" in sociological consciousness. It is a:

> built-in procedure for looking for levels of reality other than those given in the official interpretations of society, [a mandate to] look beyond the immediately given and publicly approved interpretations . . . [in order to] observe the machinery that went into the construction of the scene.

The [social analyst thus] "looks behind" the facades of social structure. (Berger 1979, pp. 9–10)

Sometimes, irony is signaled in the titles of reports, as in these examples, which combine alliteration with irony: *Reluctant Rebels* (Walton 1984), *Charismatic Capitalism* (Biggart 1989), *Polite Protesters* (J. Lofland 1993).

c. A rather more modest but nonetheless important and creative device in generic propositional framing is to discern new variations on established types of social units or aspects and on answers to the eight questions described in the previous chapter. Even though *new forms* can be associated with any of these eight questions, in practice they tend to be answers to Questions I and IV: "What type is it?" and "What is its structure?" Erving Goffman's notion of the "total institution" (discussed in Chapter 6, Section III.G and Chapter 7, Section I.A), for example, was a new form at one time.

Among "new form" answers to other questions, you might refer back to these analyses (also from Chapter 7):

- Question V: "What Are the Topic's Processes?" Defining someone as a paranoid involves a complex, self-feeding sequence of interaction in which the person's "normal" associates actually conspire against the person they fear (Lemert 1972, pp. 246–264).
- Question VI: "What Are the Topic's Causes?" Disoriented behavior and heavy drinking among the homeless appears to emerge or increase as the homeless try to cope with the stressful and difficult exigencies of their situation rather than being the reason for their situation (Snow and Anderson 1993).
- Question VII: "What Are the Topic's Consequences?" Deviant social behavior among persons in organizations serves needed but publicly unacknowledged functions that someone else would otherwise have to perform (Reed, Burnette, and Troiden 1977).
- Question VIII: "What Is Human Agency?" Managers of profit-making organizations may develop an obscurant language that defines their work in social rather than in economic terms, thus binding their employees to them by emotional as well as instrumental ties (Biggart 1989).

Creative discernment of new forms requires more familiarity with existing social analyses than does the use of metaphor or irony. Consider, for example, answering such questions as these in new form terms:

What new kind of socialization is this?

What new sort of family type is this?

What new type of organizational process is this?

You can answer these questions without being familiar with previous work on the respective subjects but, if you do so, you run the risk of rediscovering what is already quite well understood, of being faulted on the evaluative standard of newness.

As mentioned regarding the newness of sheer *data*, the churnings of the modern world are constantly throwing up new and significant variations on everything. This newness extends to new generic propositional forms of the new social structures, processes, or whatever. Persons seeking to articulate experience in this way ought, therefore, often to make discoveries. Indeed, new generic propositional articulations of new social patterns perform a quite valuable public service, as we will discuss below.

4. Developed Treatment

If two people independently research and publish reports that are substantially identical and do so at the same time, the report that is the more thoroughly developed both empirically and conceptually is considered more important and elicits a higher degree of interest. The classic case of this in the history of science is the relation between the work of Charles Darwin and Alfred Russel Wallace, the latter of whom independently formulated the theory of evolution. Indeed, Wallace might have published before Darwin except for a British gentlemanly agreement in which their respective formulations were made public simultaneously. But, nonetheless, it is Darwin, rather than Wallace, who is commonly credited with the theory. This is because Darwin, not Wallace, performed the exhaustive research, developed the theory in detail, and published several elaborate reports. Wallace's report was true and new, as far as he had gone, but he did not develop the theory in detail nor base his formulation on much data. Darwin, in great contrast, spent decades developing diverse forms of data and elaborating the theory in terms of them. Therefore, Darwin's work had a much more solid evidential base and conceptual purchase than Wallace's sketchily formulated speculations. Therefore, Darwin rather than Wallace is viewed as the inventor of the theory of evolution.

The situation is the same in social science. Indeed, publications that display all of the other framing practices relating to importance (and are also true and new) are not scarce. That is, writings of a questioning mindset that are framed with generic propositions and are resonant (discussed below) are not hard to come by. But, in the absence of empirical and conceptual development, serious social scientists regard these writings as merely skillful exercises in speculation.

What, more precisely, constitutes a "developed" treatment? While standards of this are not exact or entirely agreed upon regarding qualitative fieldstudies, we can report that many social scientists assess development along three dimensions: (1) degree of conceptual *elaboration*, (2) *balance* between conceptual elaboration and data presentation, and (3) *interpenetration* of conceptual elaboration and data presentation.

a. **Elaboration**
The dimension of conceptual elaboration refers, operationally, to the number of major conceptual or analytic divisions and subdivisions that form the main body of the report. In grounded theory language, this dimension is referred to as conceptual *density, specificity,* and interlinkage or *integration* (Strauss and Corbin 1990, pp. 109, 121, 253–254). The central concern is that the researcher provide evidence of having given detailed thought to the one or more propositions used to structure and analyze the data. The prime evidence of such detailed thought is a conceptual scheme of some reasonable complexity that works in tandem with the other two dimensions of development that we will describe in a moment.

Because particular studies and their data vary so much, it is difficult to specify precise numbers of concepts—of major divisions and subdivisions of one's report—that one ought to elaborate. There are, however, some general rules of thumb. The one we suggest is that article-length reports ought to have on the order of three to five major elements elaborating a proposition and a similar number of subdivisions within each element.

Such a general directive alerts us to the possibilities of conceptual underelaboration and overelaboration. In article-length reports, *underelaboration* refers to the absence of any organizing proposition at all or the use of only one or a very few concepts without elaboration within themselves. *Overelaboration* is seen in article-length reports where the conceptual scheme consists of dozens of concepts and distinctions, giving the impression that the researcher has become more interested in the scheme than in the data the scheme is supposed to help us understand.

b. **Balance**
The possibilities of under- and overconceptual elaboration lead into the second dimension of developed treatment: the degree of *balance* between a conceptual scheme and the presentation of data. Extremely overelaborated conceptual schemes squeeze out, so to speak, the opportunity to present data. This may be termed the error of *analytic excess.* An author making this error has become so engrossed in the logic of abstract analysis that he or she fails to report very much of the rich, concrete reality to which the analysis purportedly refers. The reader may learn a great deal about the author's mind, but very little, concretely, about what is going on in the setting. There is too little description of the many events that occurred, and the participants are almost never quoted.

The error of *descriptive excess,* in contrast, involves providing too much description relative to analysis. The author becoming so engrossed in rendering the concrete details of a setting that he or she loses connection with analytic concepts and ideas that could help to order, explain, or summarize the details. Such reports resemble simple histories or journalistic descriptions.

As with the dimension of elaboration, there are no precise rules regarding balance, only order-of-magnitude guidelines. The one we suggest is that somewhat more than half the pages of an article-length report should consist of qualitative data: accounts of episodes, incidents, events, exchanges, remarks, happenings, conversations, actions, and so forth. Somewhat less than half should be analysis: the major proposition or propositions, abstract categorizing and discussion of the meaning, application, and implications of the data, and so on.

c. Interpenetration

The dimensions of conceptual elaboration and balance come together operationally to achieve thorough development in the third dimension, that of the *interpenetration* of data and analysis. As a concrete feature of reports, interpenetration refers to the continuing and intimate *alternation* of data and analysis as text. Specifically, analytic passages do not go on very long without reporting empirical materials, and vice versa. This alternation makes the relation between the data and analysis more evident and conveys ways in which they form a whole.

This mode of appearance in the text of the report is based on—and has emerged out of—the process of the *grounded induction of analysis* we will describe in the next two chapters—a process that is also informed by all the previous chapters, as well as the one you are now reading. In this way, interpenetration is *not* merely an appearance in the report, it is the logical consequence of a thorough working through of the data in analytic terms.

Low degrees of (or the absence of) interpenetration may be thought of as *data and analysis segregation.* Such segregation is seen, for example, in reports where the researcher devotes the first and last sections to an elaborate conceptual scheme. The middle parts consist of low-level, commonsensical description that the author does not relate to the conceptual scheme reported in the first and last sections. That is, the analysis seems tacked onto the data at each end of the report rather than evolved from the data or used to analyze them. Because the two are not in intimate interplay throughout the report, the relation between the data and analysis is unknown. This failure to interpenetrate data and analysis in the report often signals, in fact, that the researcher has not actually done any analysis.

These three processes and textual practices of *elaboration, balance,* and *interpenetration* form a discipline of guiding constraints that result

Figure 8.2   Example of a Developed Treatment: Summary of Glaser and
                  Strauss on Closed Awareness Contexts

In their classic study of *Awareness of Dying,* Barney Glaser and Anselm Strauss
devote a chapter to the "closed awareness context."

Strauss's and Corbin's summary of that chapter appears below, and it nicely
illustrates the development dimensions of elaboration, balance, and interpenetration.

Text from the original publication by Glaser and Strauss is in plain text and
Strauss's and Corbin's editorial explanations of the summary are in bold.

For clarity, we have respaced the summary and numbered the major points,
using the symbols { } to indicate our editorial insertions.

There are at least five important structural conditions which contribute to the existence and maintenance of the closed awareness context. [**These are then discussed
in detail for two and a half pages.**

**Then types of interaction that occur under closed awareness conditions are pre-
sented both descriptively (with quotations) and with analytic sensitivity.**

Then, since process is important, the authors write:] Inherently, this closed awareness context tends toward instability, as the patient moves either to suspicion or
full awareness of . . . terminality. The principle reasons for the instability . . .
require only brief notation, as they have already been adumbrated.

{1} First, any breakdown in the structural conditions that make for the closed
     awareness context may lead to its disappearance. Those conditions include
     [**examples are given**] . . .

{2} Some unanticipated disclosures or tip-offs, stemming from organizational
     conditions, can also occur. [**More examples are given, including variations by
     ward.**]

{3} New symptoms understandably are likely to perplex and alarm the patient; and
     the longer his retrogressive course, the more difficult it becomes to give him
     plausible explanations, though a very complicated misrepresentational drama
     can be played for his benefit. Even so, it becomes somewhat more difficult to
     retain . . . trust over a long time. [**More comparisons and variations are
     given.**] . . .

{4} Another threat to close awareness . . . is that some treatments make little sense
     to a patient who does not recognize that he is dying. . . .

{5} At times, moreover, a patient may be unable to cope with his immensely
     deteriorating physical condition, unless nurses interpret that condition and its
     symptoms to him. To do this, nurses may feel forced to talk of his dying. Not
     to disclose . . . can torture and isolate the patient, which runs counter to a
     central value of nursing care, namely to make the patient as comfortable as
     possible. . . . The danger that staff members will give the show away also
     increases as the patient nears death, especially when the dying takes place
     slowly. . . .

This last set of conditions brings us to the question of whether, and how, personnel
actually may engineer a change of the closed awareness context. [**Examples are
given of observations of how this is done.**]

Indeed, when the family actually knows the truth, the hazards to maintaining closed
awareness probably are much increased, if only because kin are more strongly
tempted to signal the truth. [**There follows then a systematic detailing of consequences: for patients, nurses, physicians, kin, ward, and hospital.**] (Glaser &
Strauss, 1964, pp. 29–46)

Sources: Strauss and Corbin, "Grounded Theory Methodology: An Overview," 1994, p.
279; Glaser and Strauss 1964, pp. 29–46. Reprinted by permission of Sage Publications,
Inc. © 1994 by Sage Publications, Inc.

in a *developed treatment* (one example of which is presented in Figure 8.2). These stimulate—even if they do not absolutely ensure—a conscientiousness and thoroughness of work that prompt audiences to take one seriously—that is, to see one's report as important and, therefore, as interesting.

5. **Resonating Content**

Despite the peculiarity of their commitment to the scientific analysis of human life and organization, social scientists are very much like everyone else. They display the same foibles as everyone else and they are emotionally stirred by the same deep concerns as everyone else. This means that beyond the matters of social science discipline and vision described in the preceding four framing practices, social scientists participate in the common human pool of deep fears and anxieties, high ideals, and quests for meaning.

Therefore, within the vision of social science per se that is summarized in the foregoing four framing practices, social scientists are drawn to topics and conceptual substance that address fundamental human concerns and to problems that confront everyone else (and they display the same proclivity to fad and fashion in addressing these that we see in everyone else).

The frail humanity that social scientists share with everyone else means that the *specific content* or substance of one's developed, generic propositions will be assessed in terms of their felt relation to one or another common and deep human theme. We label this the dimension of *resonance*, the degree to which the content reverberates with and evokes existential concerns. In the formulation of Snow and Benford (1988, p. 207), audiences ask, "[Does it] strike a responsive chord? Does it inform understanding of events and experiences within [our] world?"

There are, however, a large number of resonant matters. How is one to select from among them? As a moral and ethical choice, rather than a research or logical decision, we cannot presume to say what you should choose. We confine ourselves, instead, to suggesting some of the factors one might take into account in making decisions about resonance.

In our view, the first and most important factor ought to be: *Is the content resonant with you?* Do you feel (and we mean *feel* rather than believe or perceive) the content is saying what you want it to say about something you deeply feel to be important? If yes, trust yourself. A liability, though, is that there may be a rather small or even nonexistent audience with whom the substance resonates. An asset, on the other side, however, is that you will at least have the satisfaction of believing in what you have done. Moreover, the fad and fashion nature of popularly resonant topics may mean that your audience has yet to arrive and that you are a pioneer of newly resonant substance.

A second factor to consider is the current resonance status of the content. There are so many matters of deep concern to people that—as a practical matter of limits on cognitive processing and coping—audiences respond to only a few topics at any given time. And it is in part because the list of "hot" resonant topics is so short that researchers (and others) tend to *research frenzy* on whatever happens to be "going" at the moment. One evident solution to the resonance problem, therefore, is to jump onto some current resonance bandwagon. A liability of this, however, is that you may jump on too late. Resonant interest may be saturated by the time you produce your report.

Third, despite fad and fashion in resonant topics, there are enduring or standing worlds of resonance. Although sometimes even obscure and marginal, they are out there, and linking up with them can be critical in shaping one's work and finding sympathy for it. In one positive scenario, your private feelings (factor number one just above) and a standing world can nicely coincide.

Because of the (1) great number and variety of resonant topics, the (2) fad and fashion manner in which given topics are "hot" or "cold," and the (3) fact that almost anything is resonant with at least some people, social scientists tend to be quite hesitant about (and ambivalent in) using resonance in assessing the importance of a report. Resonance can certainly count for much in assessing importance in a period where the content is quite fashionable. But, in a period where it is not, the tendency is to consider work important anyway *when it strongly displays the other four framing practices and is also true and new.* The obvious reason for discounting resonance and looking to other aspects of reports resides in the nature of fashionableness. Who can say when this otherwise solid piece of research will come to the fore in a wave of fashionable resonance. Or, if then fashionable, will sink into oblivion when the fashion changes. Therefore, social scientists say, let us stick with more enduring features in evaluating research.

In the foregoing, we have applied the three general criteria commonly employed in evaluating any research to qualitative fieldstudies. The generic criteria of trueness, newness, and importance therefore have the somewhat specialized meanings that we have just given. Our suggestion in applying these three criteria to reports is that the more each is met, the greater will be the interest aroused among social science audiences.

II. Social Science Value Commitments

The package of social scientific framing practices we have described above distances itself from many forms of moral and other advocacy, but it is definitely *not* value-free. Instead, by its logic, the social science approach embraces a number of specific moral and value positions. It is important that these be clearly recognized because not everyone endorses them, and, indeed, in recent years they have come increasingly under attack (sometimes from within or close to the ranks of social science itself). In our view, it is critical for social science to distinguish itself from approaches that may be superficially clothed in social scientific garb, but that are, in fact, significantly different from social science in values as well as in practice.

After sketching our understanding of the value commitments of social science in this section, we will then treat the main alternative forms in the section titled "other framings."

The value commitments we enumerate do not attach with equal clarity or strength to all of the various framing practices we have described above; rather, some particular values attach more clearly to some framing practices than to others.

A. Humanism and Liberal Science

This differential clarity and strength of association between values and framing practices is initially evident in the moral grounding of the framing practice we label the questioning mindset (Section I.C.1 above). The questioning mindset (as well as the evaluative standard of trueness, among others) is founded in the broad modern philosophical outlook commonly labeled humanism (Kurtz 1983, 1992). This is the dominant, pragmatic philosophy prevailing in the public arenas of all economically advanced democracies and it is the underpinning of organized scientific endeavor, an endeavor appropriately labeled "liberal science" (Rauch 1993).

Until recently, the value commitments embodied in humanism and liberal science were so dominant (and therefore "obvious") that hardly anyone bothered even to mention them. But, with the recent rise of attacks on them from the political, religious, and philosophical *left and right,* clear enunciation of these values has become imperative. However, since this is a research manual rather than a philosophical treatise, we will not here go beyond simply indicating that humanism and liberal science are the value perspectives in which social science is rooted. Elucidation and justification of them are abundantly available in other sources (e.g., Kurtz 1992, Rauch 1993, and the vast literatures cited therein).

In this context, we do, however, want to call attention to four value commitments within humanism and liberal science that are especially pertinent to, and embedded in, social scientific fieldstudies.

B. New Perception

Social science qualitative fieldstudy expresses and applies humanism and liberal science in its unceasing effort to turn chaotic experience into coherent perception, but coherent expression that is itself continually questioned. A signal purpose of the quest for generically framed propositions is to learn from experience by abstracting from it. To formulate a generic proposition or concept out of an historically particular instance is to strengthen our ability to recognize general patterns seen in yet other instances that we encounter. For example, to study a very unusual leader of a social movement without a concept of, say, "charisma," is to thwart our capacity to see that kind of leadership when we come upon it again. To formulate generic concepts of leadership is, in contrast, to strengthen our ability to "see" leadership in new cases by being able to compare and contrast it with our existing concepts.

The aim is to use facts to rise above facts, so to speak, and to take better control of them with the use of propositions, concepts, and the like. The quest is to move from seeing merely the trees that are the facts to seeing the forest that is composed of those trees. The alternative is to be adrift and awash in oceans of facts, drowning in information that we cannot use because we have not organized it into meaningful patterns. In the phrasing of the time-honed slogan, "There is nothing more useful than a good theory."

This quest for new perception is not, of course, uniquely the preserve of social scientists. All manner of *absolutists* (discussed above) engage in the same activity and come forth with some truly astounding generically abstracted propositions! The quests of the social scientists and the absolutists divide, however, in terms of (1) the process used to get to generic propositions (the process outlined in guides such as this and expressed in the evaluative standard of trueness) and in terms of (2) the questioning mindset that is applied to all orderings of chaotic experience into coherent perceptions. For the social scientist, the process never ends; for the absolutist, it does. And, key here, these are *different moral and value commitments*. For the social scientist, new perception is won in a hard process of inquiry and is never final. For the absolutist, as we suggest above, authority and finality stop further inquiry at some point.

C. Demystification and Reform

In complexly differentiated societies, ordinary people playing out their ordinary lives are enmeshed in devising and enacting ideas and activities that are responsive to their immediate needs. Immersed in acting, they have little time, training, or disposition for collecting information on the multiple facets of their situations. They are not in a good position to assemble such information, to reflect on its meaning, to envision larger contexts in which it might variously be interpreted, or to contemplate feasible and conceivable alternatives to their situations. Additionally, the alliances, accommodations, ruses, mutings, euphemizations, and other necessary avoidances of ordinary life lead people to miss seeing many aspects of their situations and to develop legitimizing and accommodating meanings for what they do see.

In other words, the requirements of acting weaken or nullify the capacity and honesty to reflect on the actions. Social science work that incorporates the features we have enumerated in this chapter facilitates the breakup of collective self-deceptions, the ideological "logjams" to which all social life is inherently prone. Indeed, as the situations in which people are intimately involved grow ever more specialized and arcane and are submerged in increasingly larger (even planetary) scales of social organization, *situationally induced irrationality* becomes more and more common, and its consequences more fateful for all of us. Correspondingly, social science—and the questioning mindset more broadly—come to be of greater and greater import.

Put differently, the questioning mindset both within and outside social science strives to achieve deobjectivation and demystification. As mentioned in Chapter 7, humans are the authors of all social arrangements, but after humans create them, these arrangements come, perceptually and psychologically, to have an existence of their own, to seem "wholly other" and "out there" (Berger and Luckmann 1967, p. 61).

This objectivation of social arrangements is perhaps the most fundamental form of *mystification*—the practice of shrouding social performance in an ambience of enigma, of fostering the impression that a social "show" is not fully knowable and that the performers must have very special knowledge and powers (Goffman 1959, pp. 67–70).

The questioning mindset of social science insists on the human authorship of all social arrangements—on demystifying them. Like Toto in *The Wizard of Oz,* acute social science analysis strives to pull away the curtains that hide the petty mechanisms of impressive social action.

Phrased in yet other terms, the human tendency to objectify social reality pushes from consciousness the wider appreciation that the objectified reality is only one among many possibilities. Questioning social science stimulates this recognition by rendering any "existing world . . . an object of scrutiny, not acceptance. . . . [It is only] one among many possibilities" (Gusfield 1981, p. 192). As a consequence, questioning social science "presents a world that is political rather than a world of technical necessity. If choice is possible, if new and alternative modes of acting are possible and imaginable, then the existent situation hides the conflicts and alternatives that can be imagined" (Gusfield 1981, p. 193). Social science of a questioning bent is thus a way in which "to penetrate the veil of the apolitical. . . . It makes us aware of the sheer difficulty of avoiding choice between alternatives, of having to engage in the world of politics and moralities, [of having] to take a stand without the benefits of a clear and commanding social vision" (Gusfield 1981, p. 195).

These social science aims are, of course, moral aims, the aims of widening peoples' perceptions of their situations and of enlarging their perceptions of social arrangements. Such enlargements hopefully then open the way to humane social change. And, as will become obvious, these aims and practices are very different from the *selective* demystifications preferred in other approaches.

D. Human and Moral Complexity

The species homo sapiens exhibits a quite remarkable—and perhaps dismal—propensity to divide itself into juxtaposed categories in which all virtues adhere to one or a few categories of the species ("our kind") and all vices adhere to some other category of "them" ("their kind"). We may think of this as the "good guy–bad guy" propensity of human functioning. One can easily understand the attractiveness of this form of thinking: It simplifies the task of dealing with people one encounters. You need only to "code" any new person (or topic) as a "good guy" or "bad guy" and proceed then in terms of the simple script attaching to each. In contrast, it is much more difficult to assess each new human one sees in terms of her or his own combination of specific characteristics.

Alas, many students of social situations and settings are like most everyone else in their tendency to divide the world into good guys and bad. One prominent form of this is to believe that all disadvantaged people are good guys and that all holders of power are bad guys. Another prominent form is to presume that social groups of the political left are good guys, while those of the political right are bad guys—or vice versa. Indeed, we venture to generalize that one of the most prominent themes of recent social science is that all people in advantaged social categories are bad guys and all people in disadvantaged ones are good guys.

However, our higher ethical values as humans and as humanists admonish us not to assess individuals, groups, or other social categorizations as either totally good or totally bad. Instead, all humans and their amalgamations into abstract categories exhibit both good and bad characteristics. In such appeals for appreciation of complexity, mixture, and nuance, no person or social categorical abstraction is accurately or properly analyzed as purely a "good guy" or "bad guy."

Striving for empirical truth and for application of the questioning mindset prompts an appreciation for human complexity. This appreciation, that is, derives from a serious effort to get *all* the data right and to question *every* claim one encounters. As such, depiction of moral and human complexity is a de facto value commitment that can also become a conscious one.

E. Larger, Dispassionate Understanding

The several value themes we have now described imply value-committed views of (1) the *time frame* in which to think of social science as an activity, (2) the *social frame* in which to think of its pertinence, and (3) the *emotional frame* of mind in which to do research.

1. Temporally, research is valued as a complex activity of successive and unending revisions carried out over the longer term. This is to be distinguished from framings we will describe below in which specific research efforts are conceived and valued as tactics in battle skirmishes or isolated virtuoso or prima donna performances.

2. Socially, social science more generally and fieldstudies in particular are distinctive, disciplined forms of human inquiry and knowing that are addressed to large and long-term human concerns and values. Even though the *proximate* audience for and evaluators of research must be other social scientists, the *larger* audiences are all humans who care about the topic of study. In this, social science parallels other science. The proximate audience of cancer research, for example, must be competent, evaluating cancer researchers, but the larger audience is everyone and anyone who cares about cancer.

3. Emotionally, researchers care very much about their research and the issues it may raise, but, consonant with a long and large temporal and social view, they try also to be reasonably *dispassionate*. Advocates of deep and abiding emotional engagement, of course, characterize such dispassion as emotionally distanced and uncaring. But the latter stance bears no resemblance to the attitude we are recommending, which is one of judiciousness and calm concern to examine and reexamine all data and concepts patiently and carefully.

Combined with the elements of social science framing explained in Section I of this chapter and with the values commitments we have described above in this section, these three matters of a long-term frame, a wide social reference, and a dispassionate emotional approach form the value basis on which social scientists advocate and perform *generic consolidations* of fieldstudies. By "generic consolidations" we mean the second-order activity of assembling fieldstudies (together with other relevant studies and writings) on a given generic topic and assembling them into a general statement on that topic (Prus 1987, 1994). The aim is to collate and codify findings from diverse but generically related studies. In the process of comparing and contrasting many analyses, you may discover broader themes and discern expanded domains of relevance. For example, Helen Ebaugh's *Becoming an Ex: The Process of Role Exit* (1988) brings together diverse studies of people exiting roles and depicts both the common and the variant experiences, causes, and other aspects of this generic phenomenon.

Generic consolidations such as those of Ebaugh and of a great many others are, to us, extremely valuable because they supply reliable information on and analysis of whatever phenomenon they treat, which can be achieved only with the practices and the *values* we have discussed. Such information and analysis serves interests of dispassionate understanding, certainly, but it does much more than this in the same way that cancer research does more than edify cancer researchers. Both single fieldstudies and their appearance in generic consolidations can and do *enlarge and deepen how larger audiences understand their own experiences and those of others.* At a quite practical level, people both in and after wrenching role-exit situations, for example, are able, through Ebaugh's and others' work, to situate themselves in larger terms, to cognitively and emotionally liberate themselves from the blinders of narrow knowledge and experience. They can discover, through widened knowledge, that what seems strange, eternal, threatening, atypical, or insane is actually quite familiar, brief, safe, typical, and sane.

As we have said, this is a research manual, not a moral or philosophical treatise. But, like all other human endeavors, it is founded in value commitments, and the reader has a right as well as a need to know about them. To that end, we have just sketched major values that inform this guide—and social science as we conceive it.

These value commitments would seem quite dull and even banal—and therefore not worth the time and pages to state them—had they not been challenged in recent years. We turn now to a brief review of some common forms of that challenge.

III. Other Framings

As one might expect, recent challenges to social science framing and values differ considerably among themselves and also vary in terms of which of the value commitments of social science they reject. Even so, they tend to be alike in desiring to use social science work to further the interests of one or another social category, a political or religious view advocating for such a categorization, or some combination of category and point of view. For these challenges, the question of "social science for what or whom?" is answered by advocacy for a particular grouping rather than in terms of the broader values of inquiry, knowledge, demystification, and the like that we have enumerated.

In so serving a particular grouping, the range of appropriate topics of inquiry and what to say about those topics is restricted, as is the application of the questioning mindset. Within these restrictions, an important task—if not the master frame—becomes that of performing, by means of the research, a technical or moral evaluation that serves social-categorical or specialized advocacy interests. Activist partisans, rather than social scientists and more general audiences, are therefore conceived as the most important persons in whom one desires to arouse interest.

As an abstract master template of sorts, this evaluative frame is applied in varied specific formulations. In our assessment, there are four main patterns of application: mainstream improving, radical liberating, villain pillorying, and expressive voicing. (We already met some of these in Chapter 2 and earlier in this chapter and will encounter them again in the next chapter.)

A. Mainstream Improving

Politically and socially mainstream researchers and audiences who view research as information with which to improve or control a social setting or situation in the short-term future are statistically the largest group using an evaluative frame. Often in this pattern, the aims, assumptions, and perspectives of authorities responsible for a social setting are taken as the aims, assumptions, and perspectives of the researcher. For this reason, this pattern is sometimes referred to as technocratic, meaning that the researcher is the specialized and expert investigator of questions posed by authorities, and the answers developed by researchers serve those authorities. Considerations of relative technical efficacy and efficiency figure centrally. The rubrics "applied sociology," "sociological practice," "clinical sociology," "policy research" and "evaluation research" are often employed to distinguish this pattern and its audiences. Sometimes, also, the contrast between social science and mainstream improving is expressed as the difference between the sociology *of* something and sociology *in* something, as in the well-articulated difference between "the sociology *of* medicine" and "sociology *in* medicine" (also see Hammersley 1992, Chapter 7; Shils 1961; for an example that proclaims itself to be "naturalistic inquiry," see Lincoln and Guba 1985).

B. Radical Liberating

Although the political substance and relations to authorities differ, radical-liberation audiences and researchers are like mainstream improvers in taking on and striving to further the aims, assumptions, and perspectives of another grouping. In this case, however, the researchers adopt the vantage point of a disadvantaged or otherwise mistreated set of persons and seek, by means of the research, to champion it. Paralleling the mainstream improver's aim to be helpful to authorities, radical liberationists seek to be useful to selected oppressed. In one variant on this pattern, researchers are enjoined not to report anything on an oppressed grouping that might be of use to oppressors in maintaining their oppression. In particular, practices among the oppressed that other audiences might read as negative ought not be reported. In another variant on this pattern, it is argued that some groups ought not be studied at all because anything learned would be used against them. The logical implication is, therefore, that ignorance is better than knowledge. Other terms sometimes denoting radical-liberation audiences include "liberation sociology," "participatory research," and "critical sociology." (See also Hammersley 1992, Chapter 6; Shils 1961.)

C. Villain Pillorying

The two audiences and their researchers just described feel positively about the groupings they are researching or serving and seek to frame their reports in ways that are helpful to them. An obvious next possibility (and reality) is, of course, to identity a grouping as especially reprehensible or even despicable and to frame one's research in ways that harm them. Rather than conceal facts that might be used against a category, one seeks to develop facts that injure the category. Because of the intimate familiarity entailed in fieldwork, there are few instances of villain pillorying using direct observation or interviewing methods. Instead, villain pillorying is seen more commonly in studies of the rich and powerful that utilize public records.

D. Expressive Voicing

In recent years, the topic of "voice" has come to prominence among fieldworkers and refers to two practices. First, the concept of "voice" sometimes refers to authorial voice; to the degree to which the researcher's position in her or his report is centrally and continually explicit. The author sets her or his self against "the voice from nowhere," referring to the impersonal, reportorial fashion in which much social science has, historically, been written. Critics of "the voice from nowhere" think this posture is improper and must be abandoned. In its place, there need to be voices from somewhere, which is often taken to mean that the researcher should be very "front and center" in the report and especially so in revealing the researcher's personal response to the people studied, the researcher's role, and the researcher's view of life and existence in general. Second and more commonly, the voices to be expressed are those of the people being studied, and giving them "voice" is taken to be both the moral and the disciplinary justification for the research. From this perspective, the fieldworker's task is largely limited to reporting what presumptively "voiceless" populations believe and wish to communicate about their condition. This is the fieldworker as "stenographer," to paraphrase David Snow's and Calvin Morrill's (1993) critique of this position, or the researcher as "ethnograph," to use Clinton Sanders's (1994) equally dismissive term.

These four framings (and others that might be described) are variations on the master frame of according prime importance to short-term oriented moral evaluation as this relates to authorities, oppressed groups, villain categories, or the researcher's self. While there are audiences for whom these frames make a study important, these are not audiences of serious social scientists. As laudable as these framings may be in terms of some values, practitioners of these four frames also do not engage in a number of practices that social scientists believe to be of prime importance (described in Section I of this chapter), or subscribe to many of the values we have described (in Section II of this chapter) as associated with those practices.

IV. Audiences and Interests

What, then, does all this say about arousing the interests of audiences? We think it says two things. First, if you want to catch the attention of social scientists you want to strive for trueness, newness, and importance following the meanings of these terms that we have elaborated. But, second, just as cancer researchers direct their work to one another for evaluation but *also* to wider audiences, social scientists also have larger and wider values and audiences. You therefore want to shape your work toward both social scientists and wider audiences. While being faithful to the craft of social scientific fieldstudies, you also want to think in longer and larger perspective. C. Wright Mills, an icon of social science practice and values, has put it this way:

> It is very important for any writer to have in mind just what kinds of people he is trying to speak to. . . . To write is to raise a claim to be read, but by whom? . . . One answer [is to] assume that you have been asked to give a lecture on some subject you know well, before an audience of teachers and students from all departments of a leading university, as well as an assortment of interested persons from a nearby city. Assume that such an audience is before you and that they have a right to know; assume that you want to let them know. Now write. (Mills 1959, p. 221)

V. Summary

In this chapter we have explained the third of the three major ways in which to focus data. This third way of focusing—arousing audience interest—subdivides, in turn, into the three dimensions of empirical *trueness,* data and concept *newness,* and framing *importance.* Within the dimension of importance, we described the five practices of:

- adopting a questioning mindset,
- striving for propositional framing,
- devising generic concepts,
- providing a developed treatment, and
- selecting resonant content.

In addition, we contrasted the practices and value commitments of social science framing with other and more proximately moralistic framings of qualitative field data. While these other framings also find appreciative audiences, such reports are not, in the senses we have elaborated, social scientific.

PART THREE

ANALYZING DATA

The tasks of *gathering* data (Part One) and *focusing* them (Part Two) come together in the third task of *analyzing* them. Overlapping and intertwined with the tasks of gathering and focusing data, in this third task the fieldworker begins to concentrate on:

- *developing analysis* guided by the considerations we describe in Chapter 9, and

- *writing reports* assisted by suggestions offered in Chapter 10.

CHAPTER 9

DEVELOPING ANALYSIS

In qualitative fieldstudies, analysis is conceived as an *emergent* product of a process of gradual induction. Guided by the data being gathered (as covered in Part One) and the topics, questions, and evaluative criteria that provide focus (as described in Part Two), analysis is the field-worker's *derivative ordering* of the data.

Because analysis is the product of an inductive and emergent process in which the analyst is the central agent, achieving this order is not simply a mechanical process of assembly-line steps. Even though there are several concrete and even routine activities involved in analysis (described below), the process remains, and is intended to be, significantly open-ended in character. In this way, analysis is also very much a creative act.

Because of these open-ended and creative dimensions of the analytic process, a description of the concrete operations composing it does not entirely capture what goes on. Indeed, while we do understand something of the concrete operations that facilitate analysis, the operation of the creative and open-ended dimensions is not well understood.

Referring to these open-ended and inductive features as "making it all come together," Paul Atkinson has reflected that

> Making it all come together . . . is one of the most difficult things of all. . . . Quite apart from actually achieving it, it is hard to inject the right mix of (a) *faith* that it can and will be achieved; (b) recognition that it has to be *worked* at, and isn't based on romantic inspiration; (c) that it isn't like the solution to a puzzle or math problem, but has to be *created*; (d) that you can't pack *everything* into one version, and that any one project could yield several different ways of bringing it together. (Atkinson quoted in Strauss and Corbin 1990, p. 117; emphasis in the original)

Atkinson quite correctly stresses the role of *working at* analysis in the face of creative open-endedness and not succumbing to the notion that it will arise from "romantic inspiration." For, it is this "working at"—combined with the matters we have treated in previous chapters and one's own creative impulses—that culminate in analysis. In this chapter we want, therefore, to describe major and well-established ways of "working at" analysis, ways that we can think of as *strategies* of creating analysis.

181

We want also to stress that the six categories of strategies of developing analysis we detail are not used by every analyst and do not work for every analyst all the time. Instead, this array of strategies is a storehouse of possibilities from which to devise ways of working at analysis (and from which you might devise your own new ways). This being the case, you should employ a flexible and adaptive approach. These strategies are guidelines and pointers rather than exact specifications. Said differently, *there is no single way* to achieve analysis. Therefore, read what follows and select, adapt, and combine those parts that work for you in your project.

I. Strategy One: Social Science Framing

The matters we described in previous chapters come forward and inform analysis. Most particularly, this "bringing forward" can and should take the form of conceiving your goal as that of providing a *social science framing* of your data. As detailed in the previous chapter, this general approach itself centers on devising an analysis that is empirically true, new, and important (Chapter 8, Section I). Relative to the third of these three—importance—the goal is, specifically, to formulate *generic propositions* that sum up and provide order in major portions of your data.

As described in the previous chapter, a generic proposition is an *answer* to a *question* (as discussed in Chapter 7) posed about a *topic* (as described in Chapter 6). And, as we also indicated in the last chapter, there are many other ways to phrase the quest for generic propositions, so do not feel you need to think in terms of this phrasing alone. Other phrasings we gave before and that we want to repeat here in order to drive the point home include forming a *hypothesis*, developing a *thesis*, formulating a *concept*, making an *assertion*, putting forth an *idea*, propounding a *theme*, addressing a *problem*, specifying a *story line*, constructing general *principles*, and providing a general *interpretation*.

A. Eight Forms of Propositions

And again to stress that the matters we described in the previous chapters come forth into the task of working at analysis, we here repeat that the goal of formulating a proposition can refer to *eight different formal kinds* of propositions. We describe these in detail in Chapter 7 (where we treat them as questions) and summarize them in Chapter 8, but let us nonetheless—for emphasis and convenience of reference—state them here a third (and last!) time:

1. Type: *X exists.*
2. Frequencies: *X occurs in Y units in places 1, 2, 3, n over Z periods of time.*

3. Magnitudes: *X is of Y size, strength, or intensity.*

4. Structures: *X is structured in terms of 1, 2, 3, n.*

5. Processes: *X exhibits a process with the phases or cycles of 1, 2, 3, n.*

6. Causes: *X is caused by factors 1, 2, 3, n.*

7. Consequences: *X has consequences 1, 2, 3, n.*

8. Agency: *In X, people use strategies and tactics 1, 2, 3, n.*

Chapters 6 and 7 are replete with summaries of examples of all of these eight basic types of propositions. Scanning through those chapters as you are *also* thinking about your data in propositional terms can help you to discern how you can use one or more of these forms of basic propositions to organize your data.

B. A Third Way to Contrast Propositional with Other Writing

In the previous chapter, we contrasted generic propositional framing or writing with "subject" writing and with "historically particular" writing (Chapter 8, Sections I.C.2 and 3). Let us now add a *third* way in which to think of how propositional writing is different from other writing.

Undergraduate students, especially, are schooled in the writing of what we might call the "ordinary term paper." So trained, they sometimes approach fieldwork reporting as though it were the same as writing an ordinary term paper. We must emphatically declare that fieldwork reports and ordinary term papers are *not* the same. They *are* alike in that both are constructed of sentences, paragraphs, and sections set successively on sheets of paper, but the similarity of the two pretty much ends right there.

In our experience, at least, ordinary term papers are smorgasbord or cook's tours of miscellaneous facts about their topic. Indeed, ordinary term papers seem often to be modeled on encyclopedia or other reference book articles, the sources from which much of the information in these papers has often been taken.

The principle difference between them is summed up in the contrasts between these two two-word couplets:

1. analysis–report

versus

2. review–summary.

The first couplet denotes a central focus on one or more concepts on which one is making a report. In the terminology of this guide, this analysis–report is a propositional answer to a question about a topic.

The second two-word couplet centers on surveying information available on a topic and presenting a summary of it. In the last chapter we used the terms "subject writing" and "historically particular writing" to refer to this kind of work.

The first two-word couplet denotes what one is doing in empirical inquiry and analysis—as in social science research more generally. Speaking of that more general context, Lee Cuba describes the task of the analysis–report as that of constructing "general principles from a set of observations" in which one "always sees the world in terms of the question: What is this an example of?" Such papers therefore begin with and treat some "broader, unifying theme," "general interpretation," or "larger question" (Cuba 1988, pp. 35, 36).

The moral is this: Put aside notions of ordinary term papers when starting to analyze data and develop analysis as a qualitative fieldworker.

C. Number of Propositions in a Single Fieldstudy

There is of course the question of how many propositions one ought to develop in a field project. The weaseling but accurate answer is: It depends. Among other factors, it depends on: (1) how long one is in the field and how much data one collects, (2) the stage of the project we are talking about, and (3) the number and scale of reports one plans and completes.

Brief projects, especially those done by students, quite reasonably result in but one report that centerpieces only one major proposition, with brief and subsidiary attention given to others. However, in the logic of the emergent induction of analysis, even quite small-scale projects generate, in undeveloped form, a great many possible propositions at the start and in the middle phases of the research process. These numerous propositional *possibilities* are the analytic aspects of what one's field-notes are about. They are what one creates in the coding and memoing operations to which we will come shortly. In this fashion, the single proposition or small number of propositions that your analysis finally comes down to result from a process of winnowing out of many other possible, central propositions.

Longer-term projects that collect more data and that are projected to result in several reports or a book tend to develop several (but commonly less than a half dozen) major propositions, and even books follow the model of the single report in tending to treat only one major proposition in a single chapter.

II. Strategy Two: Socializing Anxiety

As stressed in the opening paragraphs of this chapter, formulating potential major propositions from your data is an *emergently inductive* activity. You get *from* data, topics, and questions, on the one side, *to* answers or propositions, on the other, through intensive immersion in the data, allowing your data to interact with your intuition and sensibilities as these latter are informed by your knowledge of topics and questions. To do inductive analysis (more recently called "grounded theory"), you begin with an open-ended and open-minded desire to know a social situation or setting; the data and yourself as an agent of induction guide you in the task of emergently formulating one or more propositions (Glaser and Strauss 1967, Strauss and Corbin 1990).

Just below, we describe concrete activities that can help give structure to this process of emergent induction, but before coming to those activities we want to recognize that, as an inherently open-ended process, the situation of emergent induction can produce frustration and anxiety—as well as exhilaration. That is, the openness of the situation calls on the researcher to *construct* social science order and, for some, that circumstance is fearsome. Success in forging such order in what at first can seem to be chaotic materials can seem impossible. In addition, there is almost always one or another problem in data collecting per se.

Fear not! Feelings of anxiety and difficulty in the face of open-ended tasks are common and quite normal. Happily, there are some basic and successful ways of dealing with these normal feelings and fears. Let us point out three of these here and deal with many others in the rest of this chapter.

The first and most important mode of management is *to recognize and accept*—consciously and unself-consciously—the mundane fact that emergent and inductive analysis is not a mechanical and easy task. *Of course,* such a task causes fear and anxiety. This recognition and acceptance serves to normalize the anxiety and associated concerns and emotions. Therefore, relax—you are like most everyone else.

A second mode of management is *persistently to work* at the task of collecting data with an eye to an emergent and inductive analysis which can take a propositional form. The sheer accumulation of information is in itself anxiety-reducing because it ensures that you will, at minimum, be able to say *something,* even if that something is not as analytic as you might like and is not known to you at the moment.

Based on these two modes of coping, you can, third, *have faith* that you will inductively generate an analytic statement (that is, a propositional answer to one or more questions regarding one or more topics in the social situation or setting you are studying). Participation in a group of people who are doing the same thing is, we think, one major way in which you can hope to have your faith sustained and your anxiety reduced. To use a "trendy" term, the class or seminar or study group in which you are likely doing your study is a "support group" in the quest for propositions. (If you are not now part of such a circle and are doing or plan to do a fieldstudy, we urge you to find or form one forthwith. A circle as small as two or three people can do the job.)

One aspect of this faith pertains to *believing that you will be successful* in your quest and that you will achieve a significant personal and emotional reward in the form of the *joy and exhilaration of discovery.* Very much like the satisfaction felt in solving any other puzzle, finding one or more propositions in the chaos of "mere data" can be an enormously powerful and positive emotional experience—and even a "high." Reduced to a slogan, our suggestion is, "Go for the high!"

III. Strategy Three: Coding

What are commonly referred to as "coding" and "memoing" are the core physical activities of developing analysis. These are what Paul Atkinson is speaking about in the quote above in which he refers to the "recognition that [analysis] . . . has to be *worked* at, and isn't based on romantic inspiration." The most basic, continuing, concrete and mundane way one *works at* developing analysis is to ask these kinds of questions about discrete items in the incoming flow of data and about items in your corpus of information after data collection has stopped:

• Of what category is the item before me an instance?
• What can we think of this as being about?

More specific versions of these questions are:

• Of what *topic,* unit, or aspect is this an instance?
• What *question* about a topic does this item of data suggest?
• What sort of an *answer* to a question about a topic does this item of data suggest (i.e., what proposition is suggested)?

And, serving the same function, analysts ask themselves such questions as these:

• What is this? What does it represent? (Strauss and Corbin 1990, p. 63)
• What is this an example of? (Cuba 1988, p. 35)
• What do I see going on here? What are people doing? What is happening? What kind of events are at issue here? (Charmaz 1983, pp. 112, 113)

The *word* (or *short set of words*) you apply to the item of data in answering such questions is a *code.* These are labels that classify items of information as pertinent to a topic, question, answer, or whatever. Coding begins

> the process of *categorizing* and *sorting* data. Codes then serve as shorthand devices to *label, separate, compile,* and *organize* data. . . . Codes [also] serve to summarize, synthesize, and sort many observations made of the data. By providing the pivotal link between the data collection and its conceptual rendering, coding becomes the fundamental *means* of developing the analysis. (Charmaz 1983, pp. 111, 112; emphasis in the original)

Figure 9.1 Examples of Fieldnote Coding from the Charmaz Study of People with Chronic Illness

Codes	Interview Statements
	A 29-year-old man with renal failure was discussing his high school years and events that occurred long before he was diagnosed.
Self-perception	I knew I was different. I caught colds very easily and
Awareness of difference	my resistance was very low, and so I knew that
Identifying self through	generally speaking my health wasn't as good as
ill health	everybody else's, but I tried to do all the things that
Comparing health to	everybody else was doing.
others'	
	A young woman who had had a serious flare-up of colitis recalled:
	During this time I was under constant care by an intern who later thought I should see a different psychiatrist when I got out of the hospital because he thought I was coming on sexually to him and the odd thing about that was that I found him not sexually
Identifying moment	attractive at all—that was sort of an interesting twist to that thing. I mean when you are not in a very good
Critical failure of self	place to be told that you have failed with your psychiatrist is like the parting blow. You know it was awful.

Sources: Charmaz 1983, pp. 116, 119; Charmaz 1991. Reprinted by permission of Kathy Charmaz.

As Miles and Huberman express it, "Coding is analysis. . . . Codes are tags or labels for assigning units of meaning to . . . information compiled during a study" (1994, p. 56).

In even small-scale projects, the researcher is likely to devise dozens or even hundreds of code categories. The point of them is, as Kathy Charmaz indicates, to group the flow of raw reality into packages of items that are related to one another. Or, as Miles and Huberman put it, "codes are efficient data-labeling and data-retrieval devices. They empower and speed up analysis" (1994, p. 65).

Examples of this *analytic* (explained below) coding are given in Figure 9.1, where the concrete data are shown in the right-hand column of the figure and the codes that Kathy Charmaz applied are given in the left-hand column.

A. Two Physical Methods of Coding

The *cognitive* act of *assigning* a code is the *first* step in disaggregating your data, but the act is not complete until you have performed a *second* step, that of physically placing the coded data in the same place as other data that you have coded the same way. There are two major ways in which you can do this: filing and computerized, or PC, databasing.

1. Filing

Prior to the widespread availability of personal computers beginning in the late 1980s, coding frequently took the specific physical form of *filing*. The researcher established an expanding set of file folders with code names on the tabs and physically placed either the item of data itself or a note that located it in the appropriate file folder. As we noted in Chapter 5, before photocopying was easily available and cheap, some fieldworkers typed their fieldnotes with carbon paper, wrote in codes in the margins of the copies of the notes, and cut them up with scissors. They then placed the resulting slips of paper in corresponding file folders. After the advent of cheap and easily available photocopying, some fieldworkers simply made as many copies as they had codes on each fieldnote page and filed entire pages. Such physical operations created one or more file drawers of file folders containing coded data.

2. PC Databasing

As we mentioned briefly in Chapter 5, the cost and availability of appropriate hardware and software have recently made it possible for researchers to perform these same coding and filing operations on a computer. The logic of coding is the same, of course, with the possible added advantage of instantaneous "filing," thus eliminating the labor-intensive acts of physically placing items of data in different physical file folders.

PC databasing also increases the speed and complexity with which you can retrieve, recode, refile, and enumerate coded items and relate them to one another. For these reasons (and the advantages that PCs offer for data input, discussed in the context of fieldnotes in Chapter 5), we think that all fieldstudy investigators ought, at minimum, give serious consideration to employing one of the almost two dozen fieldstudy analysis programs now available. At the time of publication, the most detailed and comprehensive descriptions and discussions of these programs we have seen are Weitzman and Miles (1995) and Richards and Richards (1994). Tesch (1990) and Fielding and Lee (eds.) (1991) are earlier but continuingly helpful accounts.

We need to caution, however, that this is a very rapidly changing area and one should be alert to more recent reports of developments and experiences. In addition, some ordinary word-processing programs contain impressive coding and filing capabilities, perhaps obviating any necessity to acquire a special-purpose program. (See, for example, Hall and Marshall 1992, Ch. 9, on the use of "macros" in word-processing programs.)

Even though the use of PCs in fieldstudies has generated a great deal of interest and even enthusiastic promotion, in our view the virtues of computerized *analysis* (as distinct from data storage) programs have yet to be proven. The litmus test we apply to scholarship generated with PC data analyzers is: Are these analyses different from and better than analyses done by conventional means? The first thing we have noticed in trying to answer this question is that while there are numerous enthusiastic demonstrations of what one *might* do in analysis, few published studies claim to have been performed with such programs. We cannot see how the studies that *have* been so generated are discernibly different from or better than other studies because of PC analysis programs. If the proof of the pudding is the eating, then, on this score, we are still waiting for someone to stop fooling around in the kitchen and serve up some tasty pudding.

Indeed, our experience is that people with the strongest enthusiasm for computer fieldwork programs tend not to be the same people who are most involved in doing fieldstudies. In our conversations with this latter group, we find that while almost all of them use PCs to store data, they also view analysis inside a computer as too confining, a point that we will elaborate below with respect to flexibility.

The conclusion to these observations on the PC and fieldstudies is, then: Be exploratory and definitely use a PC to store data, but do not feel you must necessarily employ a PC analysis program to develop your own analysis.

B. Types of Coding

Issues of file-folder versus PC databasing aside, many fieldworkers find it helpful to do three basic kinds of coding. In an older terminology, they maintain three different kinds of file systems, which we label housekeeping, analytic, and fieldwork.

1. Housekeeping

While social science analysis is one's goal and the object of much of one's coding, situations and settings are also complex entities that require considerable effort to learn and get right simply in their own mundane terms. In many studies, the fieldworker is meeting dozens of new people, visiting various new locales, learning many novel historical matters and so on regarding many informational areas in which he or she is trying simply to become a knowledgeable and competent person.

Further, aside from whatever analytic story you eventually elect to tell, there are quite conventional and commonsensical stories of the sorts of things that typically go on and have gone on "around here," wherever the "around here." These are the public and shared stories that "everyone" knows but that are not less complex and necessary to know simply because "everyone" knows them. Even a study of a highly limited setting with very few people can produce a very complex set of facts, activities, and so forth. Many fieldworkers also find they need written aids to keep even more simple matters straight.

Getting and keeping a handle on local life at this mundane level is greatly assisted if you develop, maintain, and review data organized in these mundane terms. In particular, fieldworkers find it helpful to code for—to have a file on—at least each major participant in a situation or setting. Even though individuals as such may not figure in one's eventual analysis, files on persons can be enormously helpful in simply keeping the facts straight. Codes for and files on organizations and regularized events and other such major features of the situation or setting likewise help in keeping abreast of the local lay of the land. Housekeeping files can also assist in the rapid location of information otherwise buried in the chronological notes or obscurely labeled in the analytic codes. And housekeeping codes provide another angle from which to stimulate analytic coding. Reviewing the content of such codes can sometimes bring to light crucial points or patterns that had not been clear in the analytically coded materials.

2. **Analytic**
Housekeeping coding and filing aim at getting and keeping order in the basic information. As such, housekeeping coding and filing is *not* an end in itself; rather, it supports the *central* coding task, the *analytic*.

Many fieldworkers report the following kinds of practices regarding their analytic coding.

- *Emergent and Experimental Posture:* While housekeeping coding tends toward mundane fact keeping, analytic coding is emergent, venturesome, and experimental (although the coder is also prepared to classify items of information in fairly obvious terms). Especially in the early stages of a project, the worker is not particularly concerned about the eventual viability of a code or whether it will ultimately make any kind of sense. The aim, instead, is to generate as many separate codes (and files) as one is prompted to and about which one can feel reasonably excited. The task of reckoning with these emergent and venturesome analytic impulses comes later, during the period of final analysis.

- *Multiple Coding of Single Items:* Also unlike coding for mundane fact keeping where you place items in only one code category—the most commonsensically obvious (e.g., a person's name)—in analytic coding the fieldworker is prepared to code any given item of information, incident or whatever in *several* code categories. (This is exemplified in Charmaz's coding shown in Figure 9.1.)

- *Regular Coding:* The requirements of interviewing and observation, as well as other facets of life, affect the frequency with which fieldworkers can engage in coding and filing. Whatever the interval, the field wisdom is to start coding quite early in the research process and to engage in it with as much regularity and frequency as possible. Miles and Huberman go so far as to admonish: "Always code the previous set of field notes before the next trip to the site. Always—no matter how good the excuses for not doing it" (1994, p. 65). We would not be so extreme, but the spirit of their rule of thumb is well taken.

- *Amount of Coding:* Since coding is an emergent, open-ended, and, indeed, a creative activity, the question is raised of how much of it to do—how many codes should one generate overall and how many should one apply to, say, a single page of fieldnotes. Fieldworkers offer no pat answer to this question, save to counsel a "middle way" approach. If a worker finds analytic significance in only a very small part of the materials and therefore codes and files little, that fact itself ought to be made a central problem of the study. On the other hand, workers who spend an enormous amount of time coding and filing everything in sight in dozens of ways probably should ask themselves whether they have transformed a means into an end, with consequent negative effects upon the *real* end, which is to write an excellent analysis.

- *From Housekeeping to Analytic Coding:* Although there is no set pattern, some fieldworkers find they do more housekeeping than analytic coding early in a project. As time goes on and they get control of housekeeping facts, their mundane coding declines and their analytic coding increases.

- *Category Saturation and Subdivision:* Instances of some codes occur with such frequency and regularity that one develops a file with an enormous number of instances in it, far more than seem needed or manageable. Analysts proceed in one of two directions in this circumstance. On the one hand, you can inspect the instances in the code file more closely for how they vary among themselves in ways that make for more fine-grained analysis. That is, you can elaborate the code itself to identify subdivisions. On the other hand, such a closer inspection may lead to the conclusion that there is no closer analysis to do, or that what could be done is not important enough to do. In these events, you may assess the category as "saturated" and perform no further coding for it.

3. Fieldwork and Analysis

As we discussed regarding "trueness" in Chapter 8 (and will further elaborate in Chapter 10), your report should contain an account of pertinent aspects of the fieldwork itself. Coding and filing for this topic over the course of the project will greatly assist in writing this part of your report. Moveover, some fieldworkers have begun to stress the importance of documenting and analyzing the process of analysis. In one recent effort, on the order of twenty percent of time spent on analysis was devoted to describing and analyzing the process of the analysis itself (Miles and Huberman 1994, p. 286).

4. Maintaining a Chronological Record
Splitting the materials into housekeeping, analytic, and fieldwork files helps you to stay "on top" of what is happening and to develop an analysis. But it also tends to obscure that nebulous quality called "context." When you scrutinize a particular piece of filed material, the question can arise: What else was happening at the time that seemed irrelevant then but now seems important? You want, that is, to be able to look back at the more general context, and to do this easily you need an intact chronological record of the past. You should therefore keep a full set of your materials in the order in which you originally collected them.

A chronological set of materials is also useful for locating information that is not readily available in one or another of the files. And it is useful simply for reading and reviewing from beginning to end, as a stimulus to thinking about larger patterns and larger units of analysis (as outlined in Chapter 6).

C. Stages of Analytic Coding

Some fieldworkers distinguish two or more stages of coding and even distinguish among several forms of analytic coding in what are developed as exceedingly complex processes (e.g., Strauss 1987, Strauss and Corbin 1990). For present purposes, however, it suffices to call attention to the basic distinction between *initial* and *focused* coding.

1. Initial Coding
In initial coding, "researchers look for what they can define and discover in the data" (Charmaz 1983, p. 113). This is the concrete specification of the abstract term, "the *emergent induction* of analysis." This is where the rubber hits the road, as is said, and you use yourself as an instrument of the research, informed, of course, by (1) your commitments, interests, expertise and personal history (Charmaz 1983, p. 112) *and* (2) your knowledge of and skill with the topics (units, aspects), questions, and interest-arousal considerations we have discussed (Chapters 6, 7, and 8). Examples of these "rubber hitting the road" codings are given in Figure 9.1. Drawn from Kathy Charmaz's study of people with a chronic illness, the examples in the top half of Figure 9.1 are initial codings, which are distinctive in being *numerous* and *varied*.

2. Focused Coding
As a corpus of initial coding accumulates, it becomes *itself* an object that you should review in terms of which codes are being used more than others and which topics and questions are being treated more than others. That is, one begins a process of winnowing out less productive and useful codes and of focusing in on a selected number.

This selected or focused set of codes is then applied to an increasing array of data. Categories within the selected codes are elaborated. Other codes are collapsed and yet others are dropped. Some codes begin to assume the status of overarching ideas or propositions that will occupy a prominent or central place in the analysis. The bottom half of Figure 9.1 provides examples of such selected and focused codes in the Charmaz study. The two codings shown there—"identifying moment" and "critical failure of self"—are central concepts in Charmaz's published study (Charmaz 1991).

IV. Strategy Four: Memoing

Memos are the written-out counterparts or explanations and elaborations of the coding categories (i.e., the labeled ideas). Memos are prose that "tells what the code is about" (Charmaz 1983, p. 120). Miles and Huberman quote Glaser as providing the classic definition: "[A memo is] the theorizing write-up of ideas about codes and their relationships as they strike the analyst while coding. . . . [It] can be a sentence, a paragraph or a few pages. . . . [It] exhausts the analyst's momentary ideation based on data with perhaps a little conceptual elaboration" (Glaser 1978, pp. 83–84, as quoted and edited by Miles and Huberman 1994, p. 72).

Miles's and Huberman's own overview statement on memoing is equally classic in its elucidative breadth and incisiveness:

> Memos are primarily conceptual in intent. They don't just report data; they tie together different pieces of data into a recognizable cluster, often to show that those data are instances of a general concept. Memos can also go well beyond codes and their relationships to any aspect of the study—personal, methodological, and substantive. They are one of the most useful and powerful sense-making tools at hand. (Miles and Huberman 1994, p. 72)

As Glaser indicates, memos vary greatly in length. Many are simply a few sentences, others might run on for some pages; most are likely somewhere in between.

As we described in Chapter 5, codes and memos in the sense of ideas about patterns and meanings in the data appear in your fieldnotes from the very outset. As you code the data both before and after data collection has stopped, memo writing becomes a larger and larger feature of your work, even as the range of topics with which they deal becomes narrower (i.e., codes become more focused).

The effort in memoing is to develop what one hopes will eventually emerge as an interrelated set of memos that form a coherent analysis. In this spirit, some fieldworkers explicitly set out to distinguish among and to write three kinds of memos: elemental, sorting, and integrating (Charmaz 1983, pp. 121–124).

1. The *elemental* or "small piece" memo is often projected as being the lowest level of text that will appear in a final report. Running from one

to a few pages, it is a detailed analytic rendering of some relatively specific matter. Depending on the scale of the project, the worker may write from one to several dozen or more of these. Built out of selective codes and codings, these are the most basic prose cannon fodder, as it were, of the project.

It is in composing elemental memos that you come to appreciate the point of your prior codings and sortings (filings—either in folders or on a PC). For it is all these coded accumulations that provide the basis for having anything to say now.

Despite the enormous assistance of the PC in coding and filing, in coming to compose elemental memos many fieldworkers continue to print out materials and to lay out the piles of detailed codings on a table or whatever large, empty surface is available (such as the floor of a room). This makes it easier to pore over the coded data—arranging and rearranging, labeling and relabeling them. When a new piece of information or a small idea seems relevant to the current set of piles, you can retrieve it and add it. A pile that no longer seems relevant may be set aside. In poring over and thinking through such piles, analysts pose questions such as the following to themselves:

- Is this idea clear?
- Does it have a logical order?
- Which of these examples best illustrates this point?
- Is there some small scheme that would fit these piles of materials better?
- Should I recode these materials?
- Should I look at how well this projected section organization is going to fit with the next section? Will it dovetail?
- What is going to be the transition here?
- How does it fit with the previous section? Should I work more on the section preceding this one, which will make this section clearer?
- On second thought, is it possible this topic is not relevant at all and ought to be thrown out?
- Should I not work on this anymore today and work on _____ instead?

Composing elemental memos is, of course, the activity of *writing*, a topic we treat extensively in the first half of the next chapter. Therefore, for additional and more detailed guidance on the writing of elemental memos, also read the section of Chapter 10 titled "Writing Practices."

2. A second type of memo—the *sorting* memo—takes all (or many) of the elemental memos (and codings not yet developed as memos) as its topic of analysis. "By going through accumulated [elemental] memos and sorting them, researchers gain insight into . . . core variables, key phases in a process, . . . major issues" or whatever the emerging content (Char-

maz 1983, p. 122). The discoveries one makes in this sorting are then written up. As *analysis written on analysis*, these memos achieve a higher level of abstraction and generalization than do elemental memos.

This stage can be a quite critical one in the research process, for in it you are identifying the elements of a possible propositional organization for your report. This and the writing of integrating memos (described next) are likely among the hardest and most demanding of analytic tasks. While performing them, some people experience moodiness, irritability, despair, even existential crisis. But take heart! There is also the very real possibility of experiencing intense excitement over sudden insights and the rushing release and coalescence of ideas. Counterposed to analytic lows, there can be marvelous "analytic highs."

3. Third and last, this corpus of elemental and sorting memos sets the stage for *integrating* memos, which are explanations of connections and relationships among the sorting memos. Sometimes the connecting and relating integrations among sorting memos are evident, but sometimes not. Charmaz reports that "integration does not always occur spontaneously; often the researcher has to demonstrate the integration explicitly . . . [and some] analyses require the imposition of logical order" (1983, p. 123).

In many projects, the various codes and memos the fieldworker has developed may suggest *several possible modes of integration*, or, to use the terms of Part Two of this guide, several kinds of propositions that answer questions about topics. Within the limits of time and energy available, it may not be possible fully to develop and write up more than one or a very few of them. There is then a hard period of reckoning about which of several possible directions actually to take.

We must at this juncture repeat what we said at the start of this chapter on the theme we label *there is no single way*. What we have just reported about "coding" and "memoing" are elements of *one* way that some researchers get from data, topics, and questions to analysis. They are not practices that all researchers follow with great exactitude, even though many do so. Therefore, the foregoing charts strategic elements that are not the only possible such elements.

The strategies we have just reported are rendered in terms taken largely from the "grounded theory" approach to developing analysis. We need also to stress that this is not the only vocabulary and imagery that has been used to describe the process of developing analysis. Indeed, grounded theory terminology may not serve to crystalize understanding in all readers. To the end of reaching out to readers who may still not "get it" when so phrased, we now report a different linguistic and

Figure 9.2   Data-Theory Bootstrapping: Richards and Richards on Developing
Analysis

We often get going by finding little things that relate in some meaningful way—
perhaps, if our interest is in stress, that certain topics get discussed in anxious
ways. . . . So then we start looking for components in those topics that might
cause anxiety. . . . We might on a hunch start looking at text passages on people's
personal security and how they arrange it . . . to see if there is some possible connection between components occurring in the anxiety topics and security arrangements. If we find one, the theory is still thin, so we embark on a search for
others, and thereby look for a pattern.

The result of this is a little group of chunked-together coded text, ideas and hypotheses that can become an ingredient in further more abstracted or wide-ranging
explorations.

This chunk is . . . of larger "grain size" than its component codings, and it may in
turn become an ingredient of a later theorizing of larger grain size still that is
built out of existing chunks. (Big fleas are made out of smaller fleas.)

And so the web—of code, explore, relate, study the text— grows, resulting in little
explorations, little tests, little ideas hardly worth calling theories but that need
to be hung onto as wholes, to be further data for further study.

Together they link together with other theories and make the story, the understanding of the text [that is, of one's data]. The strength of this growing interpretation lies to a considerable extent in the fine grain size and tight interknitted-
ness of all these steps. . . .

This network of concepts, evidence, relations of concepts, coordinations of data, of
hierarchies of grain size where the theory/data/explanation chunks of one grain
size are the data for the work of the next grain size up [can be called] . . . *data-
theory boot-strapping.*

Source: Adapted from Richards and Richards, "Using Computers in Qualitative
Research," 1994, pp. 448–449. Reprinted by permission of Sage Publications, Inc.

cognitive depiction that might prompt a "click" of understanding. This
is Thomas J. Richards's and Lyn Richards's insightful image of "data-
theory boot-strapping," the main features of which are given in Figure
9.2. We stress, however, that when Richards and Richards speak of such
things as "grain size" codes and "chunks" in Figure 9.2 they are referring
to cognitive and physical operations that are, generically, much the same
as coding and memoing. (We should also note that their conceptualization
is informed by their intimate familiarity with PC programs for qualitative
analysis, and, in particular, their own program called NUDIST.)

Moreover, in stressing "boot-strapping," Richards and Richards do
not mean to imply that developing analysis is only "bottom-up," a
one-way data-to-theory process. Instead,

[the] researcher uses at each stage expectations, prior theories, hunches,
experience, and a good education (as with the theoretical determination
of . . . codes). The network builds up from the bottom, guided by a vision
of the structure of a larger-scale network into which . . . [the] smaller
empirical gleanings must fit. When one gets there, the larger-scale structure is likely to be different in many ways from the early ghostly vision;

were it not so, the constructed theory would be quite unempirical, quite unconditioned by one's data. And if one's prior ideas are wildly out, then that will show up in the increasingly procrustean strains of trying to build the anticipated larger structures from the small, heavily data-conditioned ones. (Richards and Richards 1994, p. 449)

For yet other depictions of the process of developing analysis, see Barzun and Graff 1977, Part II, and Huberman and Miles 1994, pp. 431–432.

V. Strategy Five: Diagramming

Generically, a *diagram* is a succinct visual presentation of the relationships among parts of something. Or, in the social science context, diagrams have been defined as "visual representations of relationships between concepts" (Strauss and Corbin 1990, p. 197). Roughly equivalent terms are chart, map, table, and design. Whatever the term, the key element is a succinct *visual* display of elements among which there is some kind of ordering line drawing or other use of physical space or distance to denote relationships. Another way to think of diagramming is as a *display*, which Miles and Huberman define as "a visual format that presents information systematically" (1994, p. 91).

The word *diagram* is both a noun and a verb. A diagram is an object or a product *of* analysis and *to* diagram is an activity or a process *in* analysis. For many fieldworkers, both *diagrams* and *diagramming* are integral and central to the analytic process.

Because we are describing the development of analysis in this chapter, we focus on diagram*ing* as an activity and, therefore, strategy of analysis. We find many fieldworkers engaging in one or more of four major forms of it as an activity or strategy: typologizing, matrix making, concept charting, and flow charting.

A. Typologizing

In Chapter 7, we discussed typologizing, the most basic and ongoing of the four types of diagramming, as an aspect of asking and answering the question, "What are the topic's types?" Its central feature is the cross-classification of two or more ideas, concepts, variables, or whatever as a visual display. A basic "two-by-two" example of one appears as Figure 7.2 in Chapter 7 ("two-by-two" is jargon for a typology of two variables with two values each).

In Chapter 7, we stress typologies as products or end results, but here we want to emphasize that they are also, in the words of C. Wright Mills, "very often genuine tools of production. They clarify the 'dimensions' of the types [you are working on], which they also help you to imagine and build" (Mills 1959, p. 213). Indeed, Mills goes on to declare that

I do not believe I have written more than a dozen pages first-draft without some little cross-classification [i.e., typology]—although, of course, I do not always or even usually display such diagrams. Most of them flop, in which case you have still learned something. When they work, they help you to think more clearly and to write more explicitly. They enable you to discover the range and the full relationships of the very terms in which you are thinking and of the facts with which you are working.

For a working sociologist, cross-classification is what diagraming a sentence is for a diligent grammarian. In many ways, cross-classification is the very grammar of the sociological imagination. (Mills 1959, p. 213; see also Miles and Huberman 1994, p. 184, on "substructing" variables)

B. Matrix Making

More complicated typologies or cross-classifications are also often referred to as *matrices,* a term Miles and Huberman define as "the 'crossing' of two lists . . . set up as rows and columns" (1994, p. 93). Indeed, these authors treat matrices as one of two major kinds of "displays" (the other being "networks," discussed below), and they have elaborated a wide array of types of such matrix displays (Miles and Huberman 1994, Chs. 5–9).

Figure 6.1 in Chapter 6 entitled "Units and Aspects Combine into Topics" is an example of such "'crossing' of two lists . . . set up as rows and columns." In that case, the list of "units" we explain in that chapter is crossed with the list of "aspects" in order to produce a matrix display of patterns of topics.

C. Concept Charting

A third strategy of visualizing and, therefore, of developing analysis is to arrange all one's working elements on a single sheet of paper, often a very large piece of paper, for the purpose of more clearly envisioning the relations among the elements. Often this can be a simple but powerful exercise in comprehending some or much of one's data. Julius Roth reports a basic strategy of charting in which he begins by assigning letters of the alphabet to each of his major concepts.

> [Then,] mechanically, [in developing a chart] this means taking a large sheet of paper, placing the letter A in the middle, examining the material under letter B and deciding whether that belongs before or after A (above and to the left or before; below and to the right or after), deciding on category C with respect to A and B and so on until all the categories have been listed. (Roth 1974, p. 354)

Concept charting need not be confined to a single sheet of paper. At what may be close to the practical limits of charting, Michael Agar reports this process of megacharting:

A couple of times during the early stages of an ethnography I'll find an empty classroom, usually in the evening when the building is deserted, a classroom with blackboards on several walls. I start writing things on the boards, erasing, and writing again, not data, but rather thought patterns. I'll stand in the middle of the room and turn slowly around, looking at the boards, then go to another board and write something else. . . . What's important is the large space that I can visualize all at once. . . . The large, simultaneously accessible visual space is critical for me in snapping the macro frame for an ethnography into focus. (Agar 1991, p. 192)

In terms of the amount of physical space they use, most analysts probably fall somewhere between Roth's letters on a sheet of paper and Agar's classroom, as in Wiseman's case: "[At the point of] preliminary analysis . . . I am usually working on a large table or, more likely, the floor" (1974, pp. 322–323). But in some instances, the diagramming task may make quite extraordinary demands on space. Speaking at a social science session on fieldwork in the early 1980s, Carol Stack reported that when doing the fieldwork for her classic *All Our Kin: Strategies for Survival in a Black Community* (1974), the need to keep her notes safe from her active child led her to pin notes on walls throughout her apartment. While the safety of her notes was the initial impetus for this, she discovered this practice was very useful in itself as a way to display her data in various configurations and to allow her easily to order and reorder them. The practice also had the benefit of exposing her to the information at various times of the day, even while she was engaged in other tasks.

Such charting adventures of course give rise to their own genre of humor, as in the "famous quote attributed to Levi-Strauss that if he had a card table big enough, he could figure out all of France" (Agar 1991, p. 192).

Often, such organizing concept charts do not appear in final reports, but sometimes the substance or complexity of the materials prompt their presentation. Such an instance is shown in Figure 9.3 (page 200), which displays forms of work behavior in a particular setting. (Figure 7.2 in Chapter 7, showing the relations among eight basic questions, is yet a further example of concept charting.)

D. Flow Charting

Flow charts, the fourth diagramming strategy, have the same basic features as concept charts except that they visualize an order of elements through *time* or in a *process* rather than as a *static structure*. The three-element chart with which we begin this guide (Figure I.1 on p. 2) is an example of a simple flow chart of concepts.

In their detailed treatment of "data displays," Miles and Huberman (1994, p. 93) speak of flow charting as *networks,* which they define as "a

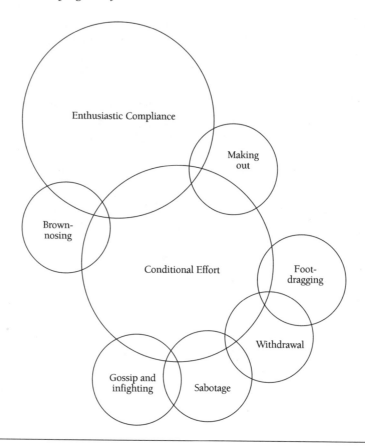

Figure 9.3   Example of a Concept Charting Diagram: Hodson on Behavioral
Modes at the Workplace. *Source:* Hodson, "The Active Worker:
Compliance and Autonomy at the Workplace," 1991, p. 53, Figure
1, "Behavioral Modes in the Workplace." Reprinted by permission
of Sage Publications, Inc. © 1991 by Sage Publications, Inc.

series of 'nodes' with links between them." As mentioned, these researchers regard networks as the second of the two major forms of data
display (the other being the matrix, as described above). As they do with
matrices, Miles and Huberman depict many forms of network display
that you might want to peruse for inspiration.

The graphing software packages that are now so abundantly available
make the kinds of diagramming we have described (as well as yet other
forms of it) relatively easy. We ought therefore to expect that diagrams

will figure ever more centrally in the analytic process and in reports of fieldwork (cf. Miles and Huberman 1994; Bernard 1994, Ch. 16).

VI. Strategy Six: Thinking Flexibly

The cognitive disposition to which we want to call attention as the strategy of "thinking flexibly" is best understood if framed by a key issue that the personal computer poses for fieldworkers.

The advent of the personal computer and its adoption in fieldstudies has forced fieldworkers to think ever more explicitly about their processes of data collection and analysis. In particular, the PC presses the question of the degree to which data collection and analysis can be codified as, or reduced to, mechanical—software driven—routines.

Following Michael Agar's reflections on this question, we can divide the answer into the two standard parts of data collection and storage versus data analysis. Much of data collection and storage does seem easily and appropriately computerized. Indeed, historically this has *always* been a mechanical process—a very labor intensive and tedious physical process. Computer applications are a great advance in this aspect of the craft. In particular, these applications offer the very useful operations of "segment-and-sort. . . . At this they are without equal, and that task will remain a core part of ethnographic work" (Agar 1991, pp. 193–194).

But, the analytic part of fieldwork "has more to do with synthesis and pattern-recognition than with" the mechanical manipulation of data (Agar 1991, p. 193). As thus far developed, at least, computer programs and electronic displays seem often to hinder rather than to help the cognitive acts of synthesis and pattern-recognition. As experienced by Michael Agar, who is among the earliest and most accomplished users of the computer (Agar 1986), existing software and technology are too physically and intellectually *confining*. With regard to detailed, microanalysis, for example, Agar reports,

> In that phase I need to lay out a couple of stretches of transcript on a table so I can look at it all at once. Then I need to mark different parts in different ways to find that pattern that holds the text together and ties it to whatever external frame I'm developing. The software problem here would be simple to solve [if one wanted to computerize this task] . . . but . . . you'd need a much bigger screen [on a computer] because simultaneous visual access to materials is what makes the ideas happen. (Agar 1991, p. 193)

Moreover, as we noted in Chapter 5, computer applications are of necessity built on their author's conceptions of the nature of some problem to be solved. In fieldstudies, though, formulating the nature of "'the problem' is exactly where ethnography shines in comparison with other social research frameworks. Figuring out the problem is part of the research process, often requiring most of the time and energy of a researcher, always involving more creativity than laying marks on a text and moving them around" (Agar 1991, p. 193). And, such creativity, Agar suggests, "comes out of numerous cycles through a little bit of data, massive amounts of thinking about that data, and slippery things like intuition and serendipity. An electronic ally doesn't have much of a role to play. . . . [Moreover,] some . . . ethnography emphasizes the interrelated detail in a small number of cases rather than the common properties across a large number. For that, you need a little bit of data and a lot of right brain" (Agar 1991, p. 193; see also Bernard 1994, p. 201).

This commentary on the cognitive and physical constraints of analysis programs sets forth both the basic limitation of the PC and of any mechanistic approach to data analysis. Computer applications and the five strategies we have described above can only take you so far. Beyond them there is, to recall Agar's terms, "intuition and serendipity." This is what we are trying to capture in the phrase "thinking flexibly." We counsel taking the foregoing five strategies *and* the PC seriously, but not *too* seriously, not seriously to the point of mechanical compulsion and ritualism. Diligence is always in order, but so is flexibility, open-mindedness, and even playfulness. Below, we enumerate some devices analysts have found helpful in encouraging their own flexible states of mind.

- *Rephrasing:* The sheer way a question (or answer) is *phrased* or worded can greatly facilitate or deter your thinking. When you are blocked, try using new words and new word orders. C. Wright Mills speaks of this as an "attitude of playfulness toward the phrase and words with which various issues are defined" (1959, p. 212). For example, instead of speaking of *causes*, you might use the related but different term *facilitants*; instead of the verb *functions,* perhaps the word *serves* might better capture the matter at hand. In this regard, a good dictionary of synonyms and antonyms is extremely useful (one of the best is Rodale 1978).

- *Changing Diagrams:* If you have already diagrammed an analysis in a form outlined above, but you do not like it, try a different form of representation, as in (1) a different kind of line drawing, (2) mathematical notations or their equivalents, or (3) physical objects from which you can construct three-dimensional models.

- *Constantly Comparing:* Constantly *comparing* items under analysis can stimulate ideas: How is this instance of X similar to or different from previous instances? How is X in this setting similar to or different from X in another setting? (Cf. Glaser and Strauss 1967, Ch. 5.)

- *Thinking in Extremes and Opposites:* Pressed fully, comparison leads to conceiving extremes and, specifically, of the extreme *opposite* of whatever is under study. C. Wright Mills counsels: "The hardest thing in the world is to study one object; when you try to contrast objects, you get a better grip on the materials and you can then sort out the dimensions in terms of which the comparisons are made" (Mills 1959, p. 214).

- *Talking with Fellow Analysts:* As mentioned above regarding the management of anxiety, the process of developing analysis ought not take place in a social vacuum. You should be in face-to-face contact with others of a similar turn of mind who have interests in your project. Aside from, and in addition to, the *morale boosting* function of being with friendly fellow analysts (discussed above), such associates can, through talk, *stimulate your thinking.* Talking with others who are knowledgeable and supportive can help to clarify in your own mind what it is that you are trying to get at.

- *Listening to Fellow Analysts:* Talk, rightly done, is a two-way street. If talking to others can help, so can *listening* to others. Other people may be able to point out critical features you had not previously noticed, even though such features were "right in front of you." Other people may suggest metaphors, ironies, or comparisons that had not occurred to you. You need, therefore, to be an active listener as well as a talker.

- *Drawing Back:* As we have emphasized previously in this chapter and will stress in the next, keep *drawing back* in order to think about the total picture. Descend into detail, to be sure, but balance that descent with self-conscious efforts to perceive a general design, overall structure, or, as phrased above, a propositional answer to a question about a topic.

- *Withholding Judgment:* Similarly, you should *withhold judgment* about the final shape of an analysis as long as it is possible, in a practical way, to do so.

We divide the third major task of doing a field study—that of analyzing data—into the two subtasks of developing analysis (discussed in this chapter) and writing reports (treated in the next chapter). This division is in one sense artificial because the analyst is clearly doing an enormous amount of writing in pursuing one or more of the six strategies we describe in this chapter. But, in another sense, developing analysis and writing reports are different and require separate discussion. Developing analysis has to do with articulating a general approach from and toward one's data, whereas writing reports is more concerned with the social psychology of writing per se and with the specific design of written reports. We now turn to these and related aspects of writing reports.

CHAPTER 10

WRITING REPORTS

In the previous chapter we were primarily concerned with procedures for generating social scientific content or substance. In contrast, in this chapter we are primarily concerned (1) with procedures for writing itself as an activity and (2) with ways to organize that activity into acceptably structured reports. We address the former first.

I. Writing Practices

Writing is a peculiar and awesome human activity. Its central feature is the physical freezing of human thought in symbols of the kind at which you are now looking. But these are not just any symbols; they are symbols with widely shared meanings that can communicate extremely complex ideas from Person A to Person B without the presence of Person A. If we pause and reflect on this quite remarkable feat, we appreciate anew how the advent and spread of writing has transformed human life and even, as a consequence, the earth itself. Writing does this, of course, by providing a means by which ideas can accumulate, develop, and spread on a scale and over distances otherwise impossible.

Curiously, despite writing's central place in and impact on human life, humans find it difficult to do. Indeed, relatively few people engage in it with any sustained regularity and the number of readers vastly outnumbers the number of writers. It is not difficult to find reasons for this imbalance. Aside from considerations of opportunity, writing is a more complicated and demanding skill than reading. Relative passivity suffices for competent reading, but intelligible writing requires active, even assertive, thinking and engagement. As such, reading is to writing as spectatorship is to participation.

But, like other skills, writing can be taught. And learning to write, like learning to participate in other undertakings, requires (1) knowledge of the basic rules and (2) practice in its procedures and routines.

In this chapter we assume that you already possess the requisite knowledge of the basic rules. We assume, that is, prior and unproblematic mastery of vocabulary, spelling, grammar, syntax, stylistic conventions, and the like—the sorts of things dealt with in handbooks of grammar and manuals of style (as in, for example, Turabian 1987; Jacobus 1989, Part IV). Here we focus on procedures, practices, or routines of writing. We draw our formulation of writing practices from our own experiences as writers and from many others who have written about the topic.

A. Have Something You Want to Say About Something

Writing is an instrument and an *instrumental activity* whose purpose is the communication of ideas. The first step in writing is therefore to form a conception of what you want to say. Writing is then simply the medium you use to communicate what you want to say. Like other media of human communication—speech, sculpture, music, or whatever—the writing medium can be cumbersome to use and recalcitrant in the face of one's best efforts. But, even so, writing is nothing but a tool in the service of reporting something.

If writing is simply a communication tool, many if not most "writing blocks" are likely not *writing* blocks at all. Instead, they are *idea* blocks. It is not that a person cannot write. Instead, the problem is that the writer has not yet formed an *idea* to write about, a something that he or she wants to report. If the purpose of writing is to report an idea, if there is no idea, there is, quite correctly, no writing.

Recall our descriptions of observing, interviewing, fieldnotes, interview transcriptions, coding, memoing, diagramming, and the like from previous chapters. All these techniques have presumably generated material that the analyst wants to say something about. If you view the substance of your communication as simply "something you want to say about something" you should begin to feel that writing is not at all fearsome. It is merely a reportorial task, a routine and mundane activity—as print journalists know very well and practice day in and day out. There is obviously more to analytic social science writing than reportorial journalism, of course, but a *reportorial attitude* is nonetheless the appropriate posture.

At the specific and quite practical level, a reportorial frame of mind is especially encouraged by having developed (or developing) diagrams of the sorts we described in Section V of the last chapter. Such viewing-all-at-once displays provide literal objects that have to be explained. As Miles and Huberman counsel: "Looking at the display helps you summarize and begin to see themes, patterns, and clusters. You write analytic text that clarifies and formalizes . . . [and] helps make sense of the display, and may suggest additional . . . [lines of analysis]" (1994, p. 101).

B. Write on Any Project Aspect, But Write

In needing something to say before you say it, the sticky part of writing is of course that you may not have anything to say about the topic before you! When that happens—and it is not uncommon—astute analysts turn to some other part of their project and see if they have anything to say about *that* part. Put more sweepingly, start (or forge ahead) with *any* part of the project that meets the key requirement of your *having something to say about it.* In turning to other writing, the topic about which you had nothing to say will be churning in your mind, both in and out of consciousness. The likelihood is that something you want to say will soon occur to you and that you will be well supplied the next time you try the topic. In making this same point, Barzun and Graff helpfully set it in the broader context of being attentive to what they term the "natural cohesion" of a project:

> Do not hesitate to write up in any order those sections of your total work that seem to have grown ripe in your mind. There is a moment in any stretch of research when all the details come together in a natural cohesion, despite small gaps and doubts. Learn to recognize that moment and seize it by composing in harmony with your inward feeling of unity. Never mind whether the portions that come out are consecutive. (1977, p. 326)

Conversely, you may have something to say about something in the context of your project but do not see how it fits into any larger scheme you are currently using. This uncertainty of pertinence may make you hesitant to sit down and work it out in writing. Overcome that hesitation. It is better to have the piece written up and not know what to do with it than to continue to carry it around in your head or leave it at the level of only coded and memoed items. While we have emphasized the need to organize what you write—to think of propositions, to compose sorting and integrating memos—it is also the case that you can become a prisoner of organization. If in doubt about pertinence, *write* anyway. Once something is written, you may find in later days or weeks that, whether it is an elemental or a larger memo, it has a perfectly logical context. The important point is that you now already have it written out and ready to place in its newly discovered context. So, don't worry about where something goes: *Write it up.* It is much easier to rearrange the written material later than to stew endlessly over how something should fit prior to actually committing it to paper.

Being flexible about what parts of the project to write about may lead to your actual report developing very unevenly. This is quite common and need be of no concern. As you continue to write parts here and there, the corpus is growing, and the fact that an increasing portion of it is *physically out there* provides *new subjects* to have something to say about! That is, your new written texts for your report are themselves new objects about which you will have something you want to say. (See again Section IV in Chapter 9 on elemental, sorting, and integrating memos.)

C. Trust in Discovery and Surprise in Writing

Even though you need to start with "something you want to say something about" this definitely does *not* mean that you know in advance *exactly* what you are going to say. Instead, using the procedures of coding, memoing, and so forth described in the last and previous chapters, an analyst typically has some data assembled under some code categories, some rough memos, and a working caption for the major topic. This is not yet true analytic writing and the writing job at hand is to tell the story to be found in those materials.

The exact words that you will use and the precise, detailed framing of the something-you-want-to-say still remain, at this point, unknown. Prototypically, an analytic writer looks through the materials yet one more time. Several similar but slightly different terms may present themselves for possible prominent use. The exact number and appropriate order of presenting components of the materials may seem unclear. Several different ways of wording and order of presentation may seem equally plausible. So sorting and stewing in the materials, many analysts simply begin to write despite the fact that there is still a lot of ambiguity about how *exactly* to say what it is they want to say. *In beginning nonetheless to write, the analyst lunges into the unknown.*

This is a fearsome but also often exhilarating moment because, frequently, *you are surprised by what you write!* Certainly, you are saying what you have to say about something, but *how* you say it, *how* you approach it, the words and concepts you use and other new matters that appear as text can all come as *news to you.* This is to say that the *physical activity of writing* can produce a *new and next level of your own discovery of what you have to say about something.*

Apropos of the reflexivity that postmodernists have urged on us of late, let us illustrate this process of discovery in writing with an account of how the first major section of this chapter was written by its initial drafter, John Lofland.

As in the abstract case I depict just above, I began with diverse source materials and with an idea. In this case, the "something I wanted to say about something" was how to organize oneself to write. My working caption was "the social psychology of writing" and I envisioned it as the title of this section. But, the more I organized, the more two other terms pressed themselves forward in my consciousness, the terms "procedures" and "practices." That is, the way I thought of ("framed") the materials shifted from "social psychology" to "practices." But, before actually writing, I could not definitely decide that this was an appropriate shift in framing. Each had to be tried out. Further, before I began to write this section, I could not see a clear and logical order in the elements that I knew I had to treat, nor did I have the exact headings you now see. Instead, I *simply began to write,* knowing I had all the materials to draw from and that I had eventually to cover each element in one way or another. It was in the process of writing itself—of rendering what I wanted to say—that the points I make about writing have taken the specific form you see and the order in which they are presented. *All the specifics of framing, captioning and order emerged in the activity of writing.* Knowing in general what I wanted to say, I simply started to say it.

Lyn Lofland is uncomfortable with the above report because of its self-congratulatory connotations, its "Oh, look at what I can do" implications. John Lofland agrees that there are dangers of self-congratulatory excesses, but thinks, nonetheless, that this risk must be taken in the interest of demystifying the writing process. To that end, he asks both Lyn Lofland's and the reader's patience with some important (but mercifully brief) elaboration on the above account:

> The two paragraphs following the heading "I. Writing Practices," above, are especially pleasing to me in content and in having been a *surprise* to me when I wrote them. At the moment I began to compose the first sentence of that first paragraph, I had no plan to begin by talking about the character of writing itself in species and historical perspective. Actually, I did not know what I was going to say in that sentence. I simply knew I wanted to begin the section and I started to write the first sentences. The sentences you see in that first paragraph are the ones that came out. (They are, however, much revised in style but not substance from their first writing.) In reading and rewriting them time and time again they have continued to seem a proper beginning, an appropriate, at-the-start encouragement for the reader to stand back and appreciate the amazing character of writing itself.

Restating the general point: *The activity of writing is a process of discovery and therefore of surprise.* Something new happens when you begin to write. It might even be true that people do not truly begin to think until they attempt to express thoughts in successive written sentences. As Wolcott puts it succinctly, "Writing *is* thinking" (1990b, p. 21). Or, stated even more extremely, and perhaps even overstated, "Writing . . . does not come after analysis; it *is* analysis, happening as the writer thinks through the meaning of data. . . . Writing is thinking, not the report of thought" (Miles and Huberman 1994, p. 101; see also Jacobus 1989, *Writing as Thinking*).

The purpose of all the elaborate prior work involved in note taking, transcribing, coding, memoing, diagramming, and the like is to provide the data that your mind can process and otherwise mysteriously interact with in the activity of writing. In so mysteriously interacting, *new* ideas, connections, framings, or whatever, are created (see also Richardson 1990, 1994).

When such a flow of discovery begins, it is important not to disrupt it with concerns over little gaps. In particular, "resist the temptation to get up and verify a fact. Leave it blank. The same holds true for the word or phrase that refuses to come to mind. It will arise much more easily on revision, and the economy in time *and momentum* are incalculable" (Barzun and Graff 1977, p. 326; emphasis in the original).

The process of thinking and (therefore) discovering while writing means that abstractly conceived outlines are not likely to be the same as the outlines of completed texts. This is as it should be. An analyst is never truly inside a topic—or on top of it—until he or she has written it up. There are, of course, degrees to which the writing process actually modifies your intentions and your outlines. You may need to modify thoroughly thought-out and already quasi-written plans and outlines only slightly. Sloppy outlines (even if well-intended) are likely to look very little like the accomplished report.

Therefore, when you start writing, be prepared for, and open to, novelty, excitement, exhilarating new lines of thought, and (perhaps) some dismay. But, don't be frightened by unexpected turns of events. In actually thinking while writing, you can only make the analysis better.

D. Admit Aversion and Write Regularly Anyway

We have now mentioned two features of writing that tell us a great deal about why so many people find it so hard and so easy to avoid. *One,* you need to have something to say about something—and sometimes you do not. *Two,* even if you do have something to say, you must face the awesome and fearful moment of the first sentence on a topic, which may or may not initiate a process of discovery and surprise in writing; often it does not. For these and other reasons, writing is difficult in the sense of being uncertain in both plan and outcome. And on top of this uncertainty, because it requires a great deal of mental concentration and sustained effort, writing is simply tiring work.

In their wonderful appendix on "a discipline for work" in *The Modern Researcher,* Barzun and Graff are even more radical and sweeping regarding problems of writing:

> Faced with the need to write, most people (including practiced writers) experience a strong and strange impulse to put off beginning. They would do anything rather than confront that blank sheet of paper. They start inventing pretexts for doing something else. . . . Let it be said once and for all: *there is no cure for this desire to escape.* It will recur as long as you live. (1977, p. 325; emphasis in the original)

But in recognizing writing as difficult and an object of avoidance, we need also to admit that *troubles of kindred if not identical sorts attend any and all serious and skilled pursuits.* Writing is like high-level athletics and risky work in that it requires *regimens of self-discipline and courage.* The self-discipline and courage required for writing are, compared to what is required for many other endeavors, quite modest, but critical nonetheless. In exercising them you recognize your "desire to escape" but counter it with what Barzun and Graff term "palliatives," some of which will hopefully be "good enough to turn the struggle virtually into a game" (1977, p. 325). Two palliatives need mention here. The discussion that follows will propose a variety of others.

First, to write well, one must write; that is, one must write *regularly.* Commonly, this means writing as a routine and daily event for some minimum and rigidly adhered to length of time. No excuses. As put by Barzun and Graff, "the palliative principle is that a regular force must be used to overcome recurrent inertia: if you can arrange to write regularly, never missing your date with yourself, no matter whether you are in the mood or not, you have won half the battle. . . . The writer's problem is the inverse of the reformed drunkard's. The latter must *never* touch a drop; the former must *always* do his stint" (1977, p. 325).

Second, this self-disciplined regularity means, as Barzun and Graff indicate, that one sits down and actually writes whether one "feels like it" or not. Novice and student writers are especially prone not to "feel like" writing. (For a perspective on this, imagine athletic teams or professional performers practicing only when they "feel like it.") Some persons want even more than simply to "feel like it." They want to be inspired. We would advise such persons to pay attention of the words of prolific social science writer Rodney Stark.

> Perhaps the most disabling myth about intellectual activity is that writing is an art that is prompted by inspiration. Some writing can be classified as art, no doubt, but the act of writing is a trade in the same sense that plumbing or automotive repair are trades. Just as plumbers and mechanics would rarely accomplish anything if they waited for inspiration to impel them to action, so writers would rarely write if they relied on inspiration. Approach the job of writing as you would approach household chores, as something you do regularly and routinely. I never have to ask myself if I feel like writing any more than I have to ask whether I feel like brushing my teeth or not. It's just what I do. (1994, p. 644)

Stark goes on to warn in particular against the student propensity to put "on a huge last-minute sprint to get a term paper completed. That's a bad way to write. It mixes writing with anxiety. When you write, you should be able to give your undivided attention to what you are saying, not to impending deadlines" (1994, p. 644).

Writing in the absence of motivation and inspiration is not simply an opportunity to display discipline and courage. Writing under these conditions also—and more importantly—conveys multiple benefits. We have mentioned some of these in the foregoing and will note others in later sections, but it seems useful to summarize them here. First, although you may find it difficult to get started, once you have started, the sense of "not feeling like it" often passes. You find yourself, instead, becoming intellectually engaged with the writing—sometimes because you've launched yourself into a process of discovery (practice C, just above). Second, writing despite your mood increases the sheer amount of writing you produce. Having and using that growing corpus is rewarding. Third, since practice makes perfect, the more you write and the more regularly you write, the better you will write. Fourth, the more you write, the more the speed with which you write is likely to increase. Fifth and finally, for a variety of reasons, including an increasing skill level, the more you write, the less anxiety about writing you will feel.

E. Do Not Seek Perfection or the One Right Way

It is not uncommon for analysts to be dissatisfied with the quality of at least a portion of their work. For some, this leads to extended periods of more data collection, more coding, memo writing, revising, and the like. In the desire to make them perfect, or almost perfect, analysts let projects drag on and on and on.

Although high standards of craft in fieldstudies are to be expected, there is no such thing as the perfect study. Once you have exercised due diligence, methodical care, analytic zeal, and careful writing, a proper sense of proportion counsels that projects must be concluded, even when they are clearly not perfect. Every reasonable person recognizes and accepts the fact that no study is without flaws. Indeed, any study claiming to be perfect is suspect for that reason! It is even part of the formal process of reporting one's inquiry to state the specific ways in which a study does or does not do particular things (these aspects are discussed in the second half of this chapter).

One form of the self-destructive quest for perfection requires particular note, that which Howard Becker (1986, Ch. 3) has described as the error of the One Right Way. Using the language of seeking a propositional answer to a question posed about a topic (Chapters 6–9), some fieldworkers embrace the idea that there must be One Right Way to do analysis in the sense that there must be one correct proposition with which to organize one's work. Uncertainty over having found it paralyzes the analyst. Or, having successfully formulated a proposition in terms of which to organize the data, the analyst believes that there must be One Right Way to provide a prose report of that organization.

Becker argues that there is no One Right Way, and we very much agree with him. There is no single, unique, obviously correct way to analyze one's data or to set forth the prose of one's report, and it is fruitless to seek one (see also Fine 1988). Becker illustrates one form of the error of One Right Way thinking with the organizational choice he faced in presenting data from his study of Chicago schoolteachers. He studied (1) *relations* teachers had with (a) students, (b) parents, (c) principals and (d) other teachers in (2) (a) slum, (b) working-class, and (c) upper-middle class *schools*. As these form a two-dimensional typology with twelve cells, should he organize his report in terms of *relations* within which he discusses schools or in terms of *schools* within which he discusses relations? Becker's answer is that there is no One Right Way. Each way has its merits and demerits. And, either way, Becker says, "I would report the same results (although in a different order) and arrive at the same conclusions (though the terms they were put in and their emphases would differ)" (Becker 1986, p. 58). Such a logic extends to other forms of seeking the One Right Way.

Lest there be misunderstanding, we need also to say that this point relates to the central propositions developed and the organization of elements in reports and *not* to empirical "trueness," as discussed in Chapter 8, Section I.A. A set of reports on the same topic can all be true to their empirical base, but still centerpiece different propositions and be organized very differently. It is in these senses that there is no One Right Way.

F. Prepare to Omit Cherished Writing

Virtually no matter how you organize your report, some of your most favored bits of analysis—codings, memos, and even fairly well-developed draft pages—will likely not fit logically into the major scheme of organization you come to use. You have then come up against the hard truth that no relatively coherent design is likely to have a pertinent place for everything you have worked on and even worked up as fairly polished writing. You must, then, live with the "agony of omission."

But take heart because there are several mechanisms of ancillary accommodation that you can sometimes use. First, you can tack on a related piece of analysis as an appendix. Second, you can insert it at some point (such as at the end of a section or chapter) as a digression and frankly label it as such. Third, you can treat it briefly in a footnote. Fourth, if it is very general, it can appear in a preface, epilogue, or afterword. There is, of course, always the possibility of an altogether separate report.

G. Have a Secluded and Indulging Place to Write

Distractions in one's physical vicinity while writing are enemies of writing. Sudden noises, irregular passersby, harsh and contrasting lighting, ringing phones, and myriad other matters disrupt thought and, thereby, the conversion of thought into words. Therefore, seek a secluded and pleasant place to write.

Such a place does more than protect you from random distractions. Entering a place that you identify as "the place to write" also serves to put you into a frame of mind for writing. In contrast, to write in places largely identified with other kinds of activities is to be prompted to think about those other activities—and prompted actually to engage in them! By design, your writing place should be outfitted so that there is nothing else you can do when you are there. Finding yourself bereft of all your favorite and distracting toys, you might as well write.

However, there is one way in which you should indulge yourself. As Barzun and Graff urge (in admonitions composed prior to the sexual revolution in language and the advent of the PC):

> A writer should as soon as possible become aware of his peculiarities and preferences regarding the mechanics of composing. He should know whether he likes the pen or typewriter, what size and color of paper he prefers, which physical arrangement of his notes and books pleases him best, even what kind of clothes and which posture he likes to assume for work. In all these matters, he is entitled to complete self-indulgence. . . . This is consistent with our underlying principle: indulge yourself so that you will have no excuses for putting off the task; and stick to your choice, so that the very presence of your favorite implements will confirm the habits of the good workman. (1977, p. 327)

We fully realize that not everyone has the luxury of a separate room or a part of a room devoted solely to writing. We also realize that even a desk or table one can call exclusively one's own is unattainable for some. Nonetheless, we urge you to strive to come as close to the ideal arrangement as your circumstances allow. If you have to bribe, threaten, or cajole children, spouses, roommates or parents to secure a little space, do it. If you have to demand, beg, or wheedle these same folks to secure a little peace, do it. On the assumption that successful completion of your project matters to you, laying claim to some peaceful space is probably the single most important thing you can do to achieve that goal.

H. Reread and Revise

One of the most useful outcomes of having written something is that the ideas are now *externalized* and therefore physically available to you as something you can scrutinize. Written analyses become objects that you can literally see. With such objects before you, you can begin to take the same actively analytic stance toward your writing as you have heretofore taken toward whatever you have been studying. You should do this at two levels: the sentence and the analytic unit.

At the sentence level, frequently reread and revise what you have written. Before the advent of the PC, this was a laboriously mechanical task of marking up text on paper and retyping. It was so laborious, in fact, that people spoke of "first," "second," and additional numbered drafts, which referred to occasions of complete retyping so as to incorporate accumulated and often scrawled changes.

With the PC, revision is a whiz and a continuous process, and the concept of discrete drafts no longer describes the reality. The following anonymous first-person account by a writer exemplifies the increasingly common process of almost continuous rereading and revising:

I begin each session of writing by reading and rewriting the six or so pages I have written in whatever number of previous days it took me to write that number of pages. This has the function of reimmersing me in whatever was my line of thought, but equally important, it means that I extensively revise virtually every sentence I have recently written, some of them many times in a single session. (Sometimes the revisions are so extensive that I have to pull up my previous day's backup set of data to find out what I said before I changed the text so much I cannot recall the original.) Further, when I eventually print out a version, this provides a fresh view of the text that I reread and revise with a red pen so that I can easily locate these handwritten revisions when I transfer them to the PC master file. Over later days and even weeks or months, there are many additional rereadings and concomitant rewritings. By the time a document is ready to be seen by colleagues, every sentence has already been reread and revised at least a dozen times. This may seem an exceedingly complicated and even tedious process. But, driven by the desire to express whatever the topic as clearly, accurately, and completely as possible, I do not experience it as either complicated or tedious. Instead, I am simply working on a very intriguing puzzle.

One key corollary of such continual revising is that you should "not be afraid of writing down something that you think may have to be changed. Paper is not granite, and in a first [or subsequent] draft you are not carving eternal words in stone. Rather, you are creating substance to be molded and remolded in successive drafts" (Barzun and Graff 1977, p. 326).

In a kind of microscopic version of the One Right Way we discussed in Section E, beginning writers are all too prone to hesitate at the sentence level, trying to form the precise, just-exactly-right way to say something they want to say. Such hesitation should be resisted—nay— ignored. As Rodney Stark has admonished:

> When you write, don't agonize over finding the best word or the best phrasing. Get the ideas down no matter how poor your prose. After you have your ideas on paper, then worry about improving the style. When you have a draft, no matter how crude, you can work on improving the writing without getting sidetracked. You do not risk forgetting where you are going as you seek a word or wrestle with a sentence. Indeed, what you are doing now is not writing but editing. (1994, p. 644)

Revision at the level of the "analytic unit" refers to revisions of paragraph or longer pieces of text, up to and including the entire report. Whatever the length of the analytic unit, you should scrutinize and revise it in any number of terms, including points overlooked, assertions undocumented, logical inconsistences, gaps or leaps, possible criticisms unanswered, transition sections unwritten, and so on.

It is our impression, indeed, that professional writers of social science reread and revise their work so much that by the time anything is actually published, its author is so familiar with it and has changed it so much that he or she is quite ready to be done with it!

I. Choose Labels Carefully

The construction of an analysis means, in a practical sense, that you need to invent or borrow a set of labels for whatever propositions, concepts, processes, or the like you propound. A wide variety of alternative labels will always be available to you. Because you have so much choice and cannot avoid making a selection, you need to consider the options and the grounds for your selections carefully. One of the truths of social analysis is that a striking (though not outlandish) set of labels gets more attention than a more mundane set, regardless of how incisive the analysis itself may be.

Nonetheless, it is also the case that you should avoid being too esoteric and should, therefore, invent few, if any, new words. Whenever possible and appropriate use common, everyday vocabulary. A review of some labels that have actually been used by social analysts (many examples are given in Part Two) should provide a sense of the inventive use that can be made of quite common language. For example, consider the genius of juxtaposing the quite ordinary words "normal" and "crime" to form a useful and self-explanatory label: "normal crime" (Sudnow 1979).

J. Let the Ego Drain Out

It is wise to complete a report well in advance of its formal presentation to an audience and then put it away for a reasonable period of time. Just prior to presentation, give it another full rereading and revision. By not looking at it for a period, the ego you have invested in it has an opportunity to "drain out" and the fixed view of it you had developed can be loosened or forgotten. We all tend to develop a cognitive set toward a piece of work we are involved in—a particular "locked-in" view of what we are doing. This view might be a very good and insightful one. Then again, it might not be. By backing off from a piece of writing for a while, getting your mind off of it and losing your commitment to what you had in mind, you can later come back with a fresh perspective. You will then be in a better frame of mind to decide whether or not your draft was really "so hot." Even if on rereading you decide it really is quite fine and that only some prose needs revision, it will at least be improved in that regard.

The phrase "well in advance" is obviously ambiguous, and its exact meaning will vary by circumstance. One such variation is the length of the report and therefore the amount of work involved in a final revision. Even with short reports, though, such as fifteen-page student papers, an interval of at least several days between completion and revision seems to us a minimum.

A similar process of letting the ego drain out and letting fixed approaches dissipate also applies to bothersome sections of a report—sections that you have trouble organizing or writing. Difficulties may mean that something is basically wrong with the section. But they may also simply mean that you have not yet discovered the most cogent thing to say about the topic or the best way to organize it. Rather than engage in prolonged stewing, turn to some other section and temporarily forget about the troublesome one. When you return to it, a fresh start may resolve the previous difficulties.

K. Find Your Own Working Style

The rather elaborate set of admonitions on writing practices we have enumerated attempts to respond to the flounderings of novices and to their pleadings for guidance. And we believe that it is altogether proper to respond in this way to these pleas. Nonetheless, the practices we describe can be unhelpful and possibly even counterproductive. This is because the assorted items we list above work well for some writers but not for others. It is inevitable that one or more of our suggestions will not be helpful to someone. That being the case, we must emphasize that the preeminent writing practice is to *find and use your own style of working*. Be aware of the kinds of things we report above as commonly productive writing practices, certainly, but do not assume that each must work for you.

We are mindful, specifically, that the underlying image of the writer embodied in the above set of practices is that of the *steady plodder*. The latent or unarticulated image is of persons who write a little each day, methodically and laboriously building up analysis. They grind out their reports slowly, writing and analyzing in detail as they go along.

While we believe this image accurately captures the largest portion of writers, we also know that it does not fit everyone. There are also what we might call the *grand sweepers*, persons who write very little actual text at first, but, instead, work out an analysis very carefully and in detail in the form of outlines and organized notes. After completing this organizing process, they then write the entire report in sequence from beginning to end in one fell swoop. Writing becomes the overriding and single governing principle of their lives for whatever period it takes to put their report into text. Let us be clear. The grand sweeper working style must not be confused with the *student goof-off* pattern. This latter refers to the practice of "goofing off" all term and then writing a thirty-page paper by staying up all night before it is due. In fundamental contrast to the student goof-off pattern, the grand sweeper has performed extremely detailed and hard analytic labor before beginning to write. The analytic effort is no different from that of the steady plodder, who is analyzing and writing at the same time. The grand sweeper has simply segregated the tasks of analytic thought and detailed writing.

In our treatment throughout this guide, it is clear that we prefer the steady plodder over the grand sweeper. But we must nonetheless acknowledge that grand sweeping works for some people and can produce true, new, and important fieldstudies. Beyond our preferences, we describe this contrast in order to make the larger point that, irrespective of all the good advice you can get, you must in the end develop your own working style, and it may not be either of these.

L. Find Your Own Prose Style

There has, of late, been a virtual explosion in "writings about writing" in social science (e.g., Agar 1990; Atkinson 1990, 1992; Becker 1986; Brown 1990; Brown, ed., 1992; Clifford and Marcus 1986; Ellis and Bochner 1992; Fine 1988; Geertz 1988; Krieger 1985, 1991; Richardson 1990, 1992; Van Maanen 1988; Wolcott 1990a, 1990b; Wolf 1992). Many of these "writings about writing" are especially concerned with prose style in fieldwork reports and, among this portion, a fair number emerge out of the feminist, postmodernist, participatory, critical or other recent approaches to naturalistic inquiry we have mentioned in preceding chapters. The advice proffered is as varied as its sources. Some authors offer suggestions for improving or for making more effective the expository prose style in which fieldworkers have traditionally rendered their reports. Others counsel adopting techniques that would transform scholarly writing into a form closer to literature—fiction, drama, or autobiography, for example. Some view their advice in strategic terms: Do what we say if it works for you. Others tend to transform strategic or aesthetic choices into blanket moral prescriptions: Do what we say because it is the only right, ethical, or virtuous way to do it.

Our advice about all this diverse advice is quite simple.

If you are a novice, stick to the expository prose style (which is our preference in all cases). It is the simplest style and the one that can be achieved even by those of us who lack "literary talent." Both Becker (1986) and Fine (1988) may be read for useful hints to help you find your personal voice within this genre.

On the other hand, if you are already a fully competent expository writer (that is, if you find it easy to convey your ideas with clarity and precision), perhaps you can risk a plunge into the thicket of stylistic alternatives and rhetorical nuance and sample more widely from the works we have cited above. But do try to avoid being seduced by the moralists. Keep in mind that the "right" style is the style that allows you to convey what you want to convey in the manner you want to convey it to the audience you want to convey it to.

II. Desirable Features of Reports: A Checklist

There are a number of conventions and standards that guide researchers in organizing and composing their research reports. Equally as important, these conventions and standards guide serious *readers* in evaluating reports. Therefore, researchers who desire positive responses from serious readers need to be aware of these conventions and standards and to employ them in composing their reports.

With the aim of increasing this awareness, we want now to describe these conventions and standards. In order to make this description maximally useful to writers, we have organized it as a checklist of questions to ask about a report. At the point of completing a final revision, a writer should be able to say "yes" in response to each italicized question on the following list. Moreover, you can also use this checklist in earlier stages of a project. Scanning this list and answering these questions at appropriate points in time provide an assessment of what has been completed and what remains to be done.

Almost all these desirable features have been discussed in detail in earlier chapters. Therefore, their appearance here as questions to ask about reports is a review and final application rather than the introduction of new material.

While this checklist is attuned to the wider world of scholarly assessment, it is drawn somewhat more broadly to take account of projects completed as part of college and university courses. Therefore, some items reflect conventions and standards more specific to that context and we will signal those that are.

In our estimation, there are nine clusters of questions that readers use to assess reports and that, therefore, can be viewed as desirable features. These are diagrammed in summary overview in Figure 10.1, where the nine are assigned alphabet letters A through I.

We can sort these nine clusters into four themes in terms of focus on:

1. *Basic Organization*—How well is the report presented?
2. *Data and Methods*—What is the quality of the data collection, analysis and presentation?
3. *Analysis*—What is the quality of the analytic effort?
4. *Overall Evaluation*—What, overall, is the value of this report?

These foci are listed in the far left-hand column of Figure 10.1, and each of the nine clusters is placed in the appropriate row.

In a very general fashion, the four cluster foci are ordered in Figure 10.1 from the more specific, concrete, and agreed-upon among audiences, in the top rows, to the more general, abstract, and contentious among audiences in the bottom rows.

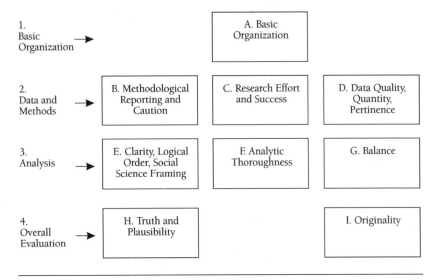

Figure 10.1   Four Types of Desired Features of Fieldstudy Reports

A. Basic Organization?

The most basic desirable features concern the presence or absence of given sections in a report and the presence or absence of very basic matters pertaining to sections and other organizational features. There are eleven of these elementary desirable features. They begin with the first thing a reader sees, the title, and end with a query about spelling and grammar.

1. Title?

Does the title contain a generic propositional referent? Research oriented to developing and reporting on social science propositions (Chapter 8, Section I.C.2; Chapter 9, Section I) should reflect that orientation in the title of the report. Therefore, irrespective of the specific situation or setting studied, the report's title or subtitle ought to include a propositional or kindred conceptual referent. One formula for this is: "[proposition or concept] in [a situation or setting]."

Examples of reports using this formula include:

"Illness Career Descent in Institutions for the Elderly" (Fisher 1987)

"Creating Cases in a Regulatory Agency" (Hawkins 1984)

"The Active Worker: Compliance and Autonomy at the Workplace" (Hodson 1991)

"The Regular: Full-Time Identities and Memberships in an Urban Bar" (Katovich and Reese 1987)

"Dogs and Their People: Pet-Facilitated Interaction in a Public Setting" (Robins, Sanders, and Cahill 1991)

In a humorous vein, one wag has offered this as the all-purpose abstract formula for fieldstudy titles: "Fundamental Aspects of Some Basic Concept/Question/Topic: A Preliminary Inquiry Conducted Someplace in the World." While phrased to be humorous, this title does contain the key elements of a proposition, concept, or question coupled with the name of the specific situation or setting studied.

2. Abstract?

Is there an abstract or a table of contents? Paper-length reports ordinarily have abstracts, and longer reports have a table of contents, which serves the same function. An abstract is a hundred word or so summary of the major arguments or findings in the paper that includes a description of the methods and an indication of the situation or setting studied. Turabian (1987), among others, gives generic instructions on the physical presentation of titles, abstracts, and other parts of a report.

3. First Paragraphs?

Is the proposition, thesis, or the like that will be used in approaching the data and the source of the data stated in the first paragraph or paragraphs? The opening paragraph or paragraphs of the report should pose a general question about some topic and state the thesis or proposition that will be developed. Here are two examples of such openings.

The first example begins a study of institutionalized elderly people:

> Declining health affects the lives of older individuals in a variety of ways. . . . Although research has shown that institutions for the aged can have positive consequences . . . , they also threaten the self-concept and self-worth of older individuals. Institutionalization entails a loss of privacy and control so that individuals have difficulty maintaining their idealized self-image. Institutionalization also renders one vulnerable to negative labels imposed by others. To cope with these social processes, people develop cognitive strategies, the subject matter of this paper.
>
> In my research [on a particular institution for the elderly] I have found it helpful to view this combined social and cognitive process as "illness career descent." (Fisher 1987, pp. 132–133, citations omitted)

The second example begins a study of a food cooperative:

> Members of groups create collective definitions of themselves. These definitions have a moral character, and individuals are expected to act in a fashion consistent with the collective typification they promote. Group members usually take great precautions to encourage this perception of consistency. . . .
>
> Members of a group are troubled when a course of conduct which appears to contradict their collective ideals is found to be necessary or

highly desirable. Participants feel constrained from engaging in such practices, lest they be discredited. Nonetheless, circumstances sometimes create great pressure on members to act with seeming disregard for what they have staked themselves to be.

In their everyday worlds, participants are frequently able to negotiate constructions through which seemingly discrediting acts are institutionalized, without team members feeling compromised. This article discusses one previously unexamined process for deftly resolving problematic situations. The process is called *discounting*. (Pestello 1991, pp. 26–27; emphasis in original, citations omitted)

4. Early Overview?

Is there an introductory section that provides an overview of what will be covered in the paper? After providing the reader with the general topic and indicating the character of the data, authors commonly provide an overview outline of how the paper is organized. Using Babbie's quotation of an "old forensic dictum," the practice here is to "tell them what you're going to tell them; tell them; and tell them what you have told them" (1995, p. A11).

5. Literature Review?

Is there an early section that reviews social science writing that is pertinent to the proposition or thesis and data being treated? A common label for this section is "review of the literature." In some research training settings, this part may be quite brief or omitted altogether. Often, though, there is a review of previous works on the general and specific topics analyzed that shows how the current inquiry relates to these earlier works.

6. Data Sources?

Is there a section that reports the sources of the data and the methods used? Does this section also indicate possible faults with the data or sources of bias and how the researcher has dealt with these? In some studies this section is called "study design and execution." Because of the central role of fieldworkers as instruments of data collection and analysis, this is an especially important section in fieldstudy reports (although it is, of course, important in *all* empirical studies). In book-length reports, an entire chapter or appendix is often devoted to describing how the data were collected. Even in short reports, such accounts may run several or more pages, depending on the complexity of events in the particular study. Because of its importance, we provide more detailed instructions on the contents of this section in Question B.1 below.

7. Subdivided Main Body?

Is there a main, data-reporting and analyzing body of the report that is divided (and subdivided, if required) with informative headings? This portion of a report is sometimes labeled the "analysis and interpretation."

This is the heart of the report. Its scheme of organization should be clear, and this clarity is facilitated by headings that communicate content and signal major elements and change of topics.

8. **Summary and Conclusion?**
   Is there a summary and conclusion section that summarizes what has been reported, draws conclusions about it, and suggests what further research is appropriate?

9. **Bibliography?**
   Is there a list of pertinent references or other appropriate bibliographic apparatus?

10. **Stylistic Conventions?**
    Are appropriate stylistic conventions employed? By stylistic conventions we mean, among other things, standard margins, numbered pages, clear and consistent placement of headings, and properly formatted references. Some of these stylistic conventions are now the default settings of many word processing programs, but many are not. One therefore needs to consult a manual of style (e.g., Turabian 1987; Cuba 1988) and adopt a consistent set of such conventions. (The graphics capabilities of some word-processing programs now also make it easy to display bad taste in one's choices of typefaces and font sizes. The wise writer will stay with widely used typeface styles and sizes.)

11. **Writing Conventions?**
    Is the writing grammatical and are the words spelled correctly? The wide availability of word processing programs with spell- and grammar-checking features means that no conscientious writer need ever again produce a report riddled with spelling and grammatical errors.

The eleven matters of basic organization we have just described make up the more routine and easily achieved side of composing and evaluating a report. We now move to the second cluster of checklist questions: aspects of data and method.

B. Methodological Reporting and Caution?

1. **Reporting?**
   Following from Question A.6, are the methodological aspects of the study adequately reported? While the character and content of methodological accounts are not highly standardized, certain items are commonly treated, and we enumerate these just below, grouped into five categories and stated as questions.

a. **Inception and Social Relations?**

- How and why did you decide to undertake interviewing and/or observation of the particular situation or setting you have studied?

- If a known observer, how did you secure cooperation from the participants? Was permission to perform the study facilitated by a prior acquaintanceship, your personal features, or your social status? Who, if anyone, sponsored your project by providing money and/or legitimacy for your work?

- If an unknown observer, what role did you occupy in the setting, and how did you come to occupy it?

- What, if any, problems did you encounter in getting along with various participants? If the setting contained marked divisions and conflicts, how did you align yourself with regard to them?

- How did you deal with any suspicion or distrust on the part of one or more participants?

- What, if any, informants did you recruit, and how did you recruit them?

- What social blunders did you commit, and how did you deal with them?

- If a known observer, what kinds of services did you provide the participants in exchange for allowing your presence?

- What ethical problems, if any, did you confront and how did you deal with them?

(In addressing these questions you may want to refer again to Chapters 3 and 4.)

b. **Private Feelings?**

- How did you privately feel about this setting and its participants at various periods during the research? Were you highly sympathetic or not? Did you experience a possible seduction or conversion effect? Did you experience, in general, other of the emotional stresses discussed in Chapter 4?

- To what extent did you find it difficult or easy, privately, to be in a setting while observing and analyzing it at the same time?

- How did you, or didn't you, protect yourself from compromising emotional involvements?

c. **Data Gathering?**

- Approximately how much time, in hours, weeks, months, or years, did you spend actually interviewing people in the setting or exposed to the situation or setting? How much time did the entire study take?

- How did you decide when to observe what, or when and whom to interview?

- When and in what manner did you take notes on events or during interviews? To what degree did you trust your memory regarding observations and interviews? Did you employ tape recorders or other devices?
- What techniques did you employ in writing up notes or interviews?
- What kinds of settings and participants were particularly difficult to observe or interview? Which ones were easily accessible? What social barriers and facilitants to gaining information did you encounter?
- Did you encounter any special ethical problems in data collection? What, if anything, did you do about them?

d. Data Focusing and Analysis?

- At what point did you begin coding, filing, memoing, or other analytic activities?
- What devices did you employ in beginning to do analysis? What was the character of your storage and retrieval system?
- What lines of analysis or perspectives, if any, did you already have before you began to study the setting? To what degree did these perspectives shift or stay the same during the course of the interviewing or observation and analysis? How clear and specific an idea did you have of what you wanted to observe or interview about at the outset?
- At what point in data collection or analysis had you more or less clearly formulated or worked out the lines of analysis now found in your report? To what degree did data collection and analysis overlap?
- What important difficulties or facilitants did you experience in doing concerted analysis?
- What was your personal, subjective experience of the analysis process?

In thinking about these questions, you will also want to review the three "canons of ethnographic validity" offered by Sanjek (discussed in Section I.A of Chapter 8).

e. Retrospect?

- Relative to all the above matters, what would you now, with the wisdom of hindsight, do differently were you to do the study over? What advice would you give to someone else studying this situation or setting, or any situation or setting?

One prominent fieldworker has commented that what typically goes into describing how the study was done are "the second worst things that happened." We are inclined to believe his generalization. What person with an eye on the future, who wishes others to think positively of her or him, is going to relate anything that is morally or professionally discrediting in any important way? This is especially the case for field-studies since they tend to be done by younger persons who have longer futures to think about and less security about them. We delude ourselves if we expect naturalistic researchers actually to "tell all" in print. *Nonetheless, a wide range of very useful, less threatening, and more neutral things can and should be committed to public print, the better to advance the craft.*

2. Caution?

In addition to cautions that may be expressed in the methods section (Question B.1, immediately above), is a concern for error and bias applied to the data and analysis throughout? It is one thing to write an appropriate section on data sources answering the questions in B.1; it is another thing to treat one's data with proper caution as an ongoing matter at the level of reporting and using data in the main body of the report. Here, readers are alert to the degree to which a writer is appropriately critical of the data and his or her own analysis as an ongoing matter in the report.

C. Research Effort and Success?

While questions about the amount of effort put into a research project and the degrees of success in collecting data more commonly come up relative to student projects, such questions are sometimes raised with regard to the projects of fully professional social scientists.

1. Effort?

Is there evidence that reasonable effort to locate data adequate to the topics treated has been expended? In fieldwork specifically, when the data seem thin, readers ask if the fieldworker has done as much as might be reasonably asked.

2. Success?

Is there evidence that those efforts were reasonably successful? Holding effort constant, exactly how successful was the fieldworker in assembling whatever data are at hand?

D. Data Quality, Quantity, Pertinence?

1. Data Quality and Quantity?

Taking account of research training versus other contexts, are the collected data of adequate quality and quantity?

2. Pertinence?

Even if quantitatively and qualitatively adequate as a general matter, are the data pertinent to the conceptual focus of the report?

The above varied aspects of data and of methods of data collection are set off from questions of how, analytically, data are treated in the report, the concern that informs clusters E, F, and G (which are shown as row three of Figure 10.1).

E. Clarity, Logical Order, Social Science Framing?

1. Clarity and Logical Order?
Even though the report displays the eleven elements listed in cluster A (basic organization), is it otherwise clearly organized? One dimension of the clarity is the degree to which the order of elements is logical, or, at least, assembled with a plausible rationale.

2. Social Science Framing?
Does the report clearly put forth one or more propositions that are answers to sociological questions? For discussion, see Section I of Chapter 8 and Section I of Chapter 9.

F. Analytic Thoroughness?

1. Elaboration?
Is the main body of the report (Question A.7) organized in terms of a detailed scheme of categories of analysis? Appropriate degrees of conceptual elaboration are discussed in Section I.C.4.a of Chapter 8.

2. Data-Analysis Interpenetration?
If there is a detailed scheme, is it interpenetrated with whatever data are used, or is the scheme presented in one place and the data in another? Interpenetration is discussed in Section I.C.4.c of Chapter 8.

3. Serious Labels?
Are the concepts used and the headings employed serious phrasings or do they run to the literary and to the stylistically "cute"?

G. Balance?

1. Descriptive-Analytic Balance?
Does the paper have a balance between description and analysis? Balance is discussed in Section I.C.4.b of Chapter 8.

2. Section Balance?
Are the sections of the paper balanced? For example, are the introduction, main body, and conclusion in proportion to one another? (Cf. Cuba 1988, pp. 71–72.)

H. Truth and Plausibility?

1. True?
To what degree are the data true? The evaluative criteria for trueness are discussed in Section I.A of Chapter 8.

2. Data-Analysis Consistency?
Are the data presented consistent with the analysis?

3. Internal-External Consistency?
Are the data and analysis presented consistent with other data and analyses?

I. Originality?

1. Newness?
Considering research instruction versus other contexts, does the report make an advance over what is already known and discussed in the particular context?

2. Importance?
Does the author state why he or she thinks the study is important and, in particular, resonant, or can we as readers see importance or resonance in this study even though it is not stated by the author? These are discussed in Chapter 8.

In this guide, we have called attention to a number of both positive and negative experiences you might have in doing a fieldstudy. Among negative experiences, we noted, for example, anxiety and fear. Among positive experiences, there can be exhilaration, playful fun, and a sense of adventure. We want now to add to these sometime accompaniments the possibility of a profound creative experience. We mean by this that you may experience the formulation or discovery of a proposition as a thrilling revelation, as a moment when the "blinders" fall from your eyes and you behold a new order in your materials and—hopefully—in social reality.

It will take further and careful checking to determine whether your discovery is original as well as creative, but your accomplishment is in no way diminished by having had predecessors. On the other hand, further checking may determine that you actually have done something new and important that deserves a very wide audience. In that case, you can add an achievement of consequence to your experience of creativity.

One oft-quoted maxim about creativity is that it is "ninety-nine percent perspiration and one percent inspiration." People experience creative insight as something that happens *to* them. But, so goes the wisdom, creative moments seem to happen more often to people who are otherwise working very hard on whatever their project. The moral is that the best way to ensure creativity is to exercise a great deal of enterprising diligence.

But even in the absence of creative flashes, one can aim for the more common but no less impressive achievement of work that is elegant, thorough, clear, and carefully organized. Such an achievement requires neither creativity nor an especially sharp intelligence. Rather, what it requires is the sustained application of methodical effort, activity, and *enterprise*. The methodical, active, enterprising researcher-analyst searches out data that less diligent colleagues overlook and carries out analysis beyond the point where less diligent colleagues stop. Such persons stand in stark contrast to those who assume a stance of passive dependence. The latter expect others to guide them each step of the way; in the face of a situation calling for get-up-and-go, they offer only stonelike immobility. Unsurprisingly, they usually fail to accomplish much of anything at all.

III. Concluding Observations

We conclude the journey we have made in this guide with observations on the fieldstudy perspective, scholarship more generally, and the hazards embodied in methodological advice.

A. The Fieldstudies Approach as a System of Parts

The ten aspects of the fieldstudies or naturalistic perspective we have expounded in this guide tend, in our assessment, toward a more or less coherent system in which any selected subset of these parts seems logically to imply the others. Most broadly, the elements of the "gathering" phase seem to cohere, in a reasonably logical fashion, with the elements of the "focusing" and "analyzing" phases.

But as we have mentioned at several points in previous chapters, not all social scientists embrace the idea that there is (or should be) a logically consistent relation among these ten parts. There are at least two major patterns or "schools" of disagreement. The first, the descriptive ethnographers, assert that one needs only the first phase, that of gathering. Focusing and analyzing are not required, and reporting is accomplished in an ordinary narrative manner. The second, the extreme grounded theorists, take the opposite view: They regard matters of focus and analysis as especially relevant but believe that the data can be gathered from almost anywhere in almost any fashion.

These and other patterns suggest, perhaps, that the ten aspects of the naturalistic approach we have presented may not, indeed, have any inherent logical interrelation. At least that interrelation is not sufficiently obvious to produce unanimity. But even if the interrelation is not inherent, there are important reasons for considering these elements a systemic package. Together they form a constraining discipline and a creative experience that begins with a deep and emotional relation to a situation or setting and proceeds by steps to articulate that personal relation in ways that are understandable and useful to wider audiences. To omit or skimp on any part is to weaken the product—to weaken the depth of the data, the precision of the focus, or the incisiveness of the analysis.

B. The Similarity of All Scholarship

It is important to conclude by recognizing that despite some distinctive features, qualitative fieldwork research and analysis are, in the respects that count most, the same as all other research and analysis. The particulars of the source materials may differ, as may difficulties in gathering material and the substance of analysis, but the essential process is identical to other kinds of intellectual endeavor. The elements of this essential similarity include tenacity, commitment, thought, reflection, critical scrutiny, methodological caution, organization, and flexibility. Happily, all these qualities can be learned. Like all learning, they are acquired through practice.

C. Technique and Impotence

The rules, guides, procedures, and other routines that constitute this guide are all quite fine and necessary. But they can themselves become problems, blinders, fetishes, or straitjackets. Therefore, draw upon and use what we say with a cautious, judicious, and selective attitude. Keep your creativity and intellectual playfulness alive. As Peter Berger has succinctly (albeit in male-centric fashion) expressed the necessary stance: "In science as in love, concentration on technique is quite likely to lead to impotence" (1963, p. 13).

DISSECTING FIELDSTUDY REPORTS

Task and Purpose

Application of ideas to an example is an important means by which one can strengthen one's understanding of both the ideas and the example. In that spirit, we have organized the instructions on fieldstudies presented in this guide as a set of questions that one can ask and answer about a published fieldstudy.

We hope this might be a fruitful analytic exercise for persons in a variety of circumstances. Most proximately, anyone undertaking his or her own fieldstudy—the audience to whom this book is most directly addressed—should find this a useful learning activity. In addition, people in courses on research methods that deal with the ideas we have covered here should find it helpful to assess their operation in an actual research report, quite apart from conducting their own studies.

Format

Operationally, the task is that of answering the questions we pose below about a research report one has read. When completing it as a requirement in a course, you might, of course, write out the answers.

Articles Versus Books

For the purpose of answering the questions below, it does not matter whether the report is a book or an article. (Of course, the former requires more work from the student than the latter.)

Research Reports

In order to be most useful, a research report selected for analysis should have many if not most or all of the following features. Put differently, it should be a report of serious research.

1. The report should be literally that—a *report* of field data—rather than a theoretical essay, review of the literature, a primarily quantitative investigation, or similar formulation.

2. The report should display the ordinary apparatus of scholarship. The following are some earmarks of that apparatus as seen in serious *books*. The more a book has of them, the more likely that it is a serious work of scholarship. (Articles should display essentially the same features except for those that are distinctive to books.)

   - It has a serious table of contents, one that avoids "cute" and metaphorical titles.

   - It has footnotes, a bibliography, and an index.

   - In the introductory chapter or chapters, the author or authors try to relate their work to what other people have written about the topics, questions, and settings under study.

   - The author or authors describe their methods of data collection and analysis.

   - The chapters are internally subdivided with headings that communicate lines of analysis.

   - There is a concluding chapter in which what has been accomplished is summarized and directions for future work are set forth.

Locating Research Reports

There are literally thousands upon thousands of fieldstudy books and articles that display the above features of serious reports of research. One must be cautious in making a selection, however, for there are many more thousands upon thousands of *journalistic* books and articles that are *not* serious reports of research. Some of these reports tend to the sensationalistic and are not based on serious efforts either to collect data or judiciously to analyze them in terms of topics and questions that are of social scientific interest.

Questions About Fieldstudy Reports

A. Identification

For books: What is the name of the author, the full title of the book, publisher, and year of publication? Indicate any complications of publication history such as a reissue by another publisher, an enlarged edition, a translation, or the like.

For articles: Give the full citation of the article.

B. Social and Personal Matters

Reports differ in the types of data they use and some data involve much more complicated social relations and personal matters than do others. If interviewing or observational data were used, the following questions are especially pertinent, although at least some of these questions arise with other kinds of data as well. Where a question is not pertinent because of the kind of data used, report that fact and the reasons why. If the report does not contain information that answers a particular question, state this.

1. What does the author say motivated the study? Who paid for it?

2. Where, geographically, was the research done? What "populations," situations, or social settings were studied?

3. In what ways was initial access to the data and/or the site problematic, if at all? Financial? Ethical? Practical? Personal? Other?

4. How were such problematic aspects (Question B.3) managed in order to get started?

5. What type of social role did the researcher occupy or assume in the research and what limitations and advantages did this role have?

6. What were special stresses in the social relations involved, if any? How were these managed? What did the research "do" to the researcher (as in getting converted or the like)?

7. Were there, in particular, ethical issues of confidentiality, disguised observation, other undercover data collection, and informed consent? Describe them. If none, explain why.

8. In what ways might the actions of the researcher have influenced either the people at the sites involved (and hence the "data") or the character of the data collected?

9. What were especially helpful and positive aspects of researcher-researched relations? (For example, were there special informants?)

10. What is your overall assessment of the ways in which and the degrees to which the researcher may or may not have been biased or less than objective in the data collection? Enumerate and document the ways and degrees.

C. Data Matters

1. What techniques of data collection were used? Participant observation? Intensive interviewing? What other sources or techniques were employed, if any (e.g., published accounts, historical archives, archived quantitative data sets, survey questionnaires, life histories)?

2. What was the relative "balance" and "mix" of data sources?

3. If pertinent, indicate the number of people observed or interviewed (and for how long), the period of time over which the study was conducted, and the number and nature of other sources located and scrutinized.

4. What technical, physical, or other devices did the author employ in moving from collected data to written analysis (for example, word processors, odd filing systems, special workplaces and practices, particular forms of coding, theoretical memoing)?

5. Where there are several and diverse "cases," how were these selected?

6. Overall, how convinced are you that the author has collected data adequate to the matter at hand? What additional data, if any, should reasonably have been collected?

D. Topics Addressed

1. What more abstract topics (units and aspects of social situations or settings) were addressed?

2. What less abstract versions of these topics does the author formulate?

3. Count the number of pages devoted to each more specific topic you have enumerated and compute the percentage of pages of the report devoted to each. Take the total number of pages in the report as your base for these percentages, count pages no finer than a half page, and round all percentages to the nearest whole number. Set the topics as a vertical column with summary labels for each aspect and report these calculations.

E. Questions Addressed

1. Which of the eight questions treated in Chapter 7 are addressed?

2. What less abstract versions of these questions does the author formulate?

3. Count the number of pages devoted to answering each of these more specific questions and compute the percentage of pages of the report devoted to each. As above for topics, use the total pages in the report as your base, count pages no finer than a half page, and round the percentages to the nearest whole number. Set the questions as a vertical column with summary labels and report these calculations.

F. Analysis Propounded

1. Enumerate and state the analytic propositions or themes the author offers about the topics and questions.

2. Count the number of pages in which these analytic themes are discussed directly (as distinct from data and the like leading up to them) and compute the percentage of pages of the report so devoted to each theme. Set as a vertical column with summary labels and report these percentages. (Once more, use the total pages as the base and round to whole numbers.)

G. Literature Context

1. Into what theoretical, conceptual, or kindred context does the author place her or his propositional answers to questions about topics?

2. What claims about the advance of knowledge, the disproof of mistaken theory, or other assertions does the author make to justify the report?

H. Data Presentation

1. What is the percentage relation between text that presents quantitative or qualitative data, on the one hand, and analytic text, on the other hand? Using whole pages as your smallest unit, count the pages devoted to each and compute and report the percentage devoted to each.

2. Focusing on only the pages presenting data, what percentage are quantitative data (i.e., presenting and discussing numbers) and what percentage are qualitative data (i.e., providing prose reports of what was studied)?

3. To what degree does the author move back and forth between presentation of data and analytic discussion of it? Extreme possibilities in this are:

    a. The first and last sections are analytic text, but everything in between is data with no analysis.

    b. Every section right down to the paragraph level moves back and forth between data and analytic text.

I. Overall

1. Overall, how clearly and logically organized is the report? Is it easy or difficult to grasp as a whole? Why?

2. How convinced or unconvinced are you by whatever is propounded by the author? Why?

3. In what ways does the work either inhibit or facilitate future work on the same or larger topics? In particular, is it set in a theoretical context sufficient to make its current and future relevance clear?

4. What are some such future relevances (Question I.3, immediately above)?

5. What consequences has the report had for the author, the people studied, opponents of the people studied, and the wider social and political world? In other words, what are (or might be) the political and social meanings of the report? (It is difficult to know these matters for many reports. For articles, some sense of consequences can be constructed from study of the report's history as reported in the *Social Science Citation Index*. For books, the same source is useful, but reviews are also available for many books; these can be located through the *Social Science Citation Index* and through indexes of book reviews.)

REFERENCES

Adler, Patricia A., and Peter Adler. 1987. *Membership Roles in Field Research.* Newbury Park, CA: Sage.

———. 1994. "Observational Techniques." Pp. 377–392 in *Handbook of Qualitative Research,* edited by N. K. Denzin and Y. S. Lincoln. Thousand Oaks, CA: Sage.

Adler, Patricia, Peter Adler, and John M. Johnson (eds.). 1992. *Street Corner Society Revisited.* Newbury Park, CA: Sage. (A special issue of the *Journal of Contemporary Ethnography* 21 [no. 1])

Agar, Michael. 1986. *Independents Declared: The Dilemmas of Independent Trucking.* Washington, DC: Smithsonian Institution Press.

———. 1990. "Text and Fieldwork: Exploring the Excluded Middle." *Journal of Contemporary Ethnography* 19 (no. 1): 73–88.

———. 1991. "The Right Brain Strikes Back." Pp. 181–194 in *Using Computers in Qualitative Research,* edited by N. G. Fielding and R. M. Lee. Newbury Park, CA: Sage.

Aldridge, Alan E. 1989. "Men, Women and Clergymen: Opinion and Authority in a Sacred Organization." *Sociological Review* 37 (no. 1): 43–64.

———. 1993. "Negotiating Status: Social Scientists and Anglican Clergy." *Journal of Contemporary Ethnography* 22 (no. 1): 97–112.

Allen, Barbara, and William L. Montess. 1981. *From Memory to History: Using Oral Sources in Local Historical Research.* Nashville, TN: American Association for State and Local History.

Allon, Natalie. 1979. "The Interrelationship of Process and Content in Field Work." *Symbolic Interaction* 2 (no. 2): 63–78.

Altheide, David L. 1987. "Ethnographic Content Analysis." *Qualitative Sociology* 10 (no. 1): 65–77.

Altheide, David L., and John M. Johnson. 1994. "Criteria for Assessing Interpretative Validity in Qualitative Research." Pp. 485–499 in *Handbook of Qualitative Research,* edited by N. K. Denzin and Y. S. Lincoln. Thousand Oaks, CA: Sage.

American Sociological Association. 1989. *Code of Ethics.* Washington, DC: American Sociological Association.

Anderson, Elijah. 1990. *Streetwise: Race, Class, and Change in an Urban Community.* Chicago: University of Chicago Press.

Anderson, Nels. 1923. *The Hobo.* Chicago: University of Chicago Press.

Angrosino, Michael V. 1989. *Documents of Interaction: Biography, Autobiography and Life History in Social Science Perspective.* Gainesville: University of Florida Press.

Arthur, P. 1987. "Elite Studies in a 'Paranocracy': The Northern Ireland Case." In *Research Methods for Elite Studies*, edited by G. Moyser and M. Wagstaffe. London: Allen and Unwin.

Atkinson, J. Maxwell, and John Heritage (eds.). 1984. *Structures of Social Action: Studies in Conversation Analysis.* Cambridge, UK: Cambridge University Press.

Atkinson, Paul. 1990. *The Ethnographic Imagination: Textual Constructions of Reality.* New York: Routledge.

————. 1992. *Understanding Ethnographic Texts.* Newbury Park, CA: Sage.

Aversa, Alfred Jr. 1990. "When Blue Collars and White Collars Meet at Play: The Case of the Yacht Club." *Qualitative Sociology* 13 (no. 1): 63–83.

Babbie, Earl R. 1995. *The Practice of Social Research* (7th ed.). Belmont, CA: Wadsworth.

Baker, Alan R. H., and Mark Bellenge (eds.). 1982. *Period and Place: Research Methods in Historical Geography.* New York: Cambridge University Press.

Baker, Therese L. 1994. *Doing Social Research* (2nd ed.). New York: McGraw-Hill.

Barley, Nigel. 1986. *The Innocent Anthropologist: Notes from a Mud Hut.* Middlesex, UK: Penguin.

Barzun, Jacques, and Henry F. Graff. 1977. *The Modern Researcher* (3rd ed.). New York: Harcourt Brace Jovanovich.

Baumgartner, M. P. 1988. *The Moral Order of the Suburb.* New York: Oxford University Press.

Beck, Jerome, and Marsha Rosenbaum. 1994. *Pursuit of Ecstasy: The MDMA Experience.* Albany: State University of New York Press.

Becker, Howard S. (with a chapter by Pamela Richards). 1986. *Writing for Social Scientists: How to Start and Finish Your Thesis, Book, or Article.* Chicago: University of Chicago Press.

Becker, Howard, and Blanche Geer. 1970. "Participant Observation and Interviewing: A Comparison." Pp. 133–142 in *Qualitative Methodology: Firsthand Involvement with the Social World*, edited by W. J. Filstead. Chicago: Markham. (Originally published in 1957)

Becker, Howard S., Blanche Geer, and Everett Hughes. 1968. *Making the Grade.* New York: Wiley.

Becker, Howard S., Blanche Geer, Everett Hughes, and Anselm Strauss. 1961. *Boys in White: Student Culture in Medical School.* Chicago: University of Chicago Press.

Beckford, James. 1983. "Talking of Apostasy: Telling Tales and 'Telling' Tales." Pp. 281–298 in *Accounting for Action*, edited by M. Muklay and N. Gilbert. London: Greenwood Press.

Bell, Robert. 1981. *Worlds of Friendship.* Beverly Hills, CA: Sage.

Benford, Robert D. 1993. "You Could Be the Hundredth Monkey: Collective Identity and Vocabularies of Motive in the Nuclear Disarmament Movement." *Sociological Quarterly* 34 (no. 2): 195–216.

Berg, Bruce L. 1989. *Qualitative Research Methods for the Social Sciences.* Boston: Allyn & Bacon.

Berger, Peter L. 1963. *Invitation to Sociology.* Garden City, NY: Doubleday.

————. 1971. "Sociology and Freedom." *American Sociologist* 6: 1–5.

————. 1979. "Sociology as a Form of Consciousness." Pp. 2–18 in *Social Interaction*, edited by H. Robboy, S. Greenblatt, and C. Clark. New York: St. Martin's Press.

Berger, Peter L., and Thomas Luckmann. 1967. *The Social Construction of Reality.* Garden City, NY: Doubleday.

Bernard, H. Russell. 1994. *Research Methods for Anthropology: Qualitative and Quantitative Approaches.* Thousand Oaks, CA: Sage.

Bernstein, Stan. 1978. "Getting It Done: Notes on Student Fritters." Pp. 17–23 in *Interaction in Everyday Life,* edited by J. Lofland. Beverly Hills, CA: Sage.

Best, Joel. 1994. "Lost in the Ozone Again: The Postmodernist Fad and Interactionist Foibles." In *Studies in Symbolic Interaction* (Vol. 17), edited by N. K. Denzin. Greenwich, CT: JAI Press.

Biernacki, Patrick, and Dan Waldorf. 1981. "Snowball Sampling: Problems and Techniques of Chain Referral Sampling." *Sociological Methods and Research* 10 (no. 2): 141–163.

Biggart, Nicole W. 1989. *Charismatic Capitalism: Direct Selling Organizations in America.* Chicago: University of Chicago Press.

Blank, Grant (ed.). 1988. *New Technology and the Nature of Sociological Work.* New Brunswick, NJ: Transaction Publishers. (Special issue of *American Sociologist* 19 [no. 1])

Bluebond-Langer, Myra. 1978. *The Private Worlds of Dying Children.* Princeton, NJ: Princeton University Press.

Blumer, Herbert. 1969. *Symbolic Interactionism: Perspective and Method.* Englewood Cliffs, NJ: Prentice-Hall.

Boden, Deidre, and Don H. Zimmerman (eds.). 1991. *Talk and Social Structure: Studies in Ethnomethodology and Conversation Analysis.* Berkeley: University of California Press.

Bogdan, Robert. 1980. "Interviewing People Labeled Retarded." Pp. 235–243 in *Fieldwork Experience: Qualitative Approaches to Social Research,* edited by W. B. Shaffir, R. A. Stebbins, and A. Turowetz. New York: St. Martin's Press.

Bok, Sissela. 1978. *Lying: Moral Choice in Public and Private Life.* New York: Pantheon.

Bosk, Charles L. 1979. *Forgive and Remember: Managing Medical Failure.* Chicago: University of Chicago Press.

———. 1985. "The Fieldworker as Watcher and Witness." *Hastings Center Report* 15 (no. 3): 10–14.

———. 1989. "The Fieldworker and the Surgeon." Pp. 135–144 in *In the Field: Readings on the Field Research Experience,* edited by C. D. Smith and W. Kornblum. New York: Praeger.

Brajuha, Mario, and Lyle Hallowell. 1986. "Legal Intrusion and the Politics of Fieldwork." *Urban Life* 14 (no. 4): 454–478.

Brewer, John, and Albert Hunter. 1989. *Multimethod Research: A Synthesis of Styles.* Newbury Park, CA: Sage.

Bronfenbrenner, Urie. 1952. "Principles of Professional Ethics." *American Psychologist* 7 (no. 8): 452–455.

Brown, Richard Harvey. 1977. *A Poetic for Sociology: Toward a Logic of Discovery for the Human Sciences.* New York: Cambridge University Press.

———. 1990. "Social Science and the Poetics of Public Truth." *Sociological Forum* 5 (no. 1): 55–74.

Brown, Richard Harvey (ed.). 1992. *Writing the Social Text: Poetics and Politics in Social Science Discourse.* Hawthorne, NY: Aldine de Gruyter.

Brunt, Lodewijk. 1975. "Anthropological Fieldwork in the Netherlands." Pp. 65–82 in *Current Anthropology in the Netherlands,* edited by P. Kloos and H. J. M. Claessen. Rotterdam: Anthropological Branch of the Netherlands Sociological and Anthropological Society.

———. 1979. "Lectori Salutem, On the Analysis of Abortion Letters in the Netherlands." *Netherlands Journal of Sociology* 15: 141–153.

Bulmer, Martin. 1982. "When Is Disguise Justified? Alternatives to Covert Participant Observation." *Qualitative Sociology* 5 (no. 4): 251–264.

Bulmer, Martin (ed.). 1982. *Social Research Ethics: An Examination of the Merits of Covert Participant Observation.* New York: Holmes & Meier.

Burawoy, Michael, Alice Burton, Ann Arnett Ferguson, Kathryn J. Fox, Joshua Gamson, Nadine Gartrell, Leslie Hurst, Charles Kurzman, Leslie Salzinger, Josepha Schiffman, and Shiori Ui. 1991. *Ethnography Unbound: Power and Resistance in the Modern Metropolis.* Berkeley: University of California Press.

Burgess, Robert G. 1984. *In the Field: An Introduction to Field Research.* London: Allen and Unwin.

Cahill, Spencer (with William Distler, Cynthia Lachowetz, Andrea Meaney, Robyn Tarallo, and Tenna Willard). 1985. "Meanwhile Backstage: Public Bathrooms and the Interaction Order." *Urban Life* 14 (no. 1): 33–58.

Cahill, Spencer. 1986. "Language Practices and Self Definition: The Case of Gender Identity Acquisition." *Sociological Quarterly* 27 (no. 3): 295–311.

———. 1989. "Fashioning Males and Females: Appearance Management and the Social Reproduction of Gender." *Symbolic Interaction* 12 (no. 2): 281–298.

———. 1990. "Childhood and Public Life: Reaffirming Biographical Divisions." *Social Problems* 37 (no. 3): 390–402.

Campbell, Colin. 1983. *Governments Under Stress: Political Executives and Key Bureaucrats in Washington, London, and Ottawa.* Toronto: University of Toronto Press.

Cancian, Francesca M. 1992. "Feminist Science: Methodologies that Challenge Inequality." *Gender and Society* 6 (no. 4): 623–642.

———. 1993. "Conflicts Between Activist Research and Academic Success: Participatory Research and Alternative Strategies." *American Sociologist* 24 (no. 1): 92–106.

Cannon, Sue. 1992. "Reflections on Fieldwork in Stressful Situations." Pp. 147–182 in *Studies in Qualitative Methodology* (Vol. 3), edited by R. G. Burgess. Greenwich, CT: JAI Press.

Caplow, Theodore, Howard M. Bahr, Bruce Chadwick, and Margaret Holmes Williamson. 1982. *Middletown Families: Fifty Years of Change and Continuity.* Minneapolis: University of Minnesota Press.

Carpenter, Cheryl, Barry Glassner, Bruce Johnson, and Julia Loughlin. 1988. *Kids, Drugs, and Crime.* Lexington, MA: Lexington Books.

Cassell, Joan (ed.). 1987. *Children in the Field: Anthropological Experiences.* Philadelphia: Temple University Press.

Cassell, Joan. 1988. "The Relationship of Observer to Observed When Studying Up." Pp. 89–108 in *Studies in Qualitative Methodology* (Vol. 1), edited by R. G. Burgess. Greenwich, CT: JAI Press.

Cassell, Joan, and Sue-Ellen Jacobs. 1987. *Handbook on Ethical Issues in Anthropology.* Washington, DC: American Anthropological Association.

Cavendish, Rebecca. 1982. *Women on the Line.* London: Routledge & Kegan Paul.

Cesara, Manda. 1982. *Reflections of a Woman Anthropologist: No Hiding Place.* New York: Academic Press.

Charmaz, Kathy. 1983. "The Grounded Theory Method: An Explication and Interpretation." Pp. 109–126 in *Contemporary Field Research: A Collection of Readings*, edited by R. M. Emerson. Boston: Little, Brown.

———. 1991. *Good Days, Bad Days: The Self in Chronic Illness and Time*. New Brunswick, NJ: Rutgers University Press.

———. 1994. "Between Postmodernism and Positivism: Implications for Methods." In *Studies in Symbolic Interaction* (Vol. 17), edited by N. K. Denzin. Greenwich, CT: JAI Press.

Christie, Agatha. 1934. *Murder in Three Acts*. New York: Popular Library. (Originally published in the United States by Dodd, Mead & Co.)

Clark, Candace. 1987. "Sympathy Biography and Sympathy Margin." *American Journal of Sociology* 93 (no. 2): 290–321.

———. 1989. "Studying Sympathy: Methodological Confessions." Pp. 137–151 in *The Sociology of Emotions: Original Essays and Research Papers*, edited by D. D. Franks and E. D. McCarthy. Greenwich, CT: JAI Press.

Clay, Grady. 1980. *How to Read an American City*. Chicago: University of Chicago Press.

Clifford, James, and George E. Marcus (eds.). 1986. *Writing Culture: The Poetics and Politics of Ethnography*. Berkeley: University of California Press.

Clough, Patricia Ticineto. 1992. *The End(s) of Ethnography: From Realism to Social Criticism*. Newbury Park, CA: Sage.

Cohn, Carol. 1987. "Sex and Death in the Rational World of Defense Intellectuals." *Signs: Journal of Women in Culture and Society* 12 (no. 4): 687–718.

Colvard, Richard. 1967. "Interaction and Identification in Reporting Field Research: A Critical Reconsideration of Protective Procedures." Pp. 319–358 in *Ethics, Politics and Social Research*, edited by G. Sjoberg. Cambridge, MA: Schenkman.

Connidis, Ingrid. 1983. "Integrating Qualitative and Quantitative Methods in Survey Research on Aging: An Assessment." *Qualitative Sociology* 6 (no. 4): 334–352.

Cooley, Charles Horton. 1926. "The Roots of Social Knowledge." *American Journal of Sociology* 32: 59–79.

Coser, Lewis. 1965. *Georg Simmel*. Englewood Cliffs, NJ: Prentice-Hall.

Cressey, Paul G. 1932. *The Taxi-Dance Hall: A Sociological Study of Commercialized Recreation and City Life*. Chicago: University of Chicago Press.

Csikszentmihalyi, Mihaly, and Eugene Rochberg-Halton. 1981. *The Meaning of Things: Domestic Symbols and the Self*. Cambridge, UK: Cambridge University Press.

Cuba, Lee J. 1988. *A Short Guide to Writing About Social Science*. Dallas, TX: HarperCollins.

Dalton, Melville. 1959. *Men Who Manage: Fusions of Feeling and Theory in Administration*. New York: Wiley.

Daniels, Arlene K. 1983. "Self-Deception and Self-Discovery in Fieldwork." *Qualitative Sociology* 6 (no. 3): 195–214.

———. 1988. *Invisible Careers: Civic Leaders from the Volunteer World*. Chicago: University of Chicago Press.

Davis, Fred. 1959. "The Cabdriver and His Fare: Facets of a Fleeting Relationship." *American Journal of Sociology* 65 (no. 2): 158–165.

———. 1960. *Interview Guide for Problems of the Handicapped in Everyday Social Situations*. (Unpublished)

———. 1961. "Comment on 'Initial Interaction of Newcomers in Alcoholics Anonymous.'" *Social Problems* 8: 35.

———. 1972. *Illness, Interaction and the Self.* Belmont, CA: Wadsworth.

———. 1973. "The Martian and the Convert: Ontological Polarities in Social Research." *Urban Life* 2 (no. 3): 333–343.

———. 1974. "Stories and Sociology." *Urban Life* 3 (no. 3): 310–316.

Davis, Murray S. 1971. "That's Interesting! Toward a Phenomenology of Sociology and a Sociology of Phenomenology." *Philosophy of Social Science* 1: 309–344.

Davis, Murray S., and Catherine J. Schmidt. 1977. "The Obnoxious and the Nice: Some Sociological Consequences of Two Psychological Types." *Sociometry* 40: 201–213.

Dawson, Lorne, and Robert Prus. 1993a. "Interactionist Ethnography and Postmodernist Discourse: Affinities and Disjunctures in Approaching Human Lived Experience." Pp. 283–297 in *Studies in Symbolic Interaction* (Vol. 15), edited by N. K. Denzin. Greenwich, CT: JAI Press.

———. 1993b. "Human Enterprise, Intersubjectivity, and the Ethnographic Other." Pp. 129–139 in *Studies in Symbolic Interaction* (Vol. 15), edited by N. K. Denzin. Greenwich, CT: JAI Press.

———. 1994. "Postmodernism and Linguistic Reality Versus Symbolic Interactionism and Obdurate Reality." In *Studies in Symbolic Interaction* (Vol. 17), edited by N. K. Denzin. Greenwich, CT: JAI Press.

Denzin, Norman K. 1971. "The Logic of Naturalistic Inquiry." *Social Forces* 50: 166–182.

———. 1984. "Toward a Phenomenology of Domestic, Family Violence." *American Journal of Sociology* 90 (no. 3): 483–513.

———. 1989. *Interpretive Interactionism.* Newbury Park, CA: Sage.

———. 1992a. *Symbolic Interactionism and Cultural Studies: The Politics of Interpretation.* Oxford, UK: Blackwell.

———. 1992b. "Whose Cornerville Is It, Anyway?" *Journal of Contemporary Ethnography* 21 (no. 1): 120–132.

Denzin, Norman K., and Yvonna S. Lincoln (eds.). 1994. *Handbook of Qualitative Research.* Thousand Oaks, CA: Sage.

Deutscher, Irwin. 1973. *What We Say/What We Do: Sentiments and Acts.* New York: Scott, Foresman.

DeVries, Raymond G. 1985. *Regulating Birth: Midwives, Medicine, & the Law.* Philadelphia: Temple University Press.

DiIorio, Judith A., and Michael R. Nusbaumer. 1993. "Securing Our Sanity: Anger Management Among Abortion Escorts." *Journal of Contemporary Ethnography* 21 (no. 4): 411–438.

Dorn, Pamela. 1986. "Gender and Personhood: Turkish Jewish Proverbs and the Politics of Reputation." *Women's Studies International Forum* 9: 295–301.

Douglas, Jack D. 1976. *Investigative Social Research: Individual and Team Field Research.* Newbury Park, CA: Sage.

Douglas, Jack, and Paul K. Rasmussen (with Carol Ann Glanagan). 1977. *The Nude Beach.* Beverly Hills, CA: Sage.

Dowdall, George, and Janet Golden. 1989. "Photographs as Data: An Analysis of Images from a Mental Hospital." *Qualitative Sociology* 12 (no. 2): 183–214.

Duneier, Mitchell. 1992. *Slim's Table: Race, Respectability, and Masculinity.* Chicago: University of Chicago Press.

Durkheim, Emile. 1951. *Suicide.* Glencoe, IL: Free Press. (Originally published in 1897)

Duster, Troy, David Matza, and David Wellman. 1979. "Field Work and the Protection of Human Subjects." *American Sociologist* 14: 136–142.

Ebaugh, Helen Rose Fuchs. 1977. *Out of the Cloister: A Study of Organizational Dilemmas.* Austin: University of Texas Press.

———. 1988. *Becoming an EX: The Process of Role Exit.* Chicago: University of Chicago Press.

Ellen, R. F. (ed.) 1984. *Ethnographic Research: A Guide to General Conduct.* Orlando, FL: Academic Press.

Ellis, Carolyn. Forthcoming. " 'There Are Survivors': Telling a Story of Sudden Death." *Sociological Quarterly.*

Ellis, Carolyn, and Arthur P. Bochner. 1992. "Telling and Performing Personal Stories: The Constraints of Choice in Abortion." Pp. 79–101 in *Investigating Subjectivity: Research on Lived Experience,* edited by C. Ellis and M. G. Flaherty. Newbury Park, CA: Sage.

Ellis, Carolyn, and Michael G. Flaherty (eds.). 1992. *Investigating Subjectivity: Research on Lived Experience.* Newbury Park, CA: Sage.

Ellis, Carolyn, and Eugene Weinstein. 1986. "Jealousy and the Social Psychology of Emotional Experience." *Journal of Social & Personal Relationships* 3 (no. 3): 337–357.

El-Or, Tamar. 1992. "Do You Really Know How They Make Love? The Limits on Intimacy with Ethnographic Informants." *Qualitative Sociology* 15 (no. 1): 53–72.

Emerson, Robert M. (ed.) 1988. *Contemporary Field Research: A Collection of Readings.* Prospect Heights, IL: Waveland Press. (Originally published in 1983)

Epstein, Barbara L. 1991. *Political Culture and Cultural Revolution: Nonviolent Direct Action in the 1970's and 1980's.* Berkeley: University of California Press.

Erikson, Kai T. 1967. "A Comment on Disguised Observation in Sociology." *Social Problems* 14 (no. 4): 366–373.

Erlandson, David A., Edward L. Harris, Barbara L. Skipper, and Steve D. Allen. 1993. *Doing Naturalistic Inquiry: A Guide to Methods.* Newbury Park, CA: Sage.

Fantasia, Rick. 1988. *Cultures of Solidarity: Consciousness, Action and Contemporary American Workers.* Berkeley: University of California Press.

Faulkner, Robert R. 1985. *Hollywood Studio Musicians: Their Work Careers in the Recording Industry.* Lanham, MD: University Press of America. (Originally published in 1971)

Fay, Brian. 1987. *Critical Social Science: Liberation and Its Limits.* Ithaca, NY: Cornell University Press.

Feagin, Joe R., Anthony M. Orum, and Gideon Sjoberg (eds.). 1991. *A Case for the Case Study.* Chapel Hill: University of North Carolina Press.

Fetterman, David M. 1989. *Ethnography Step by Step.* Newbury Park, CA: Sage.

Fielding, Nigel G., and Raymond M. Lee (eds.). 1991. *Using Computers in Qualitative Research.* Newbury Park, CA: Sage.

Fields, Echo E. 1988. "Qualitative Content Analysis of Television News: Systematic Techniques." *Qualitative Sociology* 11 (no. 3): 183–193.

Fine, Gary Alan. 1980. "Cracking Diamonds: The Observer Role in Little League Baseball Settings and the Acquisition of Social Competence." Pp. 117–132 in *Fieldwork Experience: Qualitative Approaches to Social Research,* edited by W. B. Shaffir, R. Stebbins, and A. Turowetz. New York: St. Martin's Press.

———. 1987. *With the Boys: Little League Baseball and Preadolescent Culture.* Chicago: University of Chicago Press.

———. 1988. "The Ten Commandments of Writing." *American Sociologist* 19 (no. 2): 152–157.

———. 1993. "Ten Lies of Ethnography: Moral Dilemmas In Field Research." *Journal of Contemporary Ethnography* 22 (no. 3): 267–294.

Fine, Gary Alan, and Barry Glassner. 1979. "Participant Observation with Children: Promise and Problems." *Urban Life* 8 (no. 2): 153–174.

Fine, Gary Alan, and Kent L. Sandstrom. 1988. *Knowing Children: Participant Observation with Minors.* Newbury Park, CA: Sage.

Fineman, Stephen (ed.). 1993. *Emotion in Organizations.* Newbury Park, CA: Sage.

Fisher, Bradley J. 1987. "Illness Career Descent in Institutions for the Elderly." *Qualitative Sociology* 10 (no. 2): 132–145.

Florez, Carl P., and George L. Kelling. 1984. "The Hired Hand and the Lone Wolf." *Urban Life* 12 (no. 4): 423–443.

Fontana, Andrea, and James H. Frey. 1994. "Interviewing: The Art of Science." Pp. 361–376 in *Handbook of Qualitative Research,* edited by N. K. Denzin and Y. S. Lincoln. Thousand Oaks, CA: Sage.

Fox, Greer Litton, Marie Colombo, William F. Clevenger, and Celia Ferbuson. 1988. "Parental Division of Labor in Adolescent Sexual Socialization." *Journal of Contemporary Ethnography* 17 (no. 3): 285–308.

Friedman, Norman L. 1974. "Cookies and Contests: Notes on Ordinary Occupational Deviance and Its Neutralization." *Sociological Symposium* 11 (no. 1): 1–9.

———. 1990a. "Autobiographical Sociology." *American Sociologist* 21 (no. 1): 60–66.

———. 1990b. "Conventional Covert Ethnographic Research by a Worker: Considerations from Studies Conducted as a Substitute Teacher, Hollywood Actor, and Religious School Supervisor." Pp. 99–120 in *Studies in Qualitative Methodology* (Vol. 2), edited by R. G. Burgess. Greenwich, CT: JAI Press.

Fuller, Linda. 1986. "Changes in the Relationship Among the Unions, Administration, and the Party at the Cuban Workplace, 1959–1982." *Latin American Perspectives* 13: 6–32.

———. 1987. "Power at the Workplace: The Resolution of Worker–Management Conflict in Cuba." *World Development* 15: 139–152.

———. 1988. "Fieldwork in Forbidden Terrain: The U.S. State and the Case of Cuba." *American Sociologist* 19 (no. 2): 99–120.

Gage, John T. 1987. *The Shape of Reason.* New York: Macmillan.

Gallagher, Patrick. 1967. "Games Malinowski Played." *New Republic* 17: 24–26.

Galliher, John F. 1980. "Social Scientists' Ethical Responsibilities to Superordinates: Looking Up Meekly." *Social Problems* 27 (no. 3): 298–308. (Special issue on *Ethical Problems of Fieldwork* edited by Joan Cassell and Murray Wax)

Gamson, William A. 1992. *Talking Politics.* New York: Cambridge University Press.

Gans, Herbert. 1962. *The Urban Villagers: Group and Class in the Life of Italian-Americans.* New York: Free Press.

———. 1967. *The Levittowners: Ways of Life and Politics in a New Suburban Community.* New York: Pantheon.

————. 1972. "The Positive Functions of Poverty." *American Journal of Sociology* 78: 275–289.

Gardner, Carol Brooks. 1986. "Public Aid." *Urban Life* 15 (no. 1): 37–69.

Geertz, Clifford. 1988. *Works and Lives: The Anthropologist as Author.* Stanford, CA: Stanford University Press.

George, Susan. 1976. *How the Other Half Lives: The Real Reason for World Hunger.* Harmondsworth, UK: Penguin.

Giallombardo, Rose. 1966. "Social Roles in a Prison for Women." *Social Problems* 13: 268–288.

Gibbons, Don C., and Joseph F. Jones. 1975. *The Study of Deviance: Perspectives and Problems.* Englewood Cliffs, NJ: Prentice-Hall.

Gilbert, Nigel. 1993. *Researching Social Life.* Newbury Park, CA: Sage.

Gilmore, Sam. 1991. *Is Qualitative Research Reliable?* (Unpublished)

Glaser, Barney. 1978. *Theoretical Sensitivity.* Mill Valley, CA: Sociology Press.

Glaser, Barney, and Anselm Strauss. 1965. *Awareness of Dying.* Chicago: Aldine.

————. 1967. *The Discovery of Grounded Theory: Strategies for Qualitative Research.* Chicago: Aldine.

————. 1968. *Time for Dying.* Chicago: Aldine.

Glassner, Barry, and Jonathan D. Moreno (eds.). 1989. *The Qualitative–Quantitative Distinction in the Social Sciences.* Boston: Kluwer Academic.

Glazer, Myron. 1972. *The Research Adventure: Promise and Problems of Field Work.* New York: Random House.

Gmelch, George. 1971. "Baseball Magic." *Trans-action* 9: 39–41.

Goffman, Erving. 1959. *The Presentation of Self in Everyday Life.* Garden City, NY: Doubleday.

————. 1961. *Asylums: Essays on the Social Situation of Mental Patients and Other Inmates.* Garden City, NY: Doubleday.

————. 1962. "On Cooling the Mark Out: Some Aspects of Adaptation to Failure." Pp. 482–505 in *Human Behavior and Social Processes,* edited by A. Rose. Boston: Houghton Mifflin.

————. 1983. "The Interaction Order." *American Sociological Review* 48 (no. 1): 1–17.

————. 1989. "On Fieldwork." (Transcribed and edited by Lyn H. Lofland.) *Journal of Contemporary Ethnography* 18 (no. 2): 123–132.

Gold, Steven J. 1989. "Differential Adjustment Among New Immigrant Family Members." *Journal of Contemporary Ethnography* 17 (no. 4): 408–434.

Golde, Peggy (ed.). 1986. *Women in the Field: Anthropological Experiences* (2nd ed., expanded and updated). Berkeley: University of California Press.

Gordon, David F. 1987. "Getting Close by Staying Distant: Fieldwork with Proselytizing Groups." *Qualitative Sociology* 10 (no. 3): 267–287.

Gordon, Steven L. 1981. "The Sociology of Sentiments and Emotion." Pp. 562–592 in *Social Psychology: Sociological Perspectives,* edited by M. Rosenberg and R. Turner. New York: Basic Books.

————. 1985. "Micro-sociological Theories of Emotion." Pp. 133–147 in *Microsociological Theory: Perspectives on Sociological Theory* (Vol. 2), edited by H. J. Helle and S. N. Eisenstadt. Beverly Hills, CA: Sage.

Gould, Meredit. 1985. *Innovative Sources and Uses of Qualitative Data.* (Special issue of *Qualitative Sociology* 8 [no. 4])

Gouldner, Alvin. 1979. *The Future of Intellectuals and the Rise of the New Class.* New York: Seabury Press.

Gravel, Pierre Bettez, and Robert B. Marks Ridinger. 1988. *Anthropological Fieldwork.* New York: Garland.

Greenbaum, Thomas L. 1993. *The Handbook for Focus Group Research* (revised and expanded ed.). New York: Lexington Books.

Grønbjerg, Kirsten A. 1993. *Understanding Nonprofit Funding: Managing Revenues in Social Services and Community Development Organizations.* San Francisco: Jossey-Bass.

Gubrium, Jaber F. 1986. *Oldtimers and Alzheimers: The Descriptive Organization of Senility.* Greenwich, CT: JAI Press.

————. 1988. *Analyzing Field Reality.* Newbury Park, CA: Sage.

Gurney, Joan Neff. 1985. "Not One of the Guys: The Female Researcher in a Male-Dominated Setting." *Qualitative Sociology* 8 (no. 1): 42–62.

Gusfield, Joseph. 1981. *The Culture of Public Problems: Drinking-Driving and the Symbolic Order.* Chicago: University of Chicago Press.

Gusterson, Hugh. Forthcoming. *Livermore Scientists.* Berkeley: University of California Press.

Hall, John R. 1987. *Gone from the Promised Land: Jonestown in American Cultural History.* New Brunswick, NJ: Transaction Books.

Hall, Larry D., and Kimball P. Marshall. 1992. *Computing for Social Research: Practical Approaches.* Belmont, CA: Wadsworth.

Hamilton, Gary G., and Nicole Woolsey Biggart. 1984. *Governor Reagan, Governor Brown: A Sociology of Executive Power.* New York: Columbia University Press.

Hammersley, Martyn. 1990. *Reading Ethnographic Research: A Critical Guide.* London: Longman.

————. 1992. *What's Wrong with Ethnography.* London: Routledge.

Hammersley, Martyn, and Paul Atkinson. 1983. *Ethnography: Principles in Practice.* New York: Tavistock.

Harrison, Michael. 1974. "Preparation for Life in the Spirit: The Process of Initial Commitment to a Religious Movement." *Urban Life and Culture* 2 (no. 4): 390–401.

Hawkins, Keith. 1984. "Creating Cases in a Regulatory Agency." *Urban Life* 12 (no. 4): 371–395.

Hayakawa, S. I. (in consultation with Arthur Asa Berger and Arthur Chandler). 1978. *Language in Thought and Action* (4th ed.). New York: Harcourt Brace Jovanovich.

Heider, Karl. 1991. *Grand Valley Dani: Peaceful Warriors* (2nd ed.). Fort Worth, TX: Holt, Rinehart & Winston.

Heilman, Samuel C. 1980. "Jewish Sociologist: Native-as-Stranger." *American Sociologist* 15: 100–108.

Heirich, Max. 1970. *The Beginning: Berkeley, 1964.* New York: Columbia University Press.

————. 1971. *The Spiral of Conflict: Demonstrations at Berkeley 1964–1965.* New York: Columbia University Press.

Heritage, John. 1985. "Recent Developments in Conversation Analysis." *Sociolinguistics* 15: 1–18.

Hilbert, Richard A. 1980. "Covert Participant Observation: On Its Nature and Practice." *Urban Life* 9: 51–78.

Hochschild, Arlie. 1979. "Emotion Work, Feeling Rules and Social Structure." *American Journal of Sociology* 85 (no. 3): 551–575.

———. 1983. *The Managed Heart: Commercialization of Human Feeling.* Berkeley: University of California Press.

Hodson, Randy. 1991. "The Active Worker: Compliance and Autonomy at the Workplace." *Journal of Contemporary Ethnography* 20 (no. 1): 47–78.

Hoffman, Joan Eakin. 1980. "Problems of Access in the Study of Social Elites and Boards of Directors." Pp. 45–56 in *Fieldwork Experience: Qualitative Approaches to Social Research,* edited by W. B. Shaffir, R. A. Stebbins, and A. Turowetz. New York: St. Martin's Press.

Holmes, Lowell. 1987. *Quest for the Real Samoa: The Mead/Freeman Controversy and Beyond.* South Hadley, MA: Bergin & Garvey.

Horowitz, Ruth. 1983. *Honor and the American Dream: Culture and Identity in a Chicano Community.* New Brunswick, NJ: Rutgers University Press.

———. 1986. "Remaining an Outsider: Membership as a Threat to Research Rapport." *Urban Life* 14 (no. 4): 409–430.

———. 1989. "Getting In." Pp. 45–54 in *In the Field: Readings in the Field Research Experience,* edited by C. D. Smith and W. Kornblum. New York: Praeger.

Howell, Nancy. (ed.) 1990. *Surviving Fieldwork: A Report of the Advisory Panel on Health and Safety in Fieldwork.* Washington, DC: American Anthropological Association.

Huberman, A. Michael, and Matthew B. Miles. 1994. "Data Management and Analysis Methods." Pp. 428–444 in *Handbook of Qualitative Research,* edited by N. K. Denzin and Y. S. Lincoln. Thousand Oaks, CA: Sage.

Hummon, David. 1990. *Commonplaces: Community Ideology and Identity in American Culture.* Albany: State University of New York Press.

Humphreys, Laud. 1975. *Tearoom Trade: Impersonal Sex in Public Places* (enlarged ed.). Chicago: Aldine.

Irwin, John. 1970. *The Felon.* Englewood Cliffs, NJ: Prentice-Hall.

———. 1973. "Surfing: The Natural History of an Urban Scene." *Urban Life and Culture* 2 (no. 2): 131–160.

———. 1980. *Prisons in Turmoil.* Boston: Little, Brown.

———. 1985. *The Jail: Managing the Underclass in American Society.* Berkeley: University of California Press.

Jackson, Jean E. 1990. "'Déjà Entendu': The Liminal Qualities of Anthropological Fieldnotes." *Journal of Contemporary Ethnography* 19 (no. 1): 8–43.

Jacobus, Lee. 1989. *Writing as Thinking.* New York: Macmillan.

Joffe, Carole. 1977. *Friendly Intruders: Childcare Professionals and Family Life.* Berkeley: University of California Press.

———. 1986. *The Regulation of Sexuality: Experiences of Family Planning Workers.* Philadelphia: Temple University Press.

Johnson, John M. 1975. *Doing Field Research.* New York: Free Press.

Johnson, John M., and David L. Altheide. 1993. "The Ethnographic Ethic." Pp. 95–107 in *Studies in Symbolic Interaction* (Vol. 14), edited by N. K. Denzin. Greenwich, CT: JAI Press.

Johnson, Norris R. 1987. "Panic at 'The Who' Concert Stampede: An Empirical Assessment." *Social Problems* 34 (no. 4): 362–373.

———. 1988. "Fire in a Crowded Theater: A Descriptive Investigation of the Emergence of Panic." *International Journal of Mass Emergencies and Disasters* 6 (no. 1): 7–26.

Joseph, Suad. 1978. "Women and the Neighborhood Street in Borj Hammoud, Lebanon." Pp. 541–557 in *Women in the Muslim World*, edited by E. Fernea and B. Berzirgan. Cambridge, MA: Harvard University Press.

————. 1983. "Working Class Women's Networks in a Sectarian State: A Political Paradox." *American Ethnologist* 10: 1–22.

Junker, Buford H. 1960. *Field Work: An Introduction to the Social Sciences*. Chicago: University of Chicago Press.

Kalab, Kathleen. 1987. "Student Vocabularies of Motive: Accounts for Absence." *Symbolic Interaction* 10 (no. 1): 71–83.

Kanter, Rosabeth Moss. 1977. *Men and Women of the Corporation*. New York: Basic Books.

Karp, David A. 1973. "Hiding in Pornographic Bookstores: A Reconsideration of the Nature of Urban Anonymity." *Urban Life* 1 (no. 4): 427–452.

————. 1980. "Observing Behavior in Public Places: Problems and Strategies." Pp. 82–97 in *Fieldwork Experience: Qualitative Approaches to Social Research*, edited by W. B. Shaffir, R. A. Stebbins, and A. Turowetz. New York: St. Martin's Press.

Katovich, Michael A., and William A. Reese II. 1987. "The Regular: Full-Time Identities and Memberships in an Urban Bar." *Journal of Contemporary Ethnography* 16 (no. 3): 308–343.

Kelman, Herbert C. 1970. "Deception in Social Research." Pp. 65–75 in *The Values of Social Science*, edited by N. K. Denzin. Hawthorne, NY: Aldine.

————. 1972. "The Rights of the Subject in Social Research: An Analysis in Terms of Relative Power and Legitimacy." *American Psychologist* 27: 989–1016.

Kirk, Jerome, and Marc L. Miller. 1986. *Reliability and Validity in Qualitative Research*. Newbury Park, CA: Sage.

Klapp, Orrin. 1958. "Social Types." *American Sociological Review* 23: 673–681.

Klatch, Rebecca E. 1987. *Women of the New Right*. Philadelphia: Temple University Press.

Kleinman, Sherryl. 1984. *Equals Before God: Seminarians as Humanistic Professionals*. Chicago: University of Chicago Press.

Kleinman, Sherryl, and Martha A. Copp. 1993. *Emotions and Fieldwork*. Newbury Park, CA: Sage.

Kleinman, Sherryl, Barbara Stenross, and Martha McMahon. 1994. "Privileging Fieldwork over Interviewing: Consequences for Identity and Practice." *Symbolic Interaction* 17 (no. 1): 37–50.

Kochman, Thomas. 1969. "Rapping in the Black Ghetto." *Trans-action* 6: 26–34.

Komarovsky, Mirra. 1957. "Introduction." Pp. 1–30 in *Common Frontiers of the Social Sciences*, edited by M. Komarovsky. Glencoe, IL: Free Press.

Koonz, Claudia. 1987. *Mothers in the Fatherland: Women, the Family and Nazi Politics*. New York: St. Martin's Press.

Kornblum, William. 1974. *Blue Collar Community*. Chicago: University of Chicago Press.

Kotarba, Joseph A. 1980. "Discovering Amorphous Social Experience: The Case of Chronic Pain." Pp. 57–67 in *Fieldwork Experience: Qualitative Approaches to Social Research*, edited by W. B. Shaffir, R. A. Stebbins, and A. Turowetz. New York: St. Martin's Press.

Krieger, Susan. 1983. *The Mirror Dance: Identity in a Woman's Community*. Philadelphia: Temple University Press.

————. 1985. "Beyond 'Subjectivity': The Use of the Self in Social Science." *Qualitative Sociology* 8 (no. 4): 309–324.

————. 1991. *Social Science and the Self: Personal Essays on an Art Form*. New Brunswick, NJ: Rutgers University Press.

Kriesberg, Louis. 1982. *Social Conflicts*. Englewood Cliffs, NJ: Prentice-Hall.

Kuklick, Henrika. 1991. *The Savage Within: The Social History of British Anthropology, 1885–1945*. Cambridge, UK: Cambridge University Press.

Kumar, Nita. 1992. *Friends, Brothers, and Informants: Fieldwork Memoirs of Banaras*. Berkeley: University of California Press.

Kurtz, Paul. 1983. *In Defense of Secular Humanism*. Buffalo, NY: Prometheus Books.

————. 1992. *The New Skepticism: Inquiry and Reliable Knowledge*. Buffalo, NY: Prometheus Books.

Kyvig, David E., and Myron A. Marty. 1982. *Nearby History: Exploring the Past Around You*. Nashville, TN: American Association for State and Local History.

Lareau, Annette. 1989. *Home Advantage: Social Class and Parental Intervention in Elementary Education*. London: Falmer Press.

LeCompte, Margaret D., Wendy L. Milroy, and Judith Preissle (eds.). 1992. *The Handbook of Qualitative Research in Education*. San Diego, CA: Academic Press.

Lee, Raymond. 1992. "Nobody Said It Had to Be Easy: Postgraduate Field Research in Northern Ireland." In *Studies in Qualitative Methodology* (Vol. 3), edited by R. G. Burgess. Greenwich, CT: JAI Press.

Lemert, Edwin M. 1972. *Human Deviance, Social Problems and Social Control*. Englewood Cliffs, NJ: Prentice-Hall.

Levine, Felice J. 1993. "ASA Files Amicus Brief Protecting Confidential Research Information." *Footnotes* 21 (no. 5): 2.

Levy, Robert I. 1973. *Tahitians: Mind and Experience in the Society Islands*. Chicago: University of Chicago Press.

————. 1984. "Mead, Freeman, and Samoa: The Problem of Seeing Things as They Are." *Ethos* 12 (no. 1): 85–92.

Liebow, Elliot. 1967. *Tally's Corner: A Study of Negro Streetcorner Men*. Boston: Little, Brown.

————. 1993. *Tell Them Who I Am: The Lives of Homeless Women*. New York: Free Press.

Lincoln, Yvonne S., and Egon G. Guba. 1985. *Naturalistic Inquiry*. Beverly Hills, CA: Sage.

Lofland, John. 1977. *Doomsday Cult: A Study of Conversion, Proselytization, and Maintenance of Faith* (enlarged ed.). New York: Irvington.

————. 1985. *Protest: Studies of Collective Behavior and Social Movements*. New Brunswick, NJ: Transaction Books.

————. 1993. *Polite Protesters: The American Peace Movement of the 1980s*. Syracuse, NY: Syracuse University Press.

————. 1995. "Analytic Ethnography: Features, Failures, Futures." *Journal of Contemporary Ethnography* 24 (no. 1): 25–40.

Lofland, Lyn H. (ed.). 1980. "Reminiscences of Classic Chicago: The Blumer-Hughes Talk." *Urban Life* 9 (no. 3): 251–281.

Lofland, Lyn H. 1982. "Loss and Human Connection: An Exploration into the Nature of the Social Bond." Pp. 219–242 in *Personality, Roles and Social Behavior*, edited by W. Ickes and E. Knowles. New York: Springer-Verlag.

————. 1985a. "The Social Shaping of Emotion: The Case of Grief." *Symbolic Interaction* 8 (no. 2): 171–190.

————. 1985b. *A World of Strangers: Order and Action in Urban Public Space.* Prospect Heights, IL: Waveland Press. (Originally published by Basic Books in 1973)

Lopata, Helena Z. "Interviewing American Women." Pp. 68–81 in *Fieldwork Experience: Qualitative Approaches to Social Research,* edited by W. B. Shaffir, R. A. Stebbins, and A. Turowetz. New York: St. Martin's Press.

Lopreato, Joseph, and Letitia Alston. 1970. "Ideal Types and the Idealization Strategy." *American Sociological Review* 35 (1): 88–96.

Loseke, Donileen R. 1992. *The Battered Woman and Shelters: The Construction of Wife Abuse.* Albany: State University of New York Press.

Lowry, Ritchie P. 1965. *Who's Running This Town? Community Leadership and Social Change.* New York: Harper & Row.

Lutz, Catherine A. 1988. *Unnatural Emotions: Everyday Sentiments on a Micronesian Atoll and Their Challenge to Western Theory.* Chicago: University of Chicago Press.

Lutz, Catherine A., and Geoffrey M. White. 1986. "The Anthropology of Emotions." *Annual Review of Anthropology* 15: 405–436.

Lynd, Robert S., and Helen Merrell Lynd. 1929. *Middletown: A Study in Contemporary American Culture.* New York: Harcourt Brace & Co.

Maines, David R., and Jeffrey C. Bridger. 1992. "Narratives, Community and Land Use Decisions." *Social Science Journal* 29 (no. 4): 363–408.

Maines, David R., William Shaffir, and Allan Turowetz. 1980. "Leaving the Field in Ethnographic Research: Reflections on the Entrance–Exit Hypothesis." Pp. 261–281 in *Fieldwork Experiences: Qualitative Approaches to Social Research,* edited by W. Shaffir, R. A. Stebbins, and A. Turowetz. New York: St. Martin's Press.

Malinowski, Bronislaw. 1967. *A Diary in the Strict Sense of the Term.* New York: Harcourt Brace & World.

Mandell, Nancy. 1986. "Peer Interaction in Day Care Settings: Implications for Social Cognition." Pp. 55–79 in *Sociological Studies of Child Development* (Vol. 1), edited by P. A. Adler and P. Adler. Greenwich, CT: JAI Press.

————. 1988. "The Least-Adult Role in Studying Children." *Journal of Contemporary Ethnography* 16 (no. 4): 433–467.

Manning, Peter K. 1977. *Police Work.* Cambridge, MA: MIT Press.

Margolis, Eric. 1990. "Visual Ethnography: Tools for Mapping the AIDS Epidemic." *Journal of Contemporary Ethnography* 19 (no. 3): 370–391.

Marston, Peter J., Michael L. Hecht, and Tia Robers. 1987. "True Love Ways: The Subjective Experience and Communication of Romantic Love." *Journal of Social and Personal Relationships* 4 (no. 4): 387–408.

Martin, Susan Erlich. 1978. "Sexual Politics in the Workplace: The Interactional World of Policewomen." *Symbolic Interaction* 1 (no. 2): 44–60.

————. 1980. *Breaking and Entering: Policewomen on Patrol.* Berkeley: University of California Press.

Mathews, Jay. 1983. "Tempest Over Scholar's Ouster: Faculty Discounts China Controversy in Its Decision." *Washington Post,* December 13, p. A2.

Matza, David. 1969. *Becoming Deviant.* Englewood Cliffs, NJ: Prentice-Hall.

McCracken, Grant. 1988. *The Long Interview.* Newbury Park, CA: Sage.

McGuire, Meredith B. (with the assistance of Debra Kantor). 1988. *Ritual Healing in Suburban America.* New Brunswick, NJ: Rutgers University Press.

McNaron, Toni A. (ed.). 1985. *The Sister Bond: A Feminist View of a Timeless Connection.* New York: Pergamon.

McPhail, Clark. 1995. *Acting Together: The Social Organization of Crowds.* Hawthorne, NY: Aldine de Gruyter.

Melbin, Murray. 1987. *Night As Frontier: Colonizing the World After Dark.* New York: Free Press.

Mellard, James M. 1987. *Doing Tropology: Analysis of Narrative Discourse.* Urbana: University of Illinois Press.

Mennerick, Lewis A. 1974. "Client Typologies: A Method of Coping with Conflict in the Service Worker–Client Relationship." *Sociology of Work and Occupations* 1: 396–418.

Merry, Sally Engle. 1981. *Urban Danger: Life in a Neighborhood of Strangers.* Philadelphia: Temple University Press.

Merton, Robert K. 1968. *Social Theory and Social Structure* (enlarged ed.). New York: Free Press.

Miles, Matthew B., and A. Michael Huberman. 1994. *Qualitative Data Analysis: An Expanded Sourcebook* (2nd ed.). Thousand Oaks, CA: Sage.

Mills, C. Wright. 1959. *The Sociological Imagination.* New York: Oxford University Press.

Miner, Horace. 1939. *St. Denis: A French-Canadian Parish.* Chicago: University of Chicago Press.

Mitchell, Richard G. Jr. 1993. *Secrecy and Fieldwork.* Newbury Park, CA: Sage.

Monaghan, Peter. 1993a. "Sociologist Jailed Because He 'Wouldn't Snitch' Ponders the Way Research Ought to Be Done." *The Chronicle of Higher Education,* September 1, pp. A8–A9.

———. 1993b. "Free After 6 Months: Sociologist Who Refused To Testify is Released." *The Chronicle of Higher Education,* November 3, p. A14.

Monti, Daniel J. 1992. "On the Risks and Rewards of Going Native." *Qualitative Sociology* 15 (no. 3): 325–332.

Moore, Barrington. 1963. "Strategy in Social Science." Pp. 66–95 in *Sociology on Trial,* edited by M. Stein and A. Vidich. Englewood Cliffs, NJ: Prentice-Hall.

Morales, Edmundo. 1989a. *Cocaine: White Gold Rush in Peru.* Tucson: University of Arizona Press.

———. 1989b. "Researching Peasants and Drug Producers." Pp. 115–125 in *In the Field: Readings on the Field Research Experience,* edited by C. D. Smith and W. Kornblum. New York: Praeger.

Morgan, David L. 1988. *Focus Groups as Qualitative Research.* Newbury Park, CA: Sage.

———. 1993. "Using Qualitative Methods in the Development of Surveys." *Social Psychology: Newsletter of the Social Psychology Section of the American Sociological Association* 19 (no. 1): 1–3.

Morgan, David L. (ed.). 1993. *Successful Focus Groups: Advancing the State of the Art.* Newbury Park, CA: Sage.

Morgan, David L., and Margaret T. Spanish. 1984. "Focus Groups: A New Tool for Qualitative Research." *Qualitative Sociology* 7 (no. 3): 253–270.

Morse, Janice M. (ed.). 1994. *Critical Issues in Qualitative Research Methods.* Thousand Oaks, CA: Sage.

Moyser, George. 1988. "Non-Standardized Interviewing in Elite Research." Pp. 109–136 in *Research in Qualitative Methodology* (Vol. 1), edited by R. G. Burgess. Greenwich, CT: JAI Press.

Myerhoff, Barbara. 1978. *Number Our Days: A Triumph of Continuity and Culture Among Jewish Old People in an Urban Ghetto.* New York: Simon & Schuster.

Myers, Dowell. 1992. *Analysis with Local Census Data: Portraits of Change.* Boston: Academic Press.

Myers, James E. 1969. "Unleashing the Untrained: Some Observations on Student Ethnographers." *Human Organization* 28: 155–159.

Nash, Jeffrey, and Anedith J. Nash. 1994. "The Skyway System and Urban Space: Vitality in Enclosed Public Places." Pp. 167–181 in *The Community of the Streets,* edited by S. E. Cahill and L. H. Lofland. Greenwich, CT: JAI Press.

Oakley, Ann. 1981. "Interviewing Women: A Contradiction in Terms." Pp. 243–261 in *Doing Feminist Research,* edited by H. Roberts. London: Routledge and Kegan Paul.

———. 1985. *The Sociology of Housework.* Oxford, UK: Basil Blackwell. (Originally published in 1974)

Ortiz, Steve. 1994. "Shopping for Sociability in the Mall." Pp. 183–199 in *The Community of the Streets,* edited by S. E. Cahill and L. H. Lofland. Greenwich, CT: JAI Press.

Ostrander, Susan A. 1984. *Women of the Upper Class.* Philadelphia: Temple University Press.

———. 1993. "'Surely You're Not in This Just to Be Helpful': Access, Rapport, and Interviews in Three Studies of Elites." *Journal of Contemporary Ethnography* 22 (no. 1): 1–27.

Patai, Daphne. 1994. "Sick and Tired of Scholars' Nouveau Solipsism." *The Chronicle of Higher Education,* February 23, p. A52.

Peneff, Jean. 1985. "Fieldwork in Algeria." *Qualitative Sociology* 8 (no. 1): 65–78.

Pestello, Fred P. 1991. "Discounting." *Journal of Contemporary Ethnography* 20 (no. 1): 26–46.

Platt, Jennifer. 1988. "What Can Case Studies Do?" Pp. 1–23 in *Studies in Qualitative Methodology* (Vol. 1), edited by R. G. Burgess. Greenwich, CT: JAI Press.

Posner, Judith. 1980. "On Sociology Chic: Notes on a Possible Direction for Symbolic Interactionism." *Urban Life* 9 (1): 103–112.

Powdermaker, Hortense. 1966. *Stranger and Friend: The Way of an Anthropologist.* New York: W. W. Norton.

Prus, Robert. 1987. "Generic Social Processes: Maximizing Conceptual Development in Ethnographic Research." *Journal of Contemporary Ethnography* 16 (no. 3): 250–293.

———. 1994. "Generic Social Processes and the Study of Human Lived Experiences: Achieving Transcontextuality in Ethnographic Research." Pp. 436–458 in *Symbolic Interaction: An Introduction to Social Psychology,* edited by N. J. Herman and L. T. Reynolds. Dix Hills, NY: General Hall.

Punch, Maurice. 1986. *The Politics and Ethics of Fieldwork.* Newbury Park, CA: Sage.

———. 1994. "Politics and Ethics in Qualitative Research." Pp. 83–97 in *Handbook of Qualitative Research,* edited by N. K. Denzin and Y. S. Lincoln. Thousand Oaks, CA: Sage.

Radcliffe-Brown, A. R. 1935. "On the Concept of Function in Social Science." *American Anthropologist* 37: 394–402.

Rafaeli, Anat. 1989. "When Cashiers Meet Customers: An Analysis of the Role of Supermarket Cashiers." *Academy of Management Journal* 32 (no. 2): 245–273.

Rainwater, Lee, and D. J. Pittman. 1967. "Ethical Problems in Studying a Politically Sensitive and Deviant Community." *Social Problems* 14: 357–366.

Rauch, Jonathan. 1993. *Kindly Inquisitors: The New Attacks on Free Thought.* Chicago: University of Chicago Press.

Reed, Myer S., Jerry Burnette, and R. Troiden. 1977. "Wayward Cops: The Functions of Deviance in Groups Reconsidered." *Social Problems* 24: 565–575.

Reinharz, Shulamit. 1992. *Feminist Methods in Social Research.* New York: Oxford University Press.

———. 1993. "Neglected Voices and Excessive Demands in Feminist Research." *Qualitative Sociology* 16 (no. 1): 69–76.

Richards, Thomas J., and Lyn Richards. 1994. "Using Computers in Qualitative Research." Pp. 445–462 in *Handbook of Qualitative Research,* edited by N. K. Denzin and Y. S. Lincoln. Thousand Oaks, CA: Sage.

Richardson, Laurel. 1985. *The New Other Woman: Contemporary Single Women in Affairs with Married Men.* New York: Free Press.

———. 1990. *Writing Strategies: Reaching Diverse Audiences.* Newbury Park, CA: Sage.

———. 1992. "The Consequences of Poetic Representation: Writing the Other, Rewriting the Self." In *Investigating Subjectivity: Research on Lived Experience,* edited by C. Ellis and M. G. Flaherty. Newbury Park, CA: Sage.

———. 1994. "Writing: A Method of Inquiry." Pp. 516–529 in *Handbook of Qualitative Methodology,* edited by N. K. Denzin and Y. S. Lincoln. Thousand Oaks, CA: Sage.

Riecken, Henry W. 1969. "The Unidentified Interviewer." Pp. 39–44 in *Issues in Participant Observation: A Text and Reader,* edited by G. McCall and J. L. Simmons. Reading, MA: Addison-Wesley.

Rieder, Jonathan. 1985. *Canarsie: The Jews and Italians of Brooklyn Against Liberalism.* Cambridge, MA: Harvard University Press.

Riemer, Jeffrey W. 1977. "Varieties of Opportunistic Research." *Urban Life* 5 (4): 467–477.

Riessman, Catherine Kohler. 1993. *Narrative Analysis.* Newbury Park, CA: Sage.

Robins, Douglas M., Clinton R. Sanders, and Spencer E. Cahill. 1991. "Dogs and Their People: Pet-Facilitated Interaction in a Public Setting." *Journal of Contemporary Ethnography* 20 (no. 1): 3–25.

Rodale, Jerome Irving. 1978. *The Synonym Finder.* Erasmus, PA: Rodale Press.

Romero, Mary. 1992. *Maid in the U.S.A.* New York: Routledge.

Ronai, Carol Rambo. 1992. "The Reflexive Self Through Narrative: A Night in the Life of an Erotic Dancer/Researcher." Pp. 102–124 in *Investigating Subjectivity,* edited by C. Ellis and M. G. Flaherty. Newbury Park, CA: Sage.

Rosen, Ellen Israel. 1987. *Bitter Choices: Blue-Collar Women In and Out of Work.* Chicago: University of Chicago Press.

Roth, Julius. 1966. "Hired Hand Research." *American Sociologist* 1: 190–196.

———. 1970. "Comments on 'Secret Observation.'" Pp. 278–280 in *Qualitative Methodology: Firsthand Involvement with the Social World,* edited by W. J. Filstead. Chicago: Markham.

————. 1974. "Turning Adversity to Account." *Urban Life and Culture* 3 (no. 3): 347–361.

————. 1977. "Review of D. Caplowitz, The Poor Pay More." *Contemporary Sociology* 6 (no. 1): 115.

Rothschild-Whitt, Joyce. 1979. "The Collectivist Organization: An Alternative to Rational-Bureaucratic Models." *American Sociological Review* 44 (no. 4): 509–527.

Roy, Donald F. 1976. " 'Banana Time': Job Satisfaction and Informal Interaction." Pp. 274–300 in *Doing Social Life*, edited by J. Lofland. New York: Wiley. (Originally published in 1959–1960)

Ruzek, Sherryl. 1978. *The Women's Health Movement: Feminist Alternatives to Medical Control*. New York: Praeger.

Sanders, Clinton R. 1989. *Customizing the Body: The Art and Culture of Tattooing*. Philadelphia: Temple University Press.

————. 1994. "Stranger Than Fiction: Insights in Pitfalls in Post-Modern Ethnography." In *Studies in Symbolic Interaction* (Vol. 17), edited by N. K. Denzin. Greenwich, CT: JAI Press.

Sanjek, Roger. 1990a. "On Ethnographic Validity." Pp. 385–418 in *Fieldnotes: The Makings of Anthropology*, edited by R. Sanjek. Ithaca, NY: Cornell University Press.

————. 1990b. "A Vocabulary for Fieldnotes." Pp. 92–121 in *Fieldnotes: The Makings of Anthropology*, edited by R. Sanjek. Ithaca, NY: Cornell University Press.

Sanjek, Roger (ed.). 1990. *Fieldnotes: The Makings of Anthropology*. Ithaca, NY: Cornell University Press.

Scarce, Rik. 1990. *Ecowarriors: Understanding the Radical Environmental Movement*. Chicago: Noble Press.

————. 1994. "(No) Trial (But) Tribulations: When Courts and Ethnography Conflict." *Journal of Contemporary Ethnography* 23 (no. 2): 123–149.

Schatzman, Leonard, and Anselm Strauss. 1973. *Field Research: Strategies for a Natural Sociology*. Englewood Cliffs, NJ: Prentice-Hall.

Scheper-Hughes, Nancy. 1981. "Cui Bonum—For Whose Good?: A Dialogue with Sir Raymond Firth." *Human Organization* 40 (no. 4): 371–372.

————. 1992. *Death Without Weeping: The Violence of Everyday Life in Brazil*. Berkeley: University of California Press.

Schneider, Louis. 1975. "Ironic Perspective and Sociological Thought." Pp. 323–337 in *The Idea of Social Structure*, edited by L. Coser. New York: Harcourt Brace Jovanovich.

Schutz, Alfred. 1967. *The Phenomenology of the Social World*. Evanston, IL: Northwestern University Press. (Originally published in 1932)

Schwartz, Dona. 1989. "Visual Ethnography: Using Photography in Qualitative Research." *Qualitative Sociology* 12 (no. 2): 119–154.

Scott, Gini G. 1983. *The Magicians: A Study of the Use of Power in a Black Magic Group*. New York: Irvington.

Seidman, I. E. 1991. *Interviewing as Qualitative Research: A Guide for Researchers in Education and the Social Sciences*. New York: Teachers College Press.

Selznick, Philip. 1953. *TVA and the Grassroots: A Study in the Sociology of Formal Organization*. Berkeley: University of California Press.

————. 1960. *The Organizational Weapon: A Study of Bolshevik Strategy and Tactics*. New York: Free Press.

Shaffir, William B., Victor Marshall, and Jack Haas. 1980. "Competing Commitments: Unanticipated Problems of Field Research." *Qualitative Sociology* 2: 56–71.

Shaffir, William B., and Robert A. Stebbins (eds.). 1991. *Experiencing Fieldwork: An Inside View of Qualitative Research.* Newbury Park, CA: Sage.

Shils, Edward. 1961. "The Calling of Sociology." Pp. 1405–1448 in *Theories of Society: Foundations of Modern Sociological Theory* (Vol. 2), edited by T. Parsons, E. Shils, K. D. Naegele, and J. R. Pitts. New York: Free Press.

Shupe, Anson D., and David G. Bromley. 1980. "Walking the Tightrope: Dilemmas of Participant Observation of Groups in Conflict." *Qualitative Sociology* 2: 3–21.

Silverman, David. 1993. *Interpreting Qualitative Data: Methods for Analyzing Talk, Text, and Interaction.* Newbury Park, CA: Sage.

Sjoberg, Gideon (ed.). 1967. *Ethics, Politics and Social Research.* Cambridge, MA: Schenkman.

Skocpol, Theda (ed.). 1984. *Vision and Method in Historical Sociology.* New York: Cambridge University Press.

Sluka, J. A. 1990. "Participant Observation in Violent Social Contexts." *Human Organization* 49 (no. 2): 114–126.

Smith, Allen C., and Sherryl Kleinman. 1989. "Managing Emotions in Medical School: Students' Contacts with the Living and the Dead." *Social Psychology Quarterly* 52 (no. 1): 56–69.

Smith, Carolyn D., and William Kornblum (eds.). 1989. *In the Field: Readings on the Field Research Experience.* New York: Praeger.

Snow, David A. 1980. "The Disengagement Process: A Neglected Problem in Participant Observation Research." *Qualitative Sociology* 3 (no. 2): 100–122.

Snow, David, and Leon Anderson. 1993. *Down on Their Luck: A Study of Homeless Street People.* Berkeley: University of California Press.

Snow, David A., and Robert D. Benford. 1988. "Ideology, Frame Resonance, and Participant Mobilization." Pp. 197–217 in *International Social Movement Research: A Research Annual,* edited by B. Klandermans, H. Kriesi, and S. Tarrow. Greenwich, CT: JAI Press.

Snow, David A., Robert D. Benford, and Leon Anderson. 1986. "Fieldwork Roles and Informational Yield: A Comparison of Alternative Settings and Roles." *Urban Life* 14 (no. 4): 377–408.

Snow, David A., and Calvin Morrill. 1993. "Reflections on Anthropology's Ethnographic Crisis of Faith." *Contemporary Sociology* 22 (no. 1): 8–11.

Snow, David A., Cherylon Robinson, and Patricia McCall. 1991. "Cooling Out Men in Singles Bars and Nightclubs: Observations on Survival Strategies of Women in Public Places." *Journal of Contemporary Ethnography* 19: 423–449.

Snow, David A., Louis A. Zurcher, and Gideon Sjoberg. 1982. "Interviewing by Comment: An Adjunct to the Direct Question." *Qualitative Sociology* 5 (no. 2): 285–311.

Spangler, Eve. 1986. *Lawyers for Hire: Salaried Professionals at Work.* New Haven, CT: Yale University Press.

Spector, Malcolm. 1980. "Learning to Study Public Figures." Pp. 98–110 in *Field Work Experience: Qualitative Approaches to Social Research,* edited by W. B. Shaffir, R. A. Stebbins, and A. Turowetz. New York: St. Martin's Press.

Stacey, Judith. 1988. "Can There Be a Feminist Ethnography?" *Women's Studies International Forum* 11 (no. 1): 21–27.

Stack, Carol B. 1974. *All Our Kin: Strategies for Survival in a Black Community.* New York: Harper & Row.

Staggenborg, Suzanne. 1988. " 'Hired Hand Research' Revisited." *American Sociologist* 19 (no. 3): 260–269.

Stark, Rodney. 1994. *Sociology* (5th ed.). Belmont, CA: Wadsworth.

Startt, James D., and William David Sloan. 1989. *Historical Methods in Mass Communication.* Hillsdale, NJ: Lawrence Erlbaum.

Stearns, Peter N., and Carol Z. Stearns. 1985. "Emotionology: Clarifying the History of Emotions and Emotional Standards." *American Historical Review* 90 (no. 4): 813–836.

———— (eds.). 1988. *Emotions and Social Change: Toward a New Psychohistory.* New York: Holmes and Meier.

Stebbins, Robert A. 1987. "Fitting In: The Researcher as Learner and Participant." *Quality and Quantity* 21: 103–108.

Stinchcombe, Arthur L. 1975. "Merton's Theory of Social Structure." Pp. 11–33 in *The Idea of Social Structure,* edited by L. Coser. New York: Harcourt Brace Jovanovich.

Stocking, George Jr. (ed.). 1989. *Romantic Motives: Essays on Anthropological Sensibility.* Madison: University of Wisconsin Press.

Stoecker, Randy, and Edna Bonacich (eds.). 1992. *Participatory Research, Part I.* New Brunswick, NJ: Transaction Publishers. (Special issue of *American Sociologist* 23 [no. 4])

————. (eds.). 1993. *Participatory Research, Part II.* New Brunswick, NJ: Transaction Publishers. (Special issue of *American Sociologist* 24 [no. 1])

Strauss, Anselm L. 1987. *Qualitative Analysis for Social Scientists.* New York: Cambridge University Press.

Strauss, Anselm, and Juliet Corbin. 1990. *Basics of Qualitative Research: Grounded Theory Procedures and Techniques.* Newbury Park, CA: Sage.

————. 1994. "Grounded Theory Methodology: An Overview." Pp. 273–285 in *Handbook of Qualitative Research,* edited by N. K. Denzin and Y. S. Lincoln. Thousand Oaks, CA: Sage.

Strauss, Anselm, Leonard Schatzman, Rue Bucher, Danuta Erlich, and Melvin Sabshin. 1964. *Psychiatric Ideologies and Institutions.* New York: Free Press.

Sudnow, David. 1979. "Normal Crimes: Sociological Features of a Penal Code in a Public Defender Office." Pp. 473–496 in *Social Interaction,* edited by H. Robboy, S. Greenblatt, and C. Clark. New York: St. Martin's Press. (Originally published in 1965)

Suttles, Gerald D. 1968. *The Social Order of the Slum: Ethnicity and Territory in the Inner City.* Chicago: University of Chicago Press.

————. 1990. *The Man-Made City: The Land-Use Confidence Game in Chicago.* Chicago: University of Chicago Press.

Taylor, Steven J. 1987. "Observing Abuse: Professional Ethics and Personal Morality in Field Research." *Qualitative Sociology* 10 (no. 3): 288–302.

Tesch, Renata. 1990. *Qualitative Research: Analysis Types and Software Tools.* New York: Falmer Press.

Thomas, Robert J. 1993. "Interviewing Important People in Big Companies." *Journal of Contemporary Ethnography* 22 (no.1): 80–96.

————. 1994. *What Machines Can't Do: Politics and Technology in the Industrial Enterprise.* Berkeley: University of California Press.

Thorne, Barrie. 1979. "Political Activist as Participant Observer: Conflicts of Commitment in a Study of the Draft Resistance Movement of the 1960s." *Symbolic Interaction* 2 (no. 1): 73–88.

———. 1980. " 'You Still Takin' Notes?' Fieldwork and the Problems of Informed Consent." *Social Problems* 27 (no. 1): 284–297.

———. 1993. *Gender Play: Girls and Boys in School.* New Brunswick, NJ: Rutgers University Press.

Tilly, Charles. 1984. *Big Structures, Large Processes, Huge Comparisons.* New York: Russell Sage Foundation.

Tolich, Martin B. 1993. "Alienating and Liberating Emotions at Work: Supermarket Clerks' Performance of Customer Service." *Journal of Contemporary Ethnography* 22 (no. 3): 361–381.

Turabian, Kate L. (revised and enlarged by Bonnie Birtwistle Honigsblum). 1987. *A Manual for Writers of Term Papers, Theses, and Dissertations* (5th ed.). Chicago: University of Chicago Press.

Unruh, David. 1979. "Characteristics and Types of Participation in Social Worlds." *Symbolic Interaction* 2 (no. 2): 115–129.

———. 1980. "The Nature of Social Worlds." *Pacific Sociological Review* 23 (no. 3): 271–296.

———. 1983. *Invisible Lives: Social Worlds of the Aged.* Newbury Park, CA: Sage.

van Dijk, Teun A. 1985. *Discourse and Communication: New Approaches to the Analysis of Mass Media Discourse and Communication.* New York: W. DeGruyter.

van den Berghe, Pierre. 1967. "Research in South Africa: The Story of My Experience with Tyranny." Pp. 183–197 in *Ethics, Politics and Social Research,* edited by G. Sjoberg. Cambridge, MA: Schenkman.

Van Maanen, John. 1988. *Tales of the Field: On Writing Ethnography.* Chicago: University of Chicago Press.

Van Maanen, John, and John G. Kunda. 1989. " 'Real Feelings': Emotional Expression and Organizational Culture." *Research in Organizational Behavior* 11: 43–103.

Vaughan, Diane. 1990. *Uncoupling: Turning Points in Intimate Relationships.* New York: Vintage Books. (Originally published by Oxford University Press in 1986)

Vidich, Arthur, and Joseph Bensman. 1968. *Small Town in Mass Society: Class, Power and Religion in a Rural Community* (2nd ed.). Princeton, NJ: Princeton University Press.

Vidich, Arthur J., and Stanford M. Lyman. 1994. "Qualitative Methods: Their History in Sociology and Anthropology." Pp. 23–59 in *Handbook of Qualitative Research,* edited by N. K. Denzin and Y. S. Lincoln. Thousand Oaks, CA: Sage.

Walker, Andrew, and Rosalind Kimball Moulton. 1989. "Photo Albums: Images of Time and Reflections of Self." *Qualitative Sociology* 12 (no. 2): 183–214.

Waller, Willard. 1938. *The Family: A Dynamic Interpretation.* New York: Cordon.

Wallis, Roy. 1979. *Salvation and Protest: Studies of Social and Religious Movements.* New York: St. Martin's Press.

Walton, John. 1984. *Reluctant Rebels: Comparative Studies of Revolution and Underdevelopment.* New York: Columbia University Press.

Warner, W. Lloyd. 1959. *The Living and the Dead: A Study of the Symbolic Life of Americans.* New Haven, CT: Yale University Press.

Warner, W. Lloyd, and J. O. Low. 1947. *The Social System of the Modern Factory. The Strike: A Social Analysis.* New Haven, CT: Yale University Press.

Warner, W. Lloyd, and Paul S. Lunt. 1941. *The Social Life of a Modern Community.* New Haven, CT: Yale University Press.

———. 1942. *The Status System of a Modern Community.* New Haven, CT: Yale University Press.

Warner, W. Lloyd, and Leo Srole. 1945. *The Social Systems of American Ethnic Groups.* New Haven, CT: Yale University Press.

Warren, Carol A. B. 1977. "Fieldwork in the Gay World: Issues in Phenomenological Research." *Journal of Social Issues* 33: 93–107.

———. 1988. *Gender Issues in Field Research.* Newbury Park, CA: Sage.

Warren, Carol A. B., and William G. Staples. 1989. "Fieldwork in Forbidden Terrain: The State, Privatization and Human Subjects Regulations." *American Sociologist* 20 (no. 3): 263–277.

Warwick, D. P. 1975. "Social Scientists Ought to Stop Lying." *Psychology Today* February: 38, 40, 105–106.

———. 1980. *The Teaching of Ethics in the Social Sciences.* Hastings-on-Hudson, NY: Hastings Center.

———. 1982. "Tearoom Trade: Means and Ends in Social Research." Pp. 35–58 in *Social Research Ethics,* edited by M. Bulmer. London: Macmillan.

Wasserfall, Rahel. 1993. "Reflexivity, Feminism and Difference." *Qualitative Sociology* 16 (no. 1): 23–41.

Watkins, Beverly T. 1983. "When Researcher Becomes Participant: Scholars Note the Risks and Rewards." *The Chronicle of Higher Education,* November 2, pp. 5, 8, 9.

Wax, Murray, and Joan Cassell (eds.). 1979. *Federal Regulations: Ethical Issues and Social Research.* Boulder, CO: Westview Press.

Wax, Murray, and Joan Cassell. 1981. "From Regulation to Reflection: Ethics in Social Research." *American Sociologist* 16: 224–229.

Wax, Rosalie H. 1971. *Doing Fieldwork: Warnings and Advice.* Chicago: University of Chicago Press.

———. 1979. "Gender and Age in Fieldwork and Fieldwork Education: No Good Thing Is Done by Any Man Alone." *Social Problems* 26 (no. 5): 509–522.

Webb, Eugene, Donald T. Campbell, Richard D. Schwartz, Lee Sechrest, and Janet B. Grove. 1981. *Nonreactive Measures in the Social Sciences* (2nd ed.). Boston: Houghton Mifflin.

Weber, Max. 1949. *The Methodology of the Social Sciences.* New York: Free Press. (Sections originally published in 1904, 1910, 1917)

Weinberg, Martin S., and Colin J. Williams. 1972. "Fieldwork Among Deviants: Social Relations with Subjects and Others." Pp. 165–186 in *Research on Deviance,* edited by J. D. Douglas. New York: Random House.

Weiss, Robert S. 1990. *Staying the Course: The Emotional and Social Lives of Men Who Do Well at Work.* New York: Free Press.

———. 1994. *Learning From Strangers: The Art and Method of Qualitative Interview Studies.* New York: Free Press.

Weitzman, E., and M. B. Miles. 1995. *Computer Programs for Qualitative Analysis.* Thousand Oaks, CA: Sage.

West, James. 1945. *Plainville, U.S.A.* New York: Columbia University Press.

West, W. Gordon. 1980. "Access to Adolescent Deviants and Deviance." Pp. 31–44 in *Fieldwork Experience: Qualitative Approaches to Social Research*, edited by W. B. Shaffir, R. A. Stebbins, and A. Turowetz. New York: St. Martin's Press.

Whyte, William F. 1948. *Human Relations in the Restaurant Industry*. New York: McGraw-Hill.

———. 1993. *Street Corner Society: The Social Structure of an Italian Slum* (4th ed.). Chicago: University of Chicago Press. (Fiftieth anniversary edition; originally published in 1943)

———. (with the collaboration of Kathleen King Whyte). 1984. *Learning from the Field: A Guide from Experience*. Beverly Hills: Sage.

Wiley, Juniper. 1987. "The 'Shock of Unrecognition' as a Problem in Participant Observation." *Qualitative Sociology* 10 (no. 1): 78–83.

Williams, Terry. 1989a. "Exploring the Cocaine Culture." Pp. 27–32 in *In the Field: Readings on the Field Research Experience*, edited by C. B. Smith and W. Kornblum. New York: Praeger.

———. 1989b. *The Cocaine Kids*. New York: Addison-Wesley.

Williams, Terry, Eloise Dunlap, Bruce Johnson, and Ansley Hamid. 1992. "Personal Safety in Dangerous Places." *Journal of Contemporary Ethnography* 21 (no. 3): 343–374.

Wiseman, Jacqueline P. 1974. "The Research Web." *Urban Life and Culture* 3 (no. 3): 317–328.

———. 1979. "Close Encounters of the Quasi-Primary Kind: Sociability in Urban Second-Hand Clothing Stores." *Urban Life* 8 (no. 1): 23–51.

———. 1986. "Friendship: Bonds in a Voluntary Relationship." *Journal of Social and Personal Relationships* 3 (no. 2): 191–211.

———. 1991. *The Other Half: Wives of Alcoholics and Their Social Psychological Situation*. New York: Aldine de Gruyter.

Wolcott, Harry F. 1990a. "Making a Study 'More Ethnographic.'" *Journal of Contemporary Ethnography* 19 (no. 1): 44–72.

———. 1990b. *Writing Up Qualitative Research*. Newbury Park, CA: Sage.

Wolf, Margarey. 1992. *A Thrice-Told Tale: Feminism, Postmodernism, and Ethnographic Responsibility*. Stanford, CA: Stanford University Press.

Wolfe, Diane. 1992. *Factory Daughters: Gender, Household Dynamics, and Rural Industrialization in Java*. Berkeley: University of California Press.

Workman, John P. Jr. 1992. "Use of Electronic Media in a Participant Observation Study." *Qualitative Sociology* 15 (no. 4): 419–425.

Zablocki, Benjamin. 1980. *The Joyful Community: An Account of the Bruderhof, a Communal Movement Now in Its Third Generation*. Chicago: University of Chicago Press.

Zablocki, Benjamin, and Rosabeth Moss Kanter. 1976. "The Differentiation of Life-styles." Pp. 269–298 in *Annual Review of Sociology*, edited by R. Turner. Palo Alto, CA: Annual Reviews.

Zelditch, Morris Jr. 1962. "Some Methodological Problems of Field Studies." *American Journal of Sociology* 67 (no. 2): 566–576.

Zimmerman, Don H., and D. Lawrence Wieder. 1977. "The Diary-Interview Method." *Urban Life* 5 (no. 4): 479–498.

Zukin, Sharon. 1982. *Loft Living: Culture and Capital in Urban Change*. Baltimore, MD: Johns Hopkins University Press.

INDEX

Tape-recording, 86–87, 92–93
Team research, 73–74
Tesch, Renata, 78, 188
Theoretical candor, 150–151
Thinking flexibly, 201–203
Third World, research by Westerners in, 41–42
Thorne, Barrie, 20, 29, 51–52
Topics, 123
  causes, 136
    causation and conjecture, 138–139
    forms of causal accounts, 140
    importance of auxiliary causal accounts, 139–140
    the moral, 138
    requirements of causal inference, 136–137
    situational versus dispositional causes, 140–141
  coding and, 122
  combining units and aspects into, 101, 113, 121–122
  consequences, 141
    consequences and system needs (functionalism), 143–144
    consequences of what, for what, 142–143
    distinguished from intentions, 144–145
    other wordings of the consequence question, 144
    requirements of inferring consequences, 141–142
  contexts of (substantive domains), 102
  frequencies, 127
  human agency, 145–148
  magnitudes, 128
  processes, 129–132
    cycles, 132–133
    sequences, 134–136
    spirals, 133–134
  questions about, 123–124
  structures, 128–129
  types, 124
    multiple, 125
    rules of typing, 125–126
    single, 125
    typologizing, 126–127
"Total institution," 109–110, 125
Transcribing, 87–88
Trobriand Islanders, 49–50
Typing skills, 76–77
Typologizing, 126–127, 197–198

Underelaboration, 164
Units. *See* Social settings
Unknown investigator, 32–36
Unruh, David, 112

Value commitments in social science, 168–169
  demystification and reform, 170–172
  human and moral complexity, 173
  humanism and liberal science, 169
  larger, dispassionate understanding, 172–173
  new perception, 169–170
Van Maanen, John, 118, 217
Vaughn, Diane, 12, 20, 56, 89
Vertical cliques, 108
Vertical symbiotic cliques, 108
Vidich, Arthur, 6, 30, 43, 111
Villain pillorying frame, 176

Wallace, Alfred Russel, 163
Warner, W. Lloyd, 111
Warren, Carol, 24, 42, 50, 76
Wax, Murray, 42–43
Wax, Rosalie, 23, 46, 47, 54–55, 66–67
Weber, Max, 128–129
Weiss, Robert, 79–80, 82
Whyte, William F., 59–60, 60–61, 120–121
Wiseman, Jacqueline, 12, 84, 117, 199

Zablocki, Benjamin, 104, 112, 113
Zelditch, Morris, 19
Zukin, Sharon, 12

Credits

Spencer Cahill, research published as "Childhood and Public Life: Reaffirming Biographical Divisions" 1990; material on pages 96–97 used by permission of Spencer Cahill.

Agatha Christie, *Murder in Three Acts,* New York: Popular Library, 1934; material on page 57 reprinted by permission of Dodd, Mead and Company, Inc. and Hughes Massie Limited.

Melville Dalton, *Men Who Manage,* New York: Wiley, 1959; material on page 108 reprinted by permission of John Wiley & Sons, Inc.

Erving Goffman, *Asylums,* © 1961 by Erving Goffman; material on pages 110 and 138 reprinted by permission of Doubleday & Company, Inc.

Carole Joffe, research published as *Friendly Intruders: Childcare Professionals and Family Life* 1977; material on page 97 used by permission of Carole Joffe.

Ritchie P. Lowry, *Who's Running This Town?,* New York: Harper & Row, 1965; material on page 80 reprinted by permission of Ritchie P. Lowry.

Julius Roth, "Comments on 'Secret Observation,'" *Social Problems,* Winter 1962; material on pages 34 and 36 reprinted by permission of the Society for the Study of Social Problems and Julius Roth.

Barrie Thorne, "Political Activist as Participant Observer," *Symbolic Interaction,* Spring 1979; material on pages 51–52 reprinted by permission of the Society for the Study of Symbolic Interaction.

Rosalie H. Wax, *Doing Fieldwork,* Chicago: The University of Chicago Press, 1971; material on pages 23, 40, 46, 54, 66 reprinted by permission of The University of Chicago Press.

William F. Whyte, *Street Corner Society,* 4th ed., Chicago: The University of Chicago Press, 1993; material on pages 59–60, 60–61 reprinted by permission of The University of Chicago Press.